PEARL DUST

365 pearls of wisdom for extreme teens

Robert Strand

E*ergreen
PRESS

Mobile, AL

ISBN 978-1-58169-377-5
For Worldwide Distribution
Printed in the U.S.A.

Evergreen Press
P.O. Box 191540 • Mobile, AL 36619
800-367-8203

I dedicate this book to my eight grandchildren

who are, or have been, or will be teenagers.

I thank them for their up-to-date input.

Christopher, Kristie, Sarah, Cody, Jonathan, Casey,

Benjamin, and Maxwell—you are the best.

For Cody:
Can you believe this?! Your
grandpa writing an E-book for
teens? I shall be eagerly waiting for
your critique!
Merry Christmas & a wonderful,
Exciting & Blessed New Year!
Love— Grandpa RJP
2011

INTRODUCTION

My question to you is: What do you want to BE in life and what do you want to DO with your life? Most teens have or will confront that question eventually.

Think with me a moment. God has given each of us 24 hours a day to fill with action, the time to live this short life to the fullest. Let's break it down to 1,440 minutes in each day. Whether you live seventy years or a hundred years, the total amount of time you will spend on this earth is not the most important factor in your living, but rather, what will you invest into your 1440 minutes every day.

Life is too short to be bored when you could be turned on. Life is too short to settle for average when you could reach for excellence. And perhaps, most importantly, life is too short not to make a difference in this world.

My challenge to you is to follow the most fabulous leader in all of human history. His name is Jesus Christ! It then stands to reason that the most awesome person in history can also lead you to the most fabulous, fulfilling lifestyle you can possibly live. He challenges, "Follow me and I will make you . . ." Talk about an exciting life-style filled with adventure!

This book is intended to stimulate your thinking and to help you follow with actions and become truly all that you can be. YOU can make a difference! It all starts with a total commitment to be the best you can be with His help! Let's begin this journey for the next year. with a daily discipline . . . read a pearl a day for 365 days!

1. NOTHING IS IMPOSSIBLE!

Scientists have made their declaration that, according to aerodynamic theory, bumblebees cannot fly. Why?

They say that the bees' size, weight, and body shape in relation to the wingspread and size should make it impossible for them to become airborne. Their conclusion is that the bee is too heavy, too wide, and too large to fly with such small wings! However, the bumblebee doesn't know these scientific facts. So it just flies in the face of reason and fact. The bumblebee has 130 wing-beats per second and can fly at about seven miles per hour.

Among honeybees, as among other bees, only the females have stingers. The male drones are harmless while the queen bee lays and fertilizes at least 600,000 eggs during her three to five year reign. The buzzing sound you hear is caused by their wing movements and air turbulence. The faster their wings beat, the higher the pitch.

It was God who created the bumblebee and all the other flying insects and taught them how to fly. The bees have never questioned their Creator; they just fly! Nor have the bees questioned whether God loves them or not.

When God created you and me, He gave us all the equipment we need for the lifetime flight ahead of us. He also has promised to love and be with us. God is not limited by our understanding of how things happen. Just because we might not understand how impossible things can be accomplished, it doesn't mean God the Almighty can't do it—for you or me!

I can do everything through him who gives me strength
(Philippians 4:13).

2. THE WORLD'S GREATEST HEAVYWEIGHT FIGHT

Standing in one corner is the world's undisputed heavyweight champion of all time. He's over nine feet tall and weighs more than three hundred pounds. In the other corner is a teen, well-trained and prepared, stepping into the ring for his very first heavyweight brawl. How does he measure up? He's about five feet, six inches tall and weighs almost 150 pounds.

The giant is well-protected in armor from head to foot with a shield, sword, and spear. In contrast, the outweighed teen has no armor but is armed with a slingshot and five stones. You can hear the echoes of raucous, mocking laughter coming from the giant's side of the valley, while from the other is shocked, dead silence. The odds are more than five hundred to one with the giant easily winning. What kind of a fight can this possibly be?

It's a familiar story—David versus Goliath. The stakes are unbelievably high with the future and destiny of two nations being contested. It was winner takes all—win or become enslaved!

But there's a nugget of truth often overlooked. David caught the essence of this battle; he saw the big picture. "The battle is the Lord's" was his victory cry. David knew he couldn't fail; the giant thought he couldn't be defeated!

David with his slingshot aimed at the only vulnerable spot on this giant—a patch about four inches by six inches on the giant's forehead. How many hours in practice had David spent with his slingshot? He knew his weapon and its accuracy, and he took his best shot! Goliath trusted in his size and skills, but David trusted in God. With a single stone he defeated the giant! This should be your battle plan when you face your next giant.

The battle is the Lord's, and he will give all of you into our hands
(1 Samuel 17:47).

3. WHAT'S YOUR DESTINY?

Leaders in Charlotte, North Carolina, invited their favorite son, Billy Graham, to a luncheon in his honor. Billy hesitated to accept because he was struggling with Parkinson's disease.

The Charlotte leaders said, "We don't expect a major address. Just come and let us honor you." So Dr. Graham agreed.

After wonderful things were said about him, Dr. Graham stepped to the rostrum and said, "I'm reminded today of Albert Einstein, the great physicist who this month has been honored by *TIME* magazine as the 'Man of the Century.' Einstein was once traveling from Princeton on a train when the conductor came down the aisle, punching tickets of each passenger. When he came to Einstein, Einstein searched everywhere; he couldn't find his. The conductor said, 'Dr. Einstein, I'm sure you bought a ticket. Don't worry about it.'

"Einstein nodded appreciatively. The conductor continued down the aisle. As he was ready to move to the next car, he turned and saw the famous man down on his hands and knees looking under his seat. The conductor rushed back and said, 'Dr. Einstein, don't worry. I know who you are and I'm sure you bought a ticket.' Einstein looked at him and said, 'Young man, I too know who I am. What I don't know is where I'm going!'"

Having said that, Billy Graham continued, "See the suit I'm wearing? It's a brand new suit. I went out and bought a new suit for this luncheon and one more occasion. This is the suit in which I'll be buried. But when you hear I'm dead, I don't want you to remember the suit. I want you to remember this: I not only know who I am, I also know where I'm going!"

Do you know where you are going?

Jesus answered, "I am the way and the truth and the life"
(John 14:6).

4. KEEP ON KEEPING ON!

Runner's World told the story of Beth Anne DeCiantis' attempt to qualify for the 1992 Olympic Trials marathon. A female runner is required to complete the 26-mile, 385-yard race in less than two hours and forty-five minutes in order to be able to compete at the Olympic Trials.

Beth started strong but began having trouble with her race around mile number 23. She was beginning to struggle with each step and barely reached the final straightaway at exactly two hours and forty-three minutes. Only two minutes were left in order for her to qualify.

Two hundred yards from the finish line she stumbled and fell to the ground. Dazed, she stayed down for twenty seconds. The crowd began yelling: "GET UP! GET UP! GET UP!" The clock was ticking . . . 2:44 with less than a minute to go!

Beth Anne managed to stagger to her feet and began a stumbling kind of walking. She was five yards short of the finish! Only ten seconds were left on the clock. She fell again. She began to crawl, and the crowd was cheering her on. She crossed the finish line on her hands and knees! Her time? Two hours, forty-four minutes, fifty-seven seconds! She beat the clock by three seconds, qualifying her for the Olympic Trials!

We are all in a race—a race to a finish line. You may have a lifetime in which to run a marathon, or then again it may be a sprint for you because none of us is guaranteed a certain quantity of time in which to run our individual races.

Let us run with perseverance the race marked out for us
(Hebrews 12:1).

5. IT'S A DEADLY WEAPON!

Think! Name a weapon that is more lethal than a nuclear weapon. This weapon has wounded and destroyed more people than any other weapon of destruction. You have one; we all do! It's been described as being "evil, full of deadly poison, a fire!"

It's your tongue and no, this isn't about French kissing. This is about what comes out of your mouth. Words are powerful! Words have meaning. Words can build up or destroy. You can do at least three things with your tongue.

1. *Destroy!* The Bible says it's a deadly weapon. You can gossip, you can turn it on yourself with negative talk, or make hurtful remarks to others.

Marta demeans herself when she says, "I'm ugly. I'm a failure." Yes, she has become all of these things in a self-fulfilling prophecy about herself.

2. *Change!* When Cheryl Prewitt was four and five years old, she spent

time in her dad's country grocery. Every day when the milkman came, he always greeted her with, "How's my little Miss America?" She giggled but the idea actually turned into a life goal. In 1980 she became Miss America! Positive words were planted and eventually took root in her subconscious. You have the ability to plant such visions in others as well as in yourself.

3. *Praise!* You have the power to bless others with your words. And more importantly you have the ability to praise the Lord God Almighty, the King of Kings and Lord of Lords! Before you speak, think! Will I build up or tear down?

If anyone considers himself religious and yet does not keep a tight rein on his tongue, he deceives himself and his religion is worthless
(James 1:26).

6. DREAM BIG

In his book, *Running the Amazon*, Joe Kane, a reporter from San Francisco, recounts his dream and how it was fulfilled. His dream was to take a raft trip down the almost 4000 mile length of the Amazon River, the second longest river in the world. He had been raised in the city and knew nothing about extreme river rafting. He knew less about the river, jungle insects, snakes, Marxist guerrillas, narco-traffickers, or paddling techniques to keep the raft upright and moving towards his goal.

He started at the source, a tiny little stream about 17,000 feet high up in the Alps of Peru. It was a six-month journey. He writes of his battles with rapids, tumbling through thousand-foot gorges, dodging the bullets of terrorists, horrible drinking water, the ever present stinging insects, clashes with people along the way, hunger for food without contamination, fear of the unknown especially at night, wild animals, and fatigue. All were obstacles to be overcome as he paddled the entire Amazon in six months.

Kane achieved an impressive, even awesome, feet! Obviously Joe was not afraid to dream and not afraid to take risks. His was one of those impossible dreams. No one had ever taken this trip because everyone said it couldn't be done, but he was willing to learn new techniques and overcome obstacles in his way. He tackled the world's most dangerous river!

What about you? Are you willing to dream big dreams for God? Dreams that will challenge you and test your stamina and commitment? Write down a dream. Pray about it, share it with someone else, and give it to God!

Jesus looked at them and said, "With man this is impossible, but not with God; all things are possible with God" (Mark 10:27).

COURAGE

She's barely eighteen, a junior in high school, a fabulous student, and sounds and looks like any other young Asian student who might be living in the United States. But she is not typical, for Hieu grew up in Vietnam. Her story would make a good movie or best-selling book.

Her father fought against Communistic Vietnam and was a captive for three years. When released he fled to Thailand. Then he began to fear arrest in Thailand for being thought a Communist, so he returned to Vietnam. When it appeared he was not safe there, he returned to Thailand for three more years. As he had feared, he was imprisoned by officials who believed he was a Communist. In the meantime little Hieu and the family struggled to survive. Finally, her father escaped from prison, returned to his family, and immediately made plans to come to America.

Arriving in America, the family had no contacts and no friends. They stayed a month in a church basement before finding jobs and a place to live. Hieu began high school and became an honor student. Half of her family is still in Vietnam.

If you were to ask, "Hieu, what are your plans for your future?" she would say she plans to go to college and then medical school. A young doctor with her smarts and work ethic could make lots of bucks in America; but no, after graduation she plans to return to Vietnam—not seeking revenge, not to make money, but to help her people who are caught in a system that serves the rich and ignores the poor. Her goal is to return to a nation that imprisoned her dad and left her family floundering without a father's support. What's her source of courage? She says, "Because I serve a courageous God!"

When I am afraid, I will trust in you (Psalm 56:3).

8. TURNING A TIGER INTO A TURKEY

According to *Sports Illustrated* magazine, Tiger Woods is the best golfer on the planet and perhaps the world's most famous celebrity athlete as well as the richest athlete of our day. He had led a charmed life with a gorgeous wife and two kids, and was classy, dignified, always in control, and a winner to be admired.

However, in our memory, no famous public figure has fallen so far, so fast. His carefully crafted public persona is at odds with his real person. It all came crashing down one Thanksgiving night (November 29, 2009) as he wrapped his Cadillac Escalade around a tree and fire hydrant. Domestic violence was speculated, and he was fined $164 for careless driving by the Florida Highway Patrol. This was just the beginning of revelations about his serial adultery as mistress after mistress came forward with her story of Tiger's marital infidelity. The shattering of his public image made him join a long list of other public figures who have fallen from their lofty perches.

How can a man who seemingly has everything be willing to throw it all away for fleeting, illicit pleasures? The Bible speaks of "the pleasures of sin" for a season (Hebrews 11:25). It also says that you can "be sure that your sin will find you out" (Numbers 32:23). And the finding out can be painful—if not in this life, it will happen in the world to come at an awesome place called the judgment seat of Christ. Yes, all of us—rich or poor, famous or unknown—will have our day in God's courtroom where all will be judged for the sins committed and the life that has been lived, whether good or bad! When any of us serve the devil, you can be sure that a payday is coming.

Each person is destined to die once and after that comes judgment
(Hebrews 9:27 NLT).

9. TEEN ESCAPES WITH HIS HEAD!

In the Saudi Arabian capital city of Riyadh, nineteen-year-old Jahwi Hussein Qasim Abubakr was convicted of murdering another man. For this crime, under Sharia law (the code of conduct of Islam), he received the death penalty—to be beheaded by a sword in a public execution. When the time arrived for this penalty to take place, Abubakr was blindfolded, knelt with head bowed, exposing his neck to the executioner. The sword was raised but never fell! Why? The murder victim's father stood to his feet and publicly offered forgiveness to the guilty Abubakr.

At the very last moment his life was spared! How? Saudi Arabia practices Islamic Sharia law. This law allows the family of a murder victim to spare the life of a convicted murderer by an act of forgiveness.[1]

Forgiveness is absolutely awesome when it is extended to another person. It has the ability to set a person free—in this case from a death sentence. When you offer forgiveness to another person who has wronged you, you set that person free from the bondage of the past, from the penalty for wrongdoing—and even more exciting—you set yourself free from the burden of taking revenge on another person.

Forgiveness can be expensive. You let another person go free from any penalty for their acts against you. It doesn't seem fair. But God, who is willing to forgive you, originated this entire concept. It's so cool because it works every time to heal what can't otherwise be fixed!

Forgive us our debts, as we also have forgiven our debtors
(Matthew 6:12).

10. "JEDI" WORSHIP IS NOT SANCTIONED!

In the last British census, almost 400,000 Brits wrote "Jedi" as being their official faith. However, the "British Office for National Statistics" refused to give sanction to make it an official religion in Great Britain.

The story goes like this. The census form asked all of the respondents to fill in a box for the major religions in the United Kingdom. There also was a blank space for "any other religion." More than 391,000 people filled in the blank with "Jedi" because of an intensive Internet campaign telling the Brits to claim the Star Wars related faith as their religion. A rumor had been circulating that if "Jedi" was written at least 10,000 times, it would become known as an official religion. The rumor was a huge lie. However, more English people had claimed "Jedi" as their faith than those who claimed to be Jewish, Buddhist, or Sikh in their religious faith!

What is your faith? Is it merely a religious system? Is it a belief that has turned into a religious practice? Is it based on a feeling or does it have a solid foundational base?

Let's get even more personal. On what is your faith based? The teachings of a mortal person or on the eternal Word of God? Is your faith based on evidence that doesn't change with the times? Will it survive the storms of life? Perhaps it's time to take an inventory of your faith.

Now faith is being sure of what we hope for
and certain of what we do not see (Hebrews 11:1).

11. MAKE A DIFFERENCE

A teacher in New York wanted to honor her seniors in high school by sharing with them the difference they each made that year. Using a process developed by Helice Bridges, she called each student, one at a time, before the class and shared how the student made a difference to her and the class. After presenting each one with a blue ribbon that read, "Who I Am Makes a Difference," she gave all the students three of these same ribbons to share with others in their town. They were to report back to the class with results in a week.

One student honored a junior executive for helping him with his future college planning by giving him a ribbon. Then he gave him the two extra ribbons and said, "Honor someone important in your life."

Later that day, this junior executive went to his grouchy boss, gave him a ribbon, and told him how deeply he admired him for being a creative genius. This surprised the boss, who in turn was asked to acknowledge someone else with the remaining ribbon.

That night, this cranky boss came home to his fourteen-year-old son and said, "The most incredible thing happened to me today. One of our junior executives came in and told me he admired me, and he gave me this blue ribbon for being a creative genius. Imagine! As I was driving home I started thinking about who I should honor with this other ribbon, and I thought about you. I want to honor you! I just want you to know, besides your mother, you are the most important person in my life. You're great and I love you!"

The startled son began to sob. His whole body shook. He looked up through his tears and said, "I was planning on committing suicide tomorrow, Dad, because I didn't think you loved me. Now I don't need to."

Who in your life should you honor?

A word aptly spoken is like apples of gold in settings of silver
(Proverbs 25:11).

12. HOW HIGH CAN IT FLY?

Do you remember your first helium filled balloon? You clutched it for dear life. It was fun! It always wanted to go up. Then somehow, it slipped out of your grip and you watched as it went out of sight. Did you ever wonder how high it would fly?

We have the answer provided by the "National Scientific Balloon Facility" in Palestine, Texas. That little latex balloon would reach approximately 18,000 feet. The helium would have expanded to about 80 percent more than original volume and burst the balloon. Would you like to launch a balloon higher? It can be done with specially designed experimental balloons that can reach 120,000 feet. They have cleverly designed ducts that will vent off the expansion pressure.

What's the difference in these two types of balloons? The childish latex balloon has a limited ability to adapt; the other is designed for expansion. It's much the same in life. Some of us might blow apart with a little pressure, while others who have prepared themselves will be able to climb higher because of better preparation in life.

Life holds fabulous possibilities for those who are willing to make the necessary preparations. Nobody plans to fail, especially when looking at life through young eyes.

Based on life insurance industry statistics, you can study 100 people who are now in their late teens and look ahead to age 65 and make these predictions: 1 of them will end up independently wealthy; 4 will have enough money to live comfortably; 5 will still be working to earn a living; 36 will have died; and 54 will be dependent on family, friends, or a government agency for their living at retirement age.

Forgetting what is behind and straining toward what is ahead, I press on toward the goal to win the prize" (Philippians 3:13-14).

13. RULES OF THE ROAD FOR TEENS

Do you know the number one cause of death for teens? Motor vehicle accidents! Also, a teen driver's greatest lifetime chance of a crash occurs in the first six to twelve months of getting a driver's license. Studies now show the majority of these crashes could have been prevented.

Supermodel and celebrity mom, Niki Taylor, said, "As the mother of two teenage sons and a car crash survivor, I know firsthand the gravity of this issue, and I wanted to try to do something about it." She has teamed with The Children's Hospital of Philadelphia (CHOP) and State Farm Insurance Company to develop an online resource to guide parents and teens in setting the rules most likely to protect teen drivers.

Here are the tips: 1. Use seat belts on every trip. 2. Do not use cell phones or any other electronic device when driving. 3. Follow all driving rules, including no speeding. 4. Do not drive while impaired or ride as a passenger with an impaired driver. 5. Do not ride with an unlicensed or inexperienced teen driver. 6. No peer passengers. Include siblings only after six months of experience and only if they are belted in. 7. No nighttime driving. 8. No high-speed roads.

Teens who say their parents establish rules and pay attention to their activities in a supportive way are half as likely to be in a crash.

Does the Bible say anything about cars and teens? No, but it does tell teens to obey their parents so they will live a long and fulfilling life on this earth.

Some trust in chariots and some in horses, but we trust in the name of the Lord our God (Psalm 20:7).

14. WHO IS ON YOUR WALL?

I was paging through a *Sports Illustrated* magazine, and my attention focused on the tidbit section to a story about Rico Leroy Marshall, an eighteen-year-old senior at Forestville High School in Glenarden, Maryland. Rico was a basketball star with everything going his way. He had a promising athletic scholarship to the University of South Carolina and was the first place winner in his school's talent contest.

That's background. Here's the story. Rico was driving home from a ball game on a Friday when he was stopped by a county sheriff in a patrol car. On the seat beside Rico was a plastic bag with several chunks of crack, the highly concentrated and addictive form of cocaine. So that he wouldn't be arrested for illegal possession, he swallowed the drugs as the Sheriff walked to his stopped car. Later that night, at home, he went into convulsions. His parents rushed him to the hospital. Early on Saturday morning, Rico Leroy Marshall died of an overdose.

There's another element to this story. On the wall of Rico's bedroom was a huge poster of his hero, Len Bias. Bias was the star of the University of Maryland basketball team and the number one draft pick for the NBA Boston Celtics. What Rico would never know was that on the night he was drafted, Len Bias died of an overdose of drugs!

A sad story? Yes! Are you surprised? Now my question to you: Who is your role model? Who is the poster on the wall in your bedroom? Who do you want to follow? Who will you worship? Choose well! Heroes are important, but even more important is the hero you choose to follow and worship.

Let us fix our eyes on Jesus, the author and perfecter of our faith
(Hebrews 12:2).

15. HAVE YOU EVER BEEN AFRAID?

Following the runaway success of her book, *The Joy Luck Club*, first time novelist Amy Tan feared she might be typecast. "I didn't want to be the mother-daughter expert," she said, "so I tried something else until I realized that rebellion was not a good reason to write."

Then her mother provided the inspiration for her next project. "I knew she had lived a harsh, repressive life in China. I asked about World War II and she said, 'I wasn't affected.' Then she talked about the bombs falling, 'We were always scared they would hit us.' I pointed out that she said she wasn't affected. 'I wasn't,' she replied. 'I wasn't killed.' That statement became a revelation."

Tan's goal was to understand the difference between her and her mother's perspective on life. Later during the Tiananmen Square uprising Amy wrote the book, *The Kitchen God's Wife*, based on her mother's life. Amy then said, "I wanted to know what it is like to live a life of repression, to know fear and what you must do to rise above fear!"

Did you catch that? "What you must do to rise above fear." Fear is an enemy that can reduce the best of us to jelly. What is the secret to overcoming fear? A major clue is found in God's Word, the Bible. Read through it to see if you can find the 365 written "fear nots"! There is one for every day of the year, just for you!

Fear is an enemy that you can conquer! God says to you, "Do not be afraid!"

So do not fear, for I am with you; do not be dismayed, for I am your God. I will strengthen you and help you (Isaiah 41:10).

16. KIDS GO BALD!

In Oceanside, California, in Mr. Alter's fifth grade class, it's impossible to tell which boy is undergoing chemotherapy. Nearly all the boys are bald! Thirteen of them had their heads shaved so a sick buddy wouldn't feel out of place.

"If everybody has their head shaved, sometimes people don't know who's who. They don't know who has cancer and who just shaved their head," said eleven-year-old Scott Sebelius, one of the baldies at Lake Elementary School.

For the record, Ian O'Gorman is the sick one. Doctors removed a malignant tumor from his small intestine and a week later started chemotherapy to treat the disease called lymphoma.

Ian said, "Besides surgery, I had tubes up my nose. I had butterflies in my stomach." He had eight more weeks of chemo in an effort to keep the cancer from returning. Ian decided to get his head shaved before all his hair would fall out in clumps; to his surprise, his friends wanted to join him.

"The last thing he would want is to not fit in, to be made fun of, so we just wanted to make him feel better and not left out," said ten-year-old Kyle Hanslik. Kyle started talking to the other boys, and they all went to the barbershop together. The boys teacher, Jim Alter, was so inspired by their actions that he too shaved his head![2]

The Good Book tells us that in order to have friends, we must be friendly first! Do you have any friends that could use some compassionate understanding in their lives?

A man of many companions may come to ruin, but there is a friend who sticks closer than a brother (Proverbs 18:24).

17. GREED DESTROYS
A FATHER/SON RELATIONSHIP

"Dear Abby" is a phenomenon of our day. She seems to have an answer for all kinds of human needs and problems. The following is from a reader:

Dear Abby,

The letter concerning the minister who, on receiving a pair of leather gloves for services rendered, was disappointed until he discovered a ten dollar bill stuffed into each finger reminded me of this story:

A young man from a wealthy family was about to graduate from high school. It was the custom in that neighborhood for parents to give the grad a car. "Bill" and his dad had spent months looking at cars, and the week before graduation found the perfect car! Bill was positive the car would be his on graduation night.

Imagine his disappointment when, at the celebration, Bill's dad gave him a gift-wrapped Bible! Bill was so angry he threw the Bible down and stormed out of the house. He and his father never saw each other again. It was the news of his father's death that brought Bill home again. As he was going through his father's possessions, he came across the Bible. He brushed away the dust and opened it to find a cashier's check dated the day of his graduation in the exact amount of the car they had chosen!

—Beckah Fink, Texas

Here's the response from Abby:

Dear Beckah,

I hope Bill read the Bible from cover to cover because it contains much that he needed to learn.

Greed is a passion that must be conquered early in life or it can capture you in a bondage that is a lifetime destroyer of relationships.

Such is the end of all who go after ill-gotten gain; it takes away the lives of those who get it (Proverbs 1:19).

18. THE OTHER JONAH

Do you believe the Bible story about Jonah being swallowed by a huge fish? How about a real life story about another Jonah who was swallowed and lived to tell about it?

In February 1891, a young English sailor, James Bartley, was a crew member on the whaling ship, Star of the East. It roamed the waters off the Falkland Islands in search of these marine leviathans.

About three miles off shore, they spotted a sperm whale that later proved to be eighty feet long and weighed over eighty tons! Two boats with crew members and harpooners, one of them Bartley, went after the monster. When struck by the first harpoon, the whale twisted and lashed out and slammed his tail into one of the boats, lifted it out of the water, and capsized it. Soon the whalers had subdued the whale, righted the rowboat, and discovered Bartley and another crew member were missing. They were written off as being drowned.

The crew pulled the whale alongside the boat, removed the blubber, and hoisted the carcass on deck with a derrick. According to M. deParville, science editor of *The Journal des Debats,* the crew discovered movement inside the belly of the whale. When opened they found Bartley, unconscious. They immediately bathed him in sea water, which revived him, but his mind was confused. He was confined to the captain's quarters for two weeks because he was "acting like a lunatic."

Within four weeks, Bartley fully recovered and related what it had been like to live in the belly of this whale. For the rest of his life, though, Bartley's face, neck, and hands remained white since they were bleached by the whale's gastric juices.

The Lord provided a great fish to swallow Jonah, and Jonah was inside the fish three days and three nights (Jonah 1:17).

19. WHAT IS A TITHE?

After he had been named National Football League Rookie of the Year, Barry Sanders held out for a five-year contract that included a 2.1 million dollar bonus. The fans and media accused him of greed but were silenced when they learned Sanders sent a check for $210,000 to the Baptist church he attended when he was growing up.

Sanders has tithed ever since he left home. If you don't know, a tithe is giving 10 percent of what you earn to God and His church. Skeptical Detroit Lions teammates whispered, "Just another God-squader." But Sander's un-sanctimonious style of living quickly won over his teammates.

Shortly after his holdout, Sanders left a practice drill. "I don't know if I can go back in there," he gasped to Coach Wayne Fontes. He wondered what was wrong with his prize rookie running back—in fact, the league's best running back that year.

"What's wrong?" asked the alarmed coach. "Are you hurt?"

"No! But the guys are using some awfully foul language. I don't know if I can stand it." A very few awkward moments passed. Then the fun loving, joking, happy Sanders cracked up and jogged back to the huddle.

Sanders' story highlights a number of life lessons. For one, tithing is God's plan for all of us. Tithing is a responsibility, a stewardship of handling all the things God has given us. When we tithe, we are saying we know Who really is in charge of this world.

For another, Sanders was a man who lived His relationship with God in a real world, winning the respect of the people he influenced. He lived what he believed. You should begin the discipline of being a tither in every sense of the word.

Bring the whole tithe into the storehouse [church] ... and see if I will not open the floodgates of heaven and pour out so much blessing that you will not have enough room for it (Malachi 3:10).

20. THE MOST INSPIRING PERSON OF THE YEAR

Zach Bonner is a twelve-year-old boy living in Florida who was voted "The Most Inspiring Person of the Year" in 2009 by the readers and editors at the website Beliefnet.com. This is an annual competition that included winners such notables as Chesley "Sully" Sullenberger, the hero pilot who landed his plane safely on the Hudson River, and students in Iran who risked their lives in a demonstration against a fraudulent election.

According to Laurie Sue Brockway, editor for the site, "Zach has been doing humanitarian work since he was six years old, giving out water from his little red wagon after a hurricane. I was a puddle of tears looking at photos of his efforts, like walking across the country to bring attention to causes."

Zach took time from his latest efforts to say, "It was awesome even to be in the running. Then to win was really exciting!"

You can follow his causes on his website, LittleRedWagonFoundation. com. There you will discover the simple ideas he shares that will help anyone of any age to become a philanthropist. Zach got his start following Hurricane Charley in 2004 when he saw how many people needed food, water, and supplies. "It was just something I felt I could do," he says. "When you are in preschool or kindergarten, they are teaching you to share and give to others. And I had a really good time doing it, so I wanted to continue."[3]

Wow! Zach said it all. If Zach can be a volunteer to help others, none of us is too young or too old to do the same. Zach has discovered the joy of giving! Now it's your turn!

Give, and it will be given to you. A good measure, pressed down, shaken together and running over, will be poured into your lap
(Luke 6:38).

21. BAPTIZED BY SOCRATES

It's an old story about a proud, arrogant young man who came to the noted, quite muscular philosopher, Socrates, and said, proudly, "O great Socrates, I come for knowledge." Socrates, recognizing a pompous man when he saw one, asked the young man to follow him through the streets of Athens to the shores of the Mediterranean Sea. They waded out into chest deep water. Then Socrates turned to the young man and asked, "Now, what do you want?"

"Knowledge, O wise Socrates," said the young man with a smirk. Socrates put his strong hands on the young man's shoulders and pushed him under and held him for a count to thirty. He let him up and said, "What do you want?"

"Wisdom" sputtered the young man, "O great Socrates" without a smile. Socrates crunched him under again, this time for a count of forty-five and let him up again. The young man was gasping for breath. Socrates asked again.

Between heavy, heaving breaths the young man wheezed, "Knowledge, O wise and wonder—" Socrates jammed him under again. This time he counted to fifty before he pulled the young man out of the water. "What do you want?"

"AIR!" he screeched. "I NEED AIR!"

"When you want knowledge as desperately as you have just wanted air, then you will have knowledge," said a smiling Socrates.

We live in the information age. Knowledge is today's needed quality of life. How much do you really want or need knowledge? Is it as important as your next breath?

If any of you lacks wisdom, he or she should ask God,
who gives generously to all (James 1:5).

22. A FAMOUS FATHER

"**D**ear Ann Landers . . ." began the following letter:

A great man died today. He wasn't a world leader or a famous doctor or a war hero or a sports figure. He was no business tycoon, and you will never see his name in the financial pages. But he was one of the greatest men who ever lived.

He was my father. I guess you might say he was a person who was never interested in getting credit or receiving honors. He did corny things like pay his bills on time, go to church on Sunday, and serve as an officer in the PTA (Parent Teacher Association). He helped his kids with their homework and drove his wife to do grocery shopping on Thursday nights. He got a great kick out of hauling his teenagers and their friends around to and from football games.

Dad enjoyed simple pastimes like picnics in the part and pitching horseshoes. Opera wasn't exactly his cup of tea. He liked country music, mowing the grass, and running with the dog. He didn't own a tuxedo and never tasted caviar.

Tonight is my first night without him. I don't know what to do with myself, so I am writing this to you, Ann. I am sorry now for the times I didn't show him the proper respect. But I am grateful for a lot of other things.

I am thankful that God let me have my father for fifteen years. And I am happy that I was able to let him know how much I loved him. That wonderful man died with a smile on his face and fulfillment in his heart. He knew he was a great success as a husband, father, brother, a son, and a friend. I wonder how many millionaires can say that?

The letter was signed, "Fifteen Years Old and Lonely"[4]

And whatever you do, whether in word or deed, do it all in the name of the Lord Jesus, giving thanks to God the Father (Colossians 3:17).

23. THE GOLDEN SPEECH

This is about a very creative and gutsy young lady who gave a demonstration speech. The assignment was that each student in "Beginning Speech 101" had to prepare a three- to five-minute speech based on one of four basic types of speeches.

When her speech assignment was to be given, this freshman in college was called to the front to present it. She walked to the lectern with a confident stride, turned to face the class, and planted her feet, with hands clasped in front and a pleasant look on her face. She stood there without speaking a single word for nearly the entire time allotted for her presentation, which was five minutes!

You can imagine the reactions of the students. They fidgeted, looked at her, looked at each other, shrugged their shoulders, shuffled their feet, looked out the window, glanced at the instructor, and all seemed very uncomfortable. The silence was deafening! Everyone, except this gutsy young lady, was uncomfortable. The professor didn't know what to do or say. He held the stopwatch in the palm of his hand timing her speech. She leveled her gaze at her fellow students and at the professor. She was the only one who seemed to be in control.

Finally, four minutes and forty-five seconds into her five minute "speech," she said only three words: "Silence is golden!" That was it! That was all! Everyone seemed to be stunned and in shock! By the way, her grade in presenting a demonstration type of speech was an A!

Pretty clever young lady! How about using a bit more creativity in your next presentation? You might be surprised at the outcome. And don't forget, more often than not, silence can really be golden!

Neither do men pour new wine into old wineskins. If they do, the skins will burst . . . pour new wine into new wineskins, and both are preserved (Matthew 9:17).

24. AN AFFAIR OF THE HEART

Love affairs are not unusual for teens today. Felipe Garza Jr., age fifteen, dated fourteen-year-old Donna Ashlock until she cooled it off by dating other boys. However, Felipe would not let his feelings for her cool off.

One day Donna doubled over in pain. Doctors soon discovered she was dying of a degenerative heart disease and desperately needed a heart transplant. Felipe heard about Donna's condition and told his mother, "I'm going to die and I'm going to give my heart to Donna." Fifteen-year-old boys can say some irrational things. He appeared in excellent health at this point.

Three weeks later, Felipe woke up and complained of a pain on the left side of his head. He began losing his breath and couldn't walk. He was rushed to the hospital where it was discovered a blood vessel in his brain had burst and left him brain dead. Felipe's condition mystified his doctors! While he remained on a respirator, his parents decided to allow his heart to be removed for Donna; his kidneys, eyes, and other organs were also donated to others in need.

Donna received Felipe's heart! After the transplant, Donna's father explained that Felipe had been sick for three months. "His family donated his kidneys and eyes," he said. There was a pause, then Donna added, "And I have his heart."

"Yes," said Donna's father. Her expression changed, and she asked her dad who knew.

He said, "Everybody." Donna teared up and nothing more was said.

Some days later, a funeral procession seemed to roll on forever through the fields and orchards of Patterson, California. It could have been for royalty, but it was for Felipe. His only claim to fame was his love and his heart.

Think with me a moment, what life application comes to mind for you?

Let us not love with words or tongue but with actions and in truth
(1 John 3:18).

25. DEFERRED DECISIONS

The former United States President, Ronald Reagan, told this story about himself when he was a young teen. A kind aunt of his had taken him to the local shoemaker to have a pair of shoes custom-made just for him. The shoemaker asked, among other questions, "Do you want a round toe or a square toe?"

Young Reagan hemmed and hawed and couldn't make up his mind. So the cobbler said, "Come back in a day or two and tell me what you want."

A few days later the shoemaker saw Ronald on the street and asked what he had decided about his shoes. "I haven't made up my mind yet," Reagan answered.

"Very well," said the shoemaker. "Your shoes will be ready for you to pick up late in the day tomorrow."

When Reagan picked up his shoes, one had a round toe and the other a square toe! Reagan said, "Looking at those shoes taught me a life lesson. If you don't make your own decisions, somebody else makes them for you."

Got a moment for another story? In Guyana, sixty miles up the Essequibo River in the village of Bartica, in the center of the town square, stands a huge white monument built on top of a concrete square. It's impressive! But no inscription is found on it. Ask anybody about it and no one knows why it was erected. Strange . . . a monument to nothing!

What about your life? Will it be a monument to nothing? Or will you make the decisions and choices that will make your life count for something?

Choose for yourselves this day whom you will serve . . .
But as for me . . . [I] will serve the Lord! (Joshua 24:15).

26. THE GOAL IS THE GOAL

Bobby Dodd, the former great football coach of Georgia Tech University, tells the story of a game in which his team was leading by a single point, seven to six with a minute to go. He instructed his quarterback not to pass the ball under any conditions! He said, "Whatever you do, hold on to the football and DO NOT PASS THE BALL!"

In the next few seconds of play, Tech moved the ball down the field, within ten yards of the goal line. As the quarterback began to execute the next play—with seconds ticking away—he saw an open man, he wanted another score badly, he just couldn't resist throwing the pass!

As often happens, the pass was intercepted by an opposing player. This opponent began his ninety yard run to the goal line. The entire Tech team attempted to catch him but gave up—except the quarterback who had thrown the bad pass. He continued to pursue the other player and somehow overtook him and managed to tackle him, causing a fumble that the quarterback recovered just short of their goal line! He saved a sure touchdown and avoided what would have been a heartbreaking loss. This was the last play of the game!

Georgia Tech preserved their victory—seven to six! After the game, the losing coach said to Coach Dodd, "I'll never understand how your quarterback did what he did."

Dodd explained, "Well, it's actually quite simple. Your man was running for a touchdown; my quarterback was running for his life!"

Is it just possible that important principles can be learned from a football game? How about this? Listen and obey your Coach! His name is Jesus Christ!

This is love for God: to obey his commands.
And his commands are not burdensome (1 John 5:3).

27. AN AIDS MISTAKE

At eighteen, Kay Browne (name changed) was ready for the world! This bubbly honor student was looking forward to an army career. The previous March, she had signed up at a recruiting office in Houston and took a mandatory AIDS test. One week later she learned she was HIV positive and the world was no longer a sure thing. She said, "I was really angry! My career had been snatched away from me!"

The doctors estimated she had contracted the virus recently and recommended she get in touch with anyone she had had sex with in the previous year. The list was long. "It was easy for me to number the guys I had slept with."

Brown contacted each personally. She asked each man how many partners they had had sex with before her. Each of her partners had averaged eight others with whom they had slept with the previous year. She began to calculate . . . six partners with her, and each of them had averaged ten liaisons before her. How many more had each of them had sex with others? Quickly she was up in the thousands! She said, "Each time I slept with a partner it was as though I had had sex with a thousand men!"

Brown blames only herself. "Choices I made have stolen away the choices that I might have had in the future."

The virus that causes AIDS is known as the "human immunodeficiency virus" or HIV. We do know that this virus is less infectious than others such as the virus for hepatitis B. What we also know is that certain behaviors cause HIV, AIDS, or other sexually transmitted diseases (STDs). They can be prevented by the right choices! The message from God is simple: wait until marriage! It's your choice—choose virginity and moral purity. You'll be glad you did!

It is God's will that you should . . . avoid sexual immorality; that
each of you should learn to control his own body in a way that is holy and
honorable (1 Thessalonians 4:3-5).

28. THE FREEDOMS OF ABSTINENCE

Bernice Krahn and Rita Salvadalena, volunteers at the Crisis Pregnancy Center in Everett, Washington, use the following in teaching teens to say no to sexual temptations.

1. Freedom from pregnancy and sexually transmitted disease, especially AIDS.

2. Freedom from the problems of birth control.
3. Freedom from the pressure to marry too soon.
4. Freedom from abortions.
5. Freedom from the pain of giving your baby up for adoption.
6. Freedom from exploitation by others who don't care about you.
7. Freedom from the guilt, doubt, fear, and rejection from a sexual affair.
8. Freedom to be in complete control of your own body.
9. Freedom to be able to get to know your dating partner as a person.
10. Freedom to plan a future and the kind of life you want to live.
11. Freedom to respect yourself.
12. Freedom to be unselfish, not taking pleasure at the expense of others.
13. Freedom to look forward to marriage and be chosen without past fears.
14. Freedom to enjoy being a teen with many friends—male and female.
15. Freedom from the pain of a devastating breakup.
16. Freedom to form a strong marriage bond with one person for life.
17. Freedom to remember your dating experiences with no shame![5]

These points say it all! You must make your decision to abstain and if you ask, God will give you the grace and strength to pull it off! God and abstinence are the answer.

Flee the evil desires of youth, and pursue righteousness, faith, love and peace, along with those who call on the Lord out of a pure heart
(2 Timothy 2:22).

29. A LEG TO STAND ON

Lisa Love worked hard and won a spot on the varsity cheerleading squad in her junior year in high school. About a month later, because of cancer, she had to have her leg amputated above the right knee. Over the summer, she was fitted with a prosthesis and worked hard in her physical therapy sessions, learning to maneuver and walk on it really well. She sought out her cheerleader sponsor and tried to persuade her to let her continue as a cheerleader. With some doubts still remaining, her sponsor reluctantly agreed, saying, "Okay, let's give it a try."

Lisa worked hard on her routines by herself at home before school started and then joined the other cheerleaders for the first practice. They were preparing for the first pep rally in the fall football season and all went well.

The time came for the first Thursday pep rally. The gym was packed. The squad began their routine. Lisa began her four step run and went into a somersault across the gym floor. In the middle of her somersault, her artificial leg came off and skidded across the slick floor, leaving Lisa to stumble on one leg and crash to the floor! She buried her face in her hands and cried; she thought of quitting right then and there.

Instead, she motioned for one of her cheerleading friends to retrieve her leg, and the girl helped Lisa put her prosthesis back on. All this took place in front of the bleachers packed with kids who were stunned into silence. She stood to her feet and motioned she was ready again. The squad continued their routine, and Lisa performed her part of the routine perfectly, to a rousing, enthusiastic, and long standing ovation!

Success in life is the ability to get up one more time than you have been knocked down. If you have taken a tumble, are you ready to get up again? All of heaven is ready with your standing ovation!

Since we are surrounded by such a great cloud of witnesses . . . let us run with perseverance the race marked out for us (Hebrews 12:1).

30. THE SWITCH

A young trial lawyer had developed a reputation for himself in a short time as being an accomplished and shrewd attorney. His courtroom techniques had been polished to the finest detail. His opponents feared him, and his clients loved him. He won every case. Soon he wrote in law journals, and the invitations to speak about his techniques began rolling in. He quickly developed a standard lecture for his audiences.

He traveled with a chauffeur who was also a bright young man. After several months of listening to the lawyer, he told him he could deliver the lecture himself. This intrigued the lawyer so they devised a plan. At the next lecture date, they would trade places.

So at the edge of town, they switched clothes; the lawyer was now a chauffeur and the chauffeur became the lawyer. Nobody realized the switch they had made. The chauffeur waxed eloquently, delivering the lecture without a flaw. An enthusiastic ovation followed. However, at the end the moderator opened up the floor for a question and answer time. The questioner asked about a legal precedent alluded to in the speech, a technical detail. The lawyer's heart sank . . . his chauffeur didn't know the answer. They were about to be exposed!

The chauffeur chuckled and replied, "Why, this is such a simple and well-known precedent that the common lay person could answer. To demonstrate my premise, I am going to let my chauffeur stand and give you the answer!"

How's that for quick thinking? It's just another life lesson to learn. Lots of things look easy on the surface, but what will you do with the hard questions?

Always be prepared to give an answer to everyone who asks you to give the reason for the hope that you have (1 Peter 3:15).

31. THE BULLFIGHTER'S RESOLVE

In Costa Rica the traditional Spanish/Mexican bullfight has undergone some important and specific changes that distinguish if from what a tourist would be able to see in Spain or Mexico. Costa Ricans no longer allow the toreador to kill the bull during the classic fight. A drastic plunge in the quality of Costa Rican bullfighters has resulted. No longer do any of the good bullfighters go to fight in Costa Rica. Therefore, the Costa Ricans have altered their fights to allow anyone who is eighteen or older and sober to fight the bull. It's quite a comedic spectacle!

Many of their fights begin with 100 to 150 young men dressed in bull-fighting uniforms holding their red capes. The trumpet sounds, the bull charges out of the chute snorting, pawing, mad, and looking for something to charge! Quickly, about half of the would-be toreadors scramble over the sides of the ring for safety! The bull charges and more scramble to safety! The bull charges again. Now maybe as few as five remain! From the beginning mob, just a very few are willing to face the charge. Many want the glory but few want to pay the price to learn the art when the fight begins. They have the clothes, the capes, and the wave to the crowd, but they are only pretenders!

Lots of people can talk the talk, but few walk the talk. Teddy Roosevelt said it better than I can in a famous speech he gave in France:

> The credit belongs to the man who is actually in the arena . . . who strives valiantly . . . who knows the great enthusiasms, the great devotions, and spends himself in a worthy cause; who at the best, know . . . the triumph of high achievement, and who, at worst, if he fails, at least fails while daring greatly; so that their place shall never be with those cold and timid souls who know neither victory or defeat.[6]

You need to persevere so that when you have done the will of God, you will receive what he has promised (Hebrews 10:36).

32. YOUR SINS WILL FIND YOU OUT

The following story has been making the rounds through the upper Pacific Northwest area. The truth? Maybe . . . Here it is.

On a chilly night along the Washington coast, a pathetic young man was huddled next to a fire on the beach. Lo and behold a game warden appeared out of the nearby woods, approached the fire, and asked the young man, "What are you roasting?"

He said, "A sea gull for my dinner. I haven't eaten in three days; I'm famished."

The game warden said, "What? A sea gull? You can't do that! They are protected because those birds are a crucial part of our ecosystem to keep the beaches clean. I'm going to give you a citation, and the fine is pretty hefty."

The young man pleaded, "Please, man, give me a break. I'm out of work; I'm homeless. What's one lousy sea gull compared to a starving man? Don't cite me. I have no money to pay so I will have to go to jail. Please."

The warden was touched. He weakened and said, "Okay, just this one time, but be sure it doesn't happen again." And he turned to walk away. Then he turned back and asked, "I've always wondered, what does a roasted sea gull taste like?"

The young man looked up from the sea gull carcass he was chewing on and replied, "Oh, it's a real different kind of taste—somewhere between a Snowy White Owl and an American Bald Eagle."

What more do I need to say? This is straight out of God's Word: "Be sure your sins will eventually find you out!" There is only one way a sin can be uncovered—through a God who can forgive all kinds of sin!

He who conceals his sins does not prosper, but whoever confesses and renounces them finds mercy (Proverbs 28:13).

33. LYING

The following letter was written by "Bruce" from his prison cell:

Dear Pardon/Parole Committee:

I was a compulsive liar who started young. Although my parents did all they could do to stop it, I kept lying. My problem was trying to impress people. My life never seemed glamorous enough.
The following is a short history of what happens to a liar.

I went through school lying to my friends, trying to look like a big shot. When I got out of high school, I had no friends, so I started to look for new ones. By then lying was a way of life. In order to support the lies I needed more money than I had, so I wrote checks I couldn't cover. I also impersonated a naval officer and a businessman.

My wife found out that I had totally misrepresented myself and invented friends and businesses I never had. She left me. The same thing happened with my second wife. I decided I had to change. Shortly after I married my third wife, I went to prison for passing bad checks. She divorced me while I was in prison.

This advice is for the kid who lies. Please think about the future. A lie not only hurts you, but it poisons all your relationships. I'll get out of prison someday, and when I do I vow to tell the truth. I'm twenty-six years old and by the time I'm fifty, I will have built a good reputation. A kind teacher once told me that a person's word is worth more than gold. It's too bad that it took me so long to wake up to that fact.

If you are a liar, stop while you still have friends. I hope my letter will help somebody who is where I was about fifteen years ago.
—*Bruce M., Stillwater State Prison*

Pretty sobering when we see a lifetime reduced to a tragic letter like this. If you're not a liar, don't start! If you are a liar, repent and stop!

You shall not give false testimony against your neighbor
(Exodus 20:16).

34. THE AUCTION

The very wealthy English baron, Fitzgerald, had an only son who understandably became the center of this family's attention. In his early teens, the son's mother died, bringing grief to him and his dad. Time went on, and Fitzgerald devoted himself to raising his son. Then in his late teens, the son died of cancer. In the meantime, the Fitzgerald financial holdings and investments had increased. He used much of his wealth to acquire art works of the "masters."

Eventually Fitzgerald became ill and died. Previous to his death, he had carefully prepared his will with explicit instructions on how his estate and collections were to be sold. He had directed that his considerable art collection be sold at auction at his estate. Because of the quantity and quality of the artwork, which was valued in the millions of pounds, a huge crowd assembled. Among the buyers were the curious museum curators and other collectors. The artwork was on display for two days before the auction. Among them was a painting receiving little attention; it was a poorly done portrait of Fitzgerald's son by an unknown artist.

The time came for the auction to begin. The auctioneer gaveled the crowd to silence. Before the bidding, the attorney read from the will, "The first picture to be auctioned was that of my beloved son." There were no bidders except the old groundskeeper of the estate—for sentimental reasons he bid a single pound. He bought it!

The auctioneer stopped, and the attorney continued reading from the will, "Whoever buys my son gets all of my art collection. The auction is over!"

Whoever gets the son gets it all! And whoever gets the Son of God really gets it all, including an eternal home!

God has given us eternal life, and this life is in his Son. He who has the Son has life; he who does not have the Son does not have life
(1 John 5:11-12).

35. THE BLACK DOOR

Several generations ago, during one of the most turbulent desert wars in the Middle East, a spy was captured. The general of the Persian army, a man of intelligence as well as compassion, had adopted an unusual practice in such cases. He permitted the spy to make a choice. As the moment of execution drew near, following the trial, the general always ordered the spy be brought before him for a final interview.

He concluded his exit interview with the question, "What shall it be?" He would then gesture toward the open courtyard where the firing squad was assembled for their grisly action and then point to an ominous looking black door and continued, "The firing squad or the black door?"

The condemned spies would always hesitate and finally, almost without exception, they would choose the firing squad over the black door.

It happened again, and the general stared at his boots as the sounds of the execution reach into the room. He said to his aide, "You see how it is. They always prefer the known to the unknown even though it means death."

The aide asked, "Sir, what is behind the black door?"

"Freedom," replied the general, "a walk into freedom, and I've known only a very few men brave enough to make that choice and take their freedom!"

In today's world, we face the unknown almost daily. Our choices are not always life or death, but even small choices are important and can have a lifelong impact. Life is a whole series of decisions strung together, and some are between the known and the unknown. Some choices will demand an act of faith. It's like crossing a chasm—you can't do it in steps, you must take a leap!

Without faith it is impossible to please God, because anyone who comes to him must believe that he exists (Hebrews 11:6).

36. COURAGE

Telemachus, a fourth-century Christian who lived in a remote village, tended his garden and spent much time in prayer. He was a monk. One day in prayer he heard the voice of God telling him to go to Rome, so he obeyed and walked for days. He arrived in the city at festival time. The short monk followed the crowd surging down the streets and into the Roman Colosseum.

He saw the gladiators stand before the emperor and say, "We who are about to die salute you." Then he realized these men were going to fight to the death for the entertainment of the crowd. He shouted: "In the name of Christ, stop!"

But the game began, and he pushed and shoved his way through the crowd, climbed over the wall, and dropped to the floor of the arena. When the crowd saw this small figure running to the gladiators and shouting, "In the name of Christ, stop!" they thought it was part of the show and began laughing.

When they realized it wasn't, the laughter turned to anger. As he was pleading with the gladiators to stop, one of them plunged a sword into his body. He fell to the sand. As he was dying, his last words were, "In the name of Christ, stop!"

Then a strange thing happened. The gladiators stood looking at the tiny, broken, dying figure lying there. A hush fell over the Colosseum. Way up in the upper rows, a man stood and made his way to the exit with head bowed. Others began to follow. In dead silence, everyone left the Colosseum.

The year was 391 AD. It was the last "battle to the death" between gladiators. Never again would men die for the entertainment of the crowd—all because of one tiny voice! One voice, one life who spoke the truth in God's name.

Be strong and courageous. Do not be afraid or terrified because of them, for the Lord your God goes with you (Deuteronomy 31:6).

37. THREE STUDENT DEVILS

This is the story of an old legend. Three student devils in hell were about to go with their teacher to earth for some on-the-job training as devil interns. Their internship supervisor asked them what techniques they planned to use to tempt people to sin.

The first little devil said, "I think I'll use the classical approach. I'll tell the people 'There's no God, so sin up a storm and enjoy your life.'"

The second little devil said, "I think I'll use a more subtle approach. I'll tell people, 'There's no hell, so sin up a storm and enjoy life.'"

The third little devil said, "I think I'll use a less intellectual approach. I'll tell people, 'There's no hurry, you have lots of time to get right with God, so sin up a storm and enjoy life now, and someday you can always repent of your sin.'"

Now, the question for you: Which of these little devils have you been listening to lately? Any one in particular, or are you like the young lady who said, "I can resist anything but temptation." What is it that you have been putting off in life? Temptation is only a temptation when you listen and contemplate the possibility. A temptation always presents you with the "pleasure" of sin and never the end result of sin.

A temptation is where sin begins. Without an enticement, sin has no action. The temptation may be long-lasting, it may come in an instant of time, it may happen when you are in a weakened state of mind, or it may come when you are on top of your game! It's subtle or over the top. It's a constant, but it can be overcome. You can experience a victory with the help of the Lord Jesus Christ! He was the ultimate overcomer of temptation. Ask Him to help you when temptation comes!

26

*God cannot be tempted by evil, nor does he tempt anyone; but each one is
tempted when, by his own evil desire, he is dragged away and enticed*
(James 1:13).

38. HOW TO CATCH A SPIDER MONKEY

The spider monkey is really a tiny critter native to South and Central
America. This monkey is quick as lightning and a tough one to catch in the
wild. For years hunters have tried to shoot these monkeys with tranquilizer
guns or catch them in nets but without much luck. The monkeys are faster than
the fastest net and able to dodge the tranquilizers.

Then someone made an interesting discovery. If you have a clear, narrow-
necked glass bottle, put one peanut inside the bottle and wait, you'll catch a
monkey.

How is this possible, and what happens? The monkey sees the peanut in
the bottle and reaches for the peanut. Now he can't withdraw his hand because
he grips the peanut in a death grip and will not let go! Also, the bottle is too
heavy for him to take it away, and the hunter easily snatches the monkey. The
monkey is too persistent to let go.

They have also found that you could dump a bushel of peanuts right next
to him and he still wouldn't let go of the single peanut to reach for a banquet of
peanuts. You could also place a bunch of ripe bananas alongside him and he
still refuses to let go of the peanut, losing his freedom and becoming a captive.

How many of us are like this dumb monkey? How many of us are unwilling to be flexible? How many of us are unwilling to let go of something that
we know in the long run will bring us disaster? How many of us are stubbornly
holding on to our own way no matter what?

Have you ever heard the saying, "Let go and let God"? Something much
better might be out there. Perhaps you will never lose your taste for salted
peanuts, but with God's help you can see a way out to a better way—God's way!

*One thing I do: Forgetting what is behind and straining toward what is
ahead, I press on toward the goal to win the prize for which God has called
me* (Philippians 3:13-14)

39. WHO IS YOUR LIFE MODEL?

When Nikos Kazantzakis was a young boy, the Turks invaded his village and
massacred some of the villagers. One time after such a raid, Nikos's father
took him to the spot where the massacre had taken place and made him touch
the corpses that were still hanging from the trees. He did not want the young

teen to forget, ever! He also wanted Nikos to remember how important freedom was.

Later in life Nikos wrote a book, *The Greek Passion,* a story about the people of a small village in Greece named Lycrovissi. Annually the people reenacted the Passion of Christ as a part of their Easter celebrations. The planning always took place a year in advance, and at this planning the people were chosen for the parts they would portray.

One year, a simple young man, who was a shepherd named Manolios, was selected to portray Jesus Christ. Another villager was chosen to play the part of Judas; his name was Panayotaros. The other parts were filled with other villagers. What made this unusual was that during the preceding year while they prepared for the performance, the actors began to more and more take on the characteristics of the people whose roles they were to fulfill. Manolois became more Christ-like in his attitude. Panayotaros became more and more spiteful and hateful until the villagers couldn't stand to have him near them.

During this particular year, a major conflict arose in the village. Manolios became a defender of the people in question. The conflict became more heated until it erupted on Christmas Eve. All were present in the church when Panayotaros, the man who portrayed Judas, left his seat and plunged a knife into the heart of Manolois, killing him!

Who are you becoming more like? Jesus Christ or Judas?

Blessed are you when people insult you, persecute you and falsely say all kinds of evil against you because of me. Rejoice and be glad (Matthew 5:11-12).

40. WHO AM I?

A broadcaster from Philadelphia issued a challenge: one thousand dollars would be given to anyone who could write a biblical puzzle he couldn't solve. A lady named Lucy from California won the prize for writing the following:

Adam, God made out of dust, but thought it best to make me first.
So I was made before man, to answer God's most holy plan.
A living being I became, and Adam gave to me my name.
I from his presence then withdrew, and more of Adam never knew.
I did my Maker's law obey, nor ever went from it astray.

Thousands of miles I go in fear, but seldom on earth appear.
For purpose wise which God did see, He put a living soul in me.
A soul from me God did claim and took from me the soul again!
So when from me the soul had fled, I was the same as when first made.

And without hands or feet or soul, I travel on from pole to pole.
I labor hard by day, by night, to fallen man I give great light.
Thousands of people, young and old, will by my death great light behold.

No right or wrong I can conceive, the Scripture I cannot believe.
Although my name therein is found, they are to me an empty sound.
No fear of death doth trouble me, real happiness I'll never see.
To heaven I shall never go, or to hell below.
Now when these lines you slowly read, go search your Bible with all speed.
For that my name is written there, I do honestly to you declare.
WHO AM I?

Do you give up? The answer is found in the biblical book of Jonah. You got it! It's the big fish who swallowed Jonah!

The Lord provided a great fish to swallow Jonah, and Jonah was inside the fish three days and three nights (Jonah 1:17).

41. PEARL DUST

It's an old legend . . . a wealthy king entered a room where his aides had been summoned, and he carried a gorgeous, breathtakingly beautiful pearl on a small velvet pillow. He went to his first servant and said, "What do you think this pearl is worth?"

The servant replied, "Oh, sire, many trunkfuls of gold."

"Then smash it!" the king said.

He replied, "It would be an insult to the king to destroy such a beautiful pearl."

The king moved to the second of his aides and asked, "How much is this pearl worth?"

"One cannot put a price tag on such a beautiful pearl as this."

"Then smash it!" the king said.

He went around the table, but each staff member refused to smash it. He stopped in front of the sixth man, a humble laborer who had been promoted to this position because of a favor done to the king.

"How much is this pearl worth?" he asked once again.

This servant replied, "More gold than I have ever seen in my lifetime."

"Then smash it!" the king said.

This servant took the pearl, placed it on a rock, took another rock, and instantly smashed it into worthless gray colored dust.

"The man is mad!" shouted others in the room.

The man who had smashed the pearl held up his hand for silence and said,

"Which is of greater value? A costly pearl or obedience to the king's command?"

Could it be that any disobedience to our King of all kings' commands are the result of giving things higher value than obedience to His Word?

If you are willing and obedient, you will eat the best from the land . . . but if you resist and rebel, you will be devoured (Isaiah 1:19-20).

42. HISTORY AS REWRITTEN BY HIGHSCHOOLERS

The following are some answers turned in by students to their history teachers on their tests:

- David was a Hebrew king skilled at playing the liar. Solomon, his son, had 500 wives and 500 more porcupines.
- Without the Greeks we wouldn't have any history. Socrates died from an overdose of wedlock. The Greeks invented the Olympic Games where they hurled biscuits and threw the java.
- The Romans were called Romans because they never stayed in one place and roamed everywhere. Nero was a cruel tyrant who tortured his subjects by planning the fiddle to them.
- Then came the Middle Ages when King Alfred conquered the dames and the Magna Carta proved that no free man should be hanged twice for the same crime.
- The Renaissance was the time when Martin Luther was nailed to the church door. He then died a terrible death by being excommunicated by a papal bull.
- Gutenberg invented the Bible, and Sir Walter Raleigh invented pipe tobacco. The government of England was a limited mockery. Henry VIII found walking difficult because he had abbess on his knees.
- A great writer was John Milton. He wrote Paradise Lost. Then his wife died, and he wrote Paradise Regained.

So, what more can I say? It's back to the books for more study. And, probably, the only thing we learn about history is that we don't learn from history!

There is a time for everything, and a season for every activity under heaven . . . a time to weep and a time to laugh (Ecclesiastes 3:1, 4).

43. HIT A HOME RUN FOR JOHNNY

When he was thirteen, Johnny Sylvester got kicked in the head by a horse. The wound on his forehead became badly infected and he was hospitalized. The doctors told his parents the sad news that there was no hope—Johnny would soon die!

Johnny, however, had one last wish that he told his parents and the medical staff in the hospital, "I wish I could see Babe Ruth wallop a homer before I die."

So a telegram was sent to the great slugger and the New York Yankees. Babe sent back a telegram in which he promised to hit a homer just for Johnny in the next game and that Johnny should be listening on the radio to hear it happen.

Almost overnight, Johnny Sylvester became one of the most famous teens in baseball history. The newspapers of the day picked up this story, and the radio news services featured this story. Did Babe Ruth hit a homer for Johnny in the next game?

No! He actually hit three homers in that particular game! And to top it all off, the great slugger, a few days later, made a personal visit to Johnny in the hospital. It was quite a story and was broadcast everywhere!

Well, let me tell you the rest of the story. Were the doctors right? Yes, Johnny did die. It happened in January 1990. Johnny was seventy-four years old when he died!

How long do you plan on living? You are probably not planning on dying very soon. But there's a problem. None of us knows when we will die; it happens to young and old. The best we can do is to be ready to die at any time and do the necessary preparations ahead of our death—most importantly making peace with God!

If we live, we live for the Lord; and if we die, we die for the Lord. So, whether we live or die, we belong to the Lord (Romans 14:8).

44. LIFE LESSONS FROM THE AFRICAN PLAINS

God, the Creator, has designed thousands of ways for the animal kingdom to come into existence, but the birth of a baby giraffe is likely the most dramatic and painful—for the newborn giraffe.

The mother giraffe doesn't lie down for the birthing process. She stands up to bring her calf into the world, and her hind quarters are nearly ten feet off the ground. The newborn is introduced into the world with much trauma—it falls ten feet to the hard ground!

The mother lowers her head long enough to take a quick look. Then she positions herself over her calf and does the most unreasonable thing. She swings her long leg outward and kicks her baby so hard it's sent sprawling head over hooves. When it doesn't get up, the violent process is repeated over and over. The struggle to rise is momentous. As the baby grows tired, the mother kicks it again to stimulate more effort. She does that to make sure the calf gets to its feet.

Finally, the wobbly calf stands for the first time on quivering legs. Then momma giraffe does a more unreasonable thing: she kicks it off its feet again! Why? She wants her baby to remember how it got up! In the wild, baby giraffes must be able to get up quickly in order to be able to run and stay with the herd where there is safety. Lions, hyenas, leopards, cheetahs, and wild dogs all enjoy baby giraffes for lunch; and they'd have their lunch if the momma didn't teach her calf how to get on with life. It's get up or die!

Think about this . . . any life lessons for you here? Sure, life is not easy, it's full of hard knocks. Learn how to survive or you may not be eaten, but you will be tested! When you have been knocked down, do you stay down or struggle to your feet to try again?

We have this treasure in jars of clay to show that this all-surpassing power is from God and not from us (2 Corinthians 4:7).

45. DO YOU HAVE A JOB THAT STINKS?

Do you think your part-time job really stinks? How about this. Monroe County in Pennsylvania has created a new position that pays a little bit above minimum wage and promises some limited travel in the most beautiful and scenic parts of mountainous Pennsylvania. The roads you will travel wind through the picturesque Pocono Mountains.

Are you interested? No high school diploma or college degree is needed. You will get to drive a county truck and your title will be "Roadway Sanitation Technician." If the job is not already filled, you can apply at the Monroe County offices. You will climb into a truck and drive off to spend your working days traveling from road to road in gorgeous scenery. So what will you specifically be doing? Picking up road kill!

The Pennsylvania Department of Transportation (PDOT) is responsible for the removal of dead animals along their routes on a weekly round through Monroe County. However, they couldn't keep up with the need in this heavily forested area. Therefore the county was required to create a new position and hire somebody to fill it! One bit of advice . . . please bring your own personal set of nose plugs!

All right, so it's honest hard work for an honest paycheck. Think about doing this in the summer time—whew! Is this the kind of a job you'd like to do? A job like this may be the most effective motivator to staying in school to complete your high school diploma, go on to a trade school or college to further your education, and make yourself more valuable in the job market. Since a good portion of your life will be spent working, are you giving some serious thought to this subject? Meaningful work can and should be fulfilling. God is also interested in your future in regards to work!

Whatever you do, work at it with all your heart, as working for the Lord, not for men (Colossians 3:23).

46. GOD IS THE GREATEST!

What do you think about God? Read how Dr. Lockridge describes God:

God is greater than all the superlative statements of supremacy ever shared. No far-reaching telescope can bring into focus the shoreline of His unlimited supply. No deep-digging dredge can discover the depth of His determination to deliver you. You can trust Him! He doesn't need me, He doesn't need you. He stands alone on the solitary pinnacle of His omnipotence. He is enduringly strong, He is eternally steadfast, He is impartial . . . impartially merciful. He is unparalleled and unprecedented. He is unique and inescapable. He is the cornerstone of all civilization. He is the central truth of all truthology.

He can meet all your needs and He can do it simultaneously. He gives you hope when you're hopeless, help when you're helpless, peace when you're in pain, strength when you struggle, rest when you're restless, and courage when you cry! He sees and sympathizes. He guards and He guides. He heals the sick, cleanses the leper, sets the captives free, and forgives sinners! I'm telling you, you can trust Him!

He is the key to knowledge, the wellspring of wisdom, the doorway of deliverance, and He's the pathway to peace! He's the Master of masters, the Captain of all conquerors, the Head of the heroes and the Leader of all legislators!

You can't outlive Him; you can't live without Him! Pilate couldn't stop Him, Herod couldn't kill him, death couldn't handle Him, and the grave couldn't hold Him! He is alive forevermore and you can trust Him!

He will be called Wonderful Counselor, Mighty God, Everlasting Father, Prince of Peace (Isaiah 9:6).

47. DO YOU EVER FEEL USELESS?

The next time you feel like God can't use you, just remember the following:

- Noah was a drunk! Abraham was too old. Isaac was a daydreamer.
- Jacob was a liar, Leah was ugly, and Joseph was abused.
- Moses stuttered and couldn't talk in public.
- Gideon was afraid and went to hide.
- Sampson had long hair and was a womanizer.
- Rahab was the town prostitute.
- Jeremiah and Timothy were considered too young to be useful in the ministry.
- David had an affair with Bathsheba and murdered her husband.
- Elijah was depressed and suicidal.
- Isaiah preached the Word of God while naked.
- Jonah ran away from God and ended up in the belly of a great fish.
- Naomi was a widow. Job went bankrupt and lost everything.
- John the Baptist ate bugs and honey, and dressed in wild animal skins.
- Peter denied Jesus Christ three times.
- The disciples fell asleep while they were praying.
- Martha worried about everything big and small.
- Mary Magdalene was once demon possessed.
- The Samaritan woman at the well was divorced many times.
- Zaccheus was too small so he climbed a tree to see what was happening.
- Paul was too religious. Timothy had a stomach ulcer.
- And Lazarus was dead.

No more excuses now! God's waiting to use you to your full potential because God believes in you!

Our Redeemer—the Lord Almighty is his name—is the Holy One
(Isaiah 47:4).

48. ARE WE TOO UPTIGHT?

With what is currently happening—random shootings, shootings in schools, and other acts of violence against people—maybe we are more uptight than we think.

The following story happened in Leake County, Mississippi, on a hot summer afternoon. After a lady bought her groceries, she placed them in the backseat of her car. Then remembering some things she needed from a large store, she locked her car and went to finish her shopping.

Later, she came back to her car, started the engine, and began her drive home. As she drove down the highway, to her horror, she heard three large pops and then felt something hit her on the back of her head! Holding one hand over the wound, she managed to drive herself to the emergency room of the local hospital.

After she squealed to a stop and jumped out, she screamed for help: "I've been shot! I've been shot!"

She received immediate attention.

In the examination room, the doctor said, "Please move your hand so I can see your wound."

The woman answered, "I can't! My brains will fall out!"

Finally, the doctor convinced her to let him examine the wound. As she slowly removed her hand from the back of her head, the doctor discovered that, yes, she had been hit in the back of her head but it was by canned biscuit dough and not the bullet she thought!

After much laughter and relief, the doctor noted he had seen a lot of wounds in his career, but never one inflicted by biscuit dough! Aside from acute embarrassment, the lady was sent home unharmed.

The moral of this story? Be careful but don't get uptight!

God has called us to live in peace (1 Corinthians 7:15).

49. ALASKA AIRLINES FLIGHT 261

An Alaska Airlines pilot, involved in the investigation of the horrific crash of Flight 261, has listened to the cockpit voice recorder from the downed plane. He reported that for the last nine minutes of the flight, the wife of the pastor from Monroe, Washington, can be heard sharing the gospel with the passengers over the plane's intercom system. Just before the final dive into the Pacific Ocean, she can be heard leading the sinner's prayer for salvation.

The pilot and investigators reported that the flight data recorder from the plane indicated that there is no good explanation for how the plane was able to stay in the air for those final nine minutes. But it did stay in the air until the pastor's wife had a chance to share the gospel with very attentive passengers and presumably led people to a last-minute salvation in Jesus Christ!

In the middle of this tragedy, nearly ninety people had an extraordinary opportunity to get right with their Maker just prior to meeting Him!

How about you? Where would you go if you were to die today? Knowing your sins are forgiven and you are ready for heaven is as simple as following these steps:

First, admit you have sinned. The Bible says, "For all have sinned and fall short of the glory of God" (Romans 3:23).

Second, believe in Jesus Christ. "For God so loved the world that he gave his one and only Son, that whoever believes in him shall not perish but have eternal life" (John 3:16).

Third, confess and turn away from your sin. "If we confess our sins, he is faithful and just and will forgive us our sins and purify us from all unrighteousness" (1 John 1:9).

The kingdom of God is near. Repent and believe the good news! (Mark 1:15).

50. THE FIRST VALENTINE

The story of Valentine's Day begins in the third century with an oppressive Roman Emperor, Claudius II, and the Christian martyr Valentinus. Claudius had ordered all Romans to worship twelve gods, and he made it a crime—punishable by death—for anyone who refused. Valentinus was devoted to Christ and refused to worship false gods, so he was imprisoned and sentenced to die.

During the last weeks of Valentinus' life, the jailer knew he was an educated man and asked if he could bring his daughter, Julia, for tutoring. She had been blind since birth but had a quick mind. So Valentinus read her stories of Rome's history and told her about God. For the first time, Julia began to see the world through Valentinus' eyes.

"Valentinus, does God hear our prayers?" Julia asked one day.

"Yes, my child, He hears each one," Valentinus replied.

"Do you know what I pray for every morning and night? I pray that I might be able to see. I want so much to see everything you've told me about."

"God does what is best for us if we believe in Him," he replied.

"Oh, Valentinus, I do believe," Julia said, "I do!" She grasped his hand. They sat quietly, she kneeling, he sitting, each praying. Suddenly there was a brilliant light in the prison cell! Radiant, Julia screamed, "Valentinus, I can see! I can see!"

On the eve of his death on the next day, Valentinus wrote a last note to Julia, urging her to continue her learning and encouraging her to worship God the rest of her life. He signed it: "from your Valentine."

His death sentence was carried out the next day, February 14, 270 AD.

And now these three remain: faith, hope and love. But the greatest of these is love (1 Corinthians 13:13).

51. FINISH THE RACE

It was Monday night, August 3rd, at the 1992 Olympics in Barcelona, Spain. At the track and field stadium, the gun sounded for the 400 meter semi-finals.

About 100 meters into the race, Great Britain's Derek Redmond crumpled to the track with a torn right hamstring. Medical attendants rushed to assist him, but he waved them all aside. Struggling to his feet, he stumbled and hopped in a desperate effort to finish this race. At times he was on all fours crawling toward the finish line.

Four years earlier he had qualified for the 1988 Olympics in Seoul, Korea, but had to pull out of the race because of an Achilles tendon problem. Afterward, Redmond had undergone five surgeries but he had qualified again. Now he faced another possible career-ending injury!

He said to himself, "I'm not quitting! I'm going to finish this race!" Watching his slow progress was agony for his fans. Up in the stands, a huge guy with a Nike cap with the words "Just Do It!" came barreling out of the stands, hurled aside a security guard, jumped the barrier, and ran to Derek's side and embraced him. He was Jim Redmond, Derek's father! Jim was a sports dad who had changed his life for the sake of his athlete son.

With Jim's arm around his son's waist, and Derek's arm around his dad's thick shoulders, they continued down the track. The crowd was stunned and on its feet, cheering, weeping! Back home his pregnant sister goes into false labor. Mom is weeping in the stands. Derek and his dad work their way around the track until finally, painfully, they cross the finish line together.

When I watched this on TV, my first thought was what determination, what a wonderful father. Then my thoughts turned toward God, our heavenly Father, who will help all of us who need help cross the finish line.

Forgetting what is behind and straining toward what is ahead, I press on toward the goal to win the prize for which God has called me
(Philippians 3:13-14).

52. USING YOUR TALENTS

All of Europe experienced the devastation of Adolph Hitler. During this time, Heinz was an eleven-year-old Jewish boy who lived in the Bavarian town of Furth in the 1930s. When Hitler's brown shirts and SS troopers came to occupy the village, it changed everything. Heinz's dad lost his job as a school teacher. The streets of Furth became part of the battlegrounds. The people were terrorized by the Hitler Youth who were always looking to make trouble. Always on the alert, the young Heinz managed to avoid these thugs.

One day, Heinz had a face-to-face with one of these bullies. It seemed inevitable that he would be given a brutal beating as had happened to his friends. But on this day, Heinz walked away without so much as a single punch being thrown. How? He used his persuasive skills, his logical thinking, and his language skills to convince his attacker that a fight was not necessary. This would not be the last time this young Jewish boy would be a peacemaker in Hitler-occupied Europe.

Soon after, his family managed to escape to America and safety. It was here that young Heinz would make his influence felt. In his education, he became known for his skills as a peacemaker. After his schooling, these skills were to be applied on a worldwide basis. This young boy grew up to be honored in America as well as the rest of the world. Today we know him as Henry Kissinger, former Secretary of State!

What talents do you have that could change this world for the better? At least all of us could begin by planting seeds of peace so that eventually we would harvest goodness!

Blessed are the peacemakers, for they will be called sons of God
(Matthew 5:9).

53. HE PLAYS BALL WITH NO LEGS!

People all over America as well as some people worldwide have been touched by the story of twelve-year-old Kacey McCallister. Despite losing both legs at the hip when he was run over by a truck six years ago, he plays basketball and baseball by scooting along in the gym or outdoors on the baseball field by propelling himself with his two perfectly good hands and arms.

After hearing about his story, a Little League team in North Carolina dedicated their entire season to him, and a Colorado teacher invited him to give a never-give-up pep talk to the highschoolers in his school.

The calls, emails, and letters to his house have come from Florida, Georgia, North Carolina, Ohio, California, and overseas. And these are just a few of the places from which Kacey has been contacted.

All of this attention has come after local newspapers and then nationwide newspapers and other news outlets published an Associated Press story along with photos. As a response to all this attention, Kacey smiled and said, "It's cool. It's a lot of inspiration!"[7]

Where are you getting your life inspiration from? When I read this story, I really have nothing more to complain about.

I can do everything through him who gives me strength (Philippians 4:13).

54. DO YOU EVER PRAY?

Do you ever pray? I don't mean when you are in a difficult situation and you think prayer is the only thing you can do—you know, prayer for emergencies. Do you pray on a regular basis or even on a daily basis? Prayer is absolutely for teens too! What happens when you pray? Consider the following:

THROUGH prayer there is no problem that can't be solved, no sickness that can't be healed, no burden that can't be lifted!

THROUGH prayer there is no storm that can't be weathered, no devastation that can't be relieved, and no sorrow that can't be erased!

THROUGH prayer there is no poverty cycle that can't be broken, no sinner that can't be saved, and no fallen persons that can't be lifted!

THROUGH prayer there is no hurt that can't be removed, no broken relationship that can't be mended, and no differences that can't be mended!

THROUGH prayer there is no hindrance that can't be removed, no limitation that can't be assaulted, and no mourning or sadness that can't be comforted!

THROUGH prayer there are no ashes that can't become beautiful, no thirst that can't be quenched, and no hunger that can't be filled!

THROUGH prayer there is no desert that can't blossom, no church that can't be revived, no community that can't be Christianized, and no nation that can't be changed!

Prayer—try it, you might like it! You might discover that it is the answer to all of your life's needs. Pray in the powerful name of Jesus Christ.

Do not be anxious about anything, but in everything, by prayer . . . with thanksgiving, present your requests to God (Philippians 4:6).

55. GOD AND A SPIDER

During World War II, a nineteen-year-old United States Marine was separated from his unit on a remote Pacific Ocean island. The fighting had been intense, and in the smoke, confusion, and the crossfire, he had lost touch with his unit comrades. He was now alone in the jungle and could hear enemy soldiers coming in his direction.

Scrambling for cover, he found his way up a high ridge to several small caves in the rock. Quickly he crawled inside one of the caves. Although safe for the moment, he realized that once the enemy soldiers looking for him swept up the ridge, they would quickly search all the caves and he would be killed.

As he waited, he prayed: "Lord, if it be Your will, please protect me. Whatever Your will is, though, I love You and trust You. Amen."

After praying, he lay quietly listening to the enemy coming closer. He thought, *Well, I guess the Lord isn't going to help me out of this one.* Then he saw a large jungle spider begin to build a web over the front of his cave. As he watched the spider, he also heard the enemy searching for him; all the while the spider layered strand after strand of web across the opening of the cave.

Hah, he thought. *What I need is a stone wall and what He has sent me is a spider building a web. God sure does have a sense of humor.* As the enemy approached, he watched from the darkness of his shallow cave as they searched cave after cave. When they came to his, he got ready do make his last stand. Then to his amazement, after glancing in the direction of his cave, they moved on! Suddenly he realized that with the spider web over the entrance, his cave looked as if no one had entered for a long time!

"Lord, forgive me," prayed the young man. "I had forgotten that in You a spider's web is stronger than a rock wall!"

With man this is impossible, but not with God;
all things are possible with God (Mark 10:26-28).

56. MY TOP TEN PREDICTIONS FOR YOU

The world you live in can sometimes be scary! Almost daily you can hear reports of terrorism, bombings, random shootings, disasters, divorces, family breakups, school shootings, global change, and much more. How are you to live? Is there any hope, are there any answers? In spite of all of this, I give you my top ten predictions for you today and tomorrow.

1. The Bible will still have all of life's answers for you.
2. Prayer still works and will always work no matter what your need.
3. The Holy Spirit of God is still at work in your world.
4. God will still live in the praises of young people.
5. There will still be God-anointed youth leaders and teachers.
6. Young people will still be singing praises to a wonderful God.
7. God will still be pouring out His blessings on the young.
8. There is always room at the cross for you.
9. Jesus will still love you no matter what you do or where you go.
10. Jesus still has wonderful life plans for you no matter how much you have messed up!

God whispers into your soul and spirit, and still speaks to your mind. Sometimes, when you don't think you have time to listen, He has a brick to throw at you. It's your response to what is happening to you that is important, not what happens to you. Always remember how bad it seems, God is still alive and well!

Jesus Christ is the same yesterday and today and forever (Hebrews 13:8).

57. DARK TRAIN . . . A KISS AND A SLAP

A young soldier and his commanding officer had to ride a train from their base to a conference in Europe. They found their seats and discovered they were in a compartment with a beautiful young woman and her grandmother.

Within the first hour everyone realized that the young woman and the young soldier were attracted to each other. Then the train entered a long dark tunnel; while in the tunnel, everyone heard a loud kissing sound followed by a crisp, sharp slap!

On the other side of the tunnel, the officer thought, *I'm glad my soldier was creative enough to get a kiss, but I wish she hadn't missed him and slapped me!*

The grandmother thought, *Hmmph! The nerve of that young man to kiss my granddaughter! Well at least he got what he deserved when she slapped him!*

The granddaughter thought, *That was nice of him to kiss me, but I wish my grandmother hadn't slapped him for giving me a kiss!*

The young soldier is the only one who really knew what happened. He thought, *Wow! I got to kiss a beautiful girl and slap real hard my unreasonable, demanding, unpopular commanding officer all at once!*

There is more than one life lesson here. For example, if you're creative and quick thinking enough, you can always make the most of a difficult situation. We always travel without knowing what lies ahead. It may be a dark tunnel of testings, of trials, of misunderstanding, of helplessness, but know there is always an answer. Perhaps it's your opportunity of a lifetime to take action!

Be wise, my son, and bring joy to my heart (Proverbs 27:11).

58. ARE EMOTIONS ENOUGH?

The concept, "If it feels good, just do it" seems to be everywhere in our twenty-first century world. Teens are being told to allow their impulses to be the main factor in making life choices. This concept brings to mind a story told by Dr. James Dobson of *Focus on the Family* fame about his mother's high school football team.

This high school had one of the worst football teams in the history of Oklahoma. They hadn't won a game in years. It became almost a scandal to the town. Finally, a wealthy oil producer in the town asked to speak to the team in the locker room following another dismal defeat. He offered to buy every player and coach a brand new Ford of their choice—if they would simply defeat their bitter rivals in the next Friday's game.

The team and coaches went crazy! For seven days they thought about nothing but football and new Fords. They were so excited they couldn't sleep at nights. Talk about motivation! Just one win and receive a new Ford! It couldn't get any better.

Finally, the big night arrived and the team was frantic with anticipation. They assembled around their coaches on the sideline. They slapped high fives. They shouted encouragement to each other. Then they ran on the field and were smashed once more: thirty-eight to nothing![8]

No amount of excitement could compensate for the players' lack of discipline, conditioning, practice, study, coaching, running drills, experience, and character. Such is the nature of emotion. It has a definite place in your life, but it is not a substitute for intelligence, character, preparation, or self-control.

Choose my instruction instead of silver, knowledge rather than choice gold,
for wisdom is more precious than rubies, and nothing you desire can compare
with her (Proverbs 8:10-11).

59. QUICK THINKING

It happened on Saturday, January 17, 1990. Carrie Heiman and a bunch of friends were hiking on a snow-covered hillside in the Angeles National Forest when an avalanche swept them off their feet. Frantically they grabbed for trees, branches, even each other—anything that could keep them from being buried in the cascading wall of snow. Carrie was quickly buried in what promised to be an icy grave.

The survivors did a quick count and were one short: Carrie was nowhere in sight! They began digging, shouting for her to answer while others ran for help. Soon eighty students and fifteen chaperones were racing against time to find her. The area's professional ski patrol rescue team arrived about twenty minutes later and began leading a thorough search. Nearly ninety minutes later, after searching with long poles, one step at a time, a ski patrol near the top shouted, "We found her! She's conscious!" She was dug out and rushed to a nearby hospital. She was treated for frostbite on her toes and amazingly was quickly released from the hospital in great shape.

How had she survived? She later explained how she had avoided suffocation. She described being tumbled in the snow while she kept her hands on her face. Before the snow piled its massive weight tightly on her, she had quickly pushed her hands in front of her face as far as she could. This created a pocket of air to breathe in until she was found and rescued. This was the difference between life and death!

Would you have been prepared to handle this disaster as Carrie did? Perhaps it's time to dig deeper into God's Word because it's as vital to your relationship to Jesus Christ as oxygen is to your lungs.

I have hidden your word in my heart that I might not sin against you
(Psalm 119:11).

60. DONT BOTHER ME; EVERYTHING'S OKAY

If you are like most teens, you believe everybody lives somewhere forever. According to surveys, many American teens believe in heaven, and a smaller group believes in hell. In other parts of the world, there's a strong belief that the soul never dies but comes back to live all over again, as someone or something.

There are lots of differences in religions, but all seem to have one thing in common. How you live your life here determines what will happen after death. Some believe all good people go to heaven; others believe good people come back as better people or the possibility of becoming a better person.

Think about it. If God asked you, "Why should I let you into My heaven?" how would you answer that? If you're like a whole lot of kids, you'd say, "I always tried to be good." Or it might go like this, "I never did anything really bad."

Okay. Talk to Muslims, Hindus, or even Christians and you get much the same answer: most believe that good people go to heaven or come back. The moral of this situation is simply, behave yourself here and now and you don't need to worry about what comes next! Am I right?

Gandhi of India said, "In the realm of the political and social and economic, we can be sufficiently certain to convert; but in the realm of religion there is not sufficient certainty to convert anybody, and therefore, there can be no conversions in religions."

If Gandhi wasn't certain about his religion, can you be certain about yours? I am so glad that Jesus gave us certainty about how we can get to heaven, and it doesn't depend on my good deeds. He said, "I am the way and the truth and the life. No one comes to the Father except through me" (John 14:6). That's a certainty that will really take you to heaven!

You may ask me for anything in my name, and I will do it (John 14:14).

61. ME FIRST

License plates on cars can say some of the most profound things. I've seen a couple that have made me stop and think. How about this one—"ME FIRST," or another one proudly proclaimed, "IM NUMBER ONE." It seems to me that we are caught up in a "me first" kind of world. We are all searching for more personal gratification. We are in a world that is more occupied with "me" or "I" as being the most important person or thing in the whole world.

Did you hear about the seventeen-year-old guy who was stabbed to death by two thugs on a New York City subway car? What is even more tragic is that eleven—that's right, eleven—people watched it happen and nobody helped, not even at the next stop as he lay in a pool of blood. Or take this incident that happened in Orange County, California, where a woman was raped and brutally beaten. She shrieked and screamed for her life for thirty minutes until she was so hoarse she couldn't scream any more. Thirty-eight neighbors in that apartment complex heard her screams, but no one bothered to help or even call the police for help! She died the next day. Talk about being self-centered!

Granted, these two stories may be extreme ones, but this sickness is everywhere. Is there a cure? How can this attitude be turned around? The answer is simple: put others first!

The life and call of Jesus Christ is to follow Him as our example. He didn't only talk about this, He washed the dirty feet of His followers! He said He came to serve. He came so He could die for others so they could have eternal life. He always put others first. Now it's your turn!

Now that I, your Lord and Teacher, have washed your feet, you also should wash one another's feet (John 13:14).

62. COACH CORYELL TELLS HIS SECRET

D on Coryell diagrammed the plays that helped him become the only coach in football to win 100 games on both the college and professional levels. But sixty years ago, standing at a blackboard in his Seattle junior high school, Coryell couldn't diagram a sentence if his life depended on it.

In an emotional speech in South Bend during his induction into the College Football Hall of Fame, Coryell revealed that he suffers from dyslexia, a learning disorder that made him stutter and have difficulty reading and spelling as a junior high student. At this induction Coryell was seventy-four years old and credited sports and football with allowing him to live a very productive life.

"I was always this dumb kid who talked funny," said Coryell, who fine-tuned his "Air Coryell" passing attack as the head coach of San Diego State from 1961 to 1972, where he went on to win 104 games while losing only 19. In three of the seasons the team went undefeated. Then he was hired by a professional team to bring his brand of football to the National Football League.

"It was embarrassing for me to talk about an imperfection," Coryell said of his Hall of Fame speech to a crowd that included fellow inductees Bo Jackson and Tom Osborne. "I was scared. But we were supposed to talk about how the sport has affected our lives, and football was the one thing that gave me the self-esteem to pick up my grades, go to college, and become a coach. Maybe someone with a disability will look at me and say 'If that guy did it, why can't I?'"

Don't let anyone look down on you because you are young, but set an example
for the believers in speech, in life, in love, in faith and in purity
(1 Timothy 4:12).

63. QUIET TIME

Are you one of those teens who are connected 24/7? We are living in an amazing time! No generation in world history has had the communication possibilities we enjoy today. The possibilities are almost endless. Who else has had Facebook, iPods, MP3 players, iPads, Sony PSPs, tweeting, texting, online IMs, smart phones, satellite TV, blogging, and emails all at the same time! Yes, it's possible to stay connected 24/7.

Absolutely we are a generation of multitaskers. Perhaps this might sound a bit like an old fogey talking, but multitasking isn't always a good thing! Have your parents ever said, "Quit talking on the phone, turn off the TV, and quit tweeting while you are doing your homework!"?

Multitasking can also be very deadly. Did you hear the news story about six teenagers who were killed because the driver of their van was texting, crossed the median, and crashed head-on with an eighteen wheeler? Driving is never a good time to text or tweet.

Living with constant multitasking, connectivity, and media overload can also put a barrier between us and our Creator. When home do you ever turn off the TV? Do you ever go anywhere without your cell phone or iPod? Are you afraid of silence?

When looking at the life of Jesus Christ, have you noticed how often He went away and spent time in solitude with His heavenly Father? Solitude and silence take time and space. How about setting aside some time each day for quiet time with yourself and with your Lord, Jesus Christ? Today is not too soon to start!

Be still, and know that I am God (Psalm 46:10).

64. DO YOU WANT TO BE A MISSIONARY?

I listened as she spoke, passionately, "I'm in high school and I'm going to college. When I graduate I want to be a missionary, but how do I get started?"

A great question! Thank you for being honest and open. Your desire is commendable. The really cool thing is that you can be a missionary right now! You don't have to wait until you graduate.

Are you aware that the middle school and high school campus is one of the greatest mission fields in America and in other parts of the world? Every day

45

on your campus you have a unique challenge to make an impact on lots of people. You can do what no adult can do—you have the freedom to share Jesus Christ at your school. How about starting today by making a decision to become your school's campus missionary? There are lots of things you can do but I suggest the following:

You can PRAY! Pray for fellow Christians. Pray for at least five people who do not know Jesus Christ as their Savior . . . yet.

You can LIVE! Live your lifestyle in such a way so that others will be able to see a real Christian on good days as well as bad days. Live it before you talk it.

You can SHARE! Tell your own personal story of how Jesus changed your life and how He can change their lives too.

You can SERVE! It's at this point where you help others to see that your living for Christ is more than words or talk. Here is Christianity lived out in serving others.

You can GIVE! Here is an opportunity to help other missionaries in other parts of the world. Give through your local church. Give in your neighborhood. Give to others in your school.

Therefore, since we are receiving a kingdom that cannot be shaken, let us be thankful, and so worship God acceptably with reverence and awe
(Hebrews 12:28).

65. OVERCOMING LONG ODDS

He was born in Eritrea—a small, poor country of about half a million people in East Africa, just north of Ethiopia and east of Sudan on the Red Sea. He and his family immigrated to San Diego in 1987. About two years ago, Meb Keflezighi could not walk; even moving in his bed required help. His problem came as a result of fracturing a hip on November 3, 2007, at the Olympic Marathon Trials in New York. He finished eighth in spite of breaking his hip, which was a huge disappointment because he had won the silver medal at the 2004 Olympics. He needed to qualify in the top three for the 2008 games. He didn't know he'd fractured his right hip until weeks later.

Fast forward to November 1, 2009, to the New York City Marathon—the world's largest—and this time also included the United States Marathon Championship. Keflezighi, now thirty-four years old, was sort of an afterthought. He was viewed as being too old for a marathon as well as not being able because of his fractured hip.

However, 26.2 miles later, he proved all the pundits wrong and crossed the finish line in a personal best time of 2 hours, 9 minutes, 15 seconds to win and defeat the four-time Boston Marathon champion, Robert Cheruiyot, and became the first American to win this event since 1982![9]

After the race in an interview, Keflezighi said, "Nobody ran their best time but me." He had spent the last two miles of the race talking to God. "It just showed the power of God was huge on my success." He always talks about faith and work when talking about his running. "You live and learn, in God's time. Whatever it takes, you have to work hard!"

Show me your faith without deeds, and I will show you
my faith by what I do (James 2:18).

66. ENCOURAGEMENT—THE GIFT FOR EVERYONE

The song "Home on the Range" has been called the anthem of the West. Life's realities or words are not always quite as encouraging as the lyrics tell us, and not all days are cloudless. We live in a world where too many people only seem to be interested in the negative in all situations. Read some discouraging words:

- After famous dancer and choreographer, Fred Astaire, had his first screen test, a 1933 memo from the testing director at MGM read: "Can't act. Slightly bald. Can dance a little." Astaire framed that memo and hung it over his fireplace. Oh yes, this director is nameless.
- An "expert" wrote about the legendary football coach, Vince Lombardi, "He possesses minimal football knowledge. Lacks motivation."
- Louisa May Alcott, author of the famous *Little Women* books was advised by her family to give up writing and find real work as a servant or seamstress.
- Beethoven played the violin awkwardly and preferred playing his own compositions instead of improving his technique. His violin teacher called him "hopeless as a composer."
- Walt Disney was fired by a newspaper because "he lacked ideas." He went bankrupt several times before building Disneyland.

The people just named persevered in the face of discouragement. On the other side of the coin, think of the people who have accomplished much in life with and because of words of encouragement! Encouragement is a positive part of our human existence. So I ask you, are you a discourager or an encourager?

For you know that we dealt with each of you . . . encouraging, comforting
and urging you to live lives worthy of God (1 Thessalonians 2:11-12).

67. TO SAVE A LIFE

Teen movies have been around along time. These really began with the rantings and rebellion of James Dean in *Rebel Without a Cause* in 1955. This was later followed by the comedic antics of Zak Efron in *Seventeen Again* in 2009. These two flicks illustrate and reflect each generation's style and show the teen rebellion of the day.

In the 50s and 60s, teen rebellion was shown by smoking cigarettes and disobeying parents. In the 60s through 80s, alcohol, drug abuse, and sex were added to these teen vices. In the 90s and into the 2000s, debauchery reached new lows. The teen movie today has become a sordid mix of booze, drugs, losing one's virginity, and same sex encounters, while the level of intensity has grown. However, a common desire seems to remain in all of these movies—acceptance by peers and acceptance in the right clique.

Actor Sean Afable in his 2010 movie *To Save a Life* has some attributes of a teen movie but may be the first Hollywood film that deals with and confronts such teen issues as drinking, drug use, premarital sex, abortion, self-injury, and parental infidelity for what they are—sin!

This production is not preachy but shares an approach that promises a much better life without giving in to these entanglements. Sean grew up in a Christian home and accepted Jesus as his personal Savior at a young age.

Sean says, "I am defined by Jesus and what He has done for me on the cross." This film is a positive presentation and encouragement to the fact that real answers to a real world of fatal choices exist. The answer is in a relationship with Jesus Christ!

Trust in the Lord with all your heart and lean not on your own understanding; in all your ways acknowledge him, and he will make your paths straight (Proverbs 3:5-6).

68. HAVE YOU BEEN TO A FUNERAL LATELY?

Have you been to a funeral lately? I almost forgot, most teens don't make a habit of attending funerals. Elderly folks attend lots of funerals because all of their friends are dying. However, you might learn something at a contemporary funeral.

A healthy trend is happening in modern funerals. Many friends or family members will stand at a podium and one by one tell stories about their late friend. If you listen carefully, a theme may emerge. For example, at one funeral I attended, the outstanding trait was the willingness of their friend to serve and help others. He was always ready to lend a helping hand no matter what the problem was. One of these friends went into detail about how everywhere he went, he kept a toolbox in the trunk of his car "just in case somebody needed something fixed."

You can learn a whole lot about people after their life has been completed. Have you ever given thought to what people might say about you after you are gone? Life can really be lived after you have decided what you would like to have written on your tombstone. *Morbid!* you may be thinking. Perhaps, but how many of us are taking the long look. How will your life be lived and how will you be remembered?

The great Christian missionary, Albert Schweitzer, was asked to name the greatest living person in the world. He replied, "The greatest person in the world is some unknown individual who at this very moment has gone in love to help another."

Just for today and maybe for tomorrow, as you go about doing what teens do, you could also be someone's hero!

Dear friend, you are faithful in what you are doing for the brothers, even though they are strangers to you (3 John 1:5).

69. TOO MUCH CHANGE

This story is about a very young man who was preparing for the ministry. The pastor invited him to give a short sermon as part of a service. His text was "Thou shalt not steal." The next morning he boarded a city bus, handed the driver a dollar bill, and was given some change. He walked to the rear of the bus because no seats were open. Once at the back, he braced himself and the bus took off. Then he counted his change and realized it was a dime too much. His first thought was, *It's only a thin dime and the bus company will not miss it.*

By this time, the bus had made another stop, and the aisle was crowded with people. Then he thought, *This is not right, I cannot kept this dime which isn't mine.* He started back to the front and the driver. After a dozen or more apologizes and some sour looks later, he stood next to the driver, offered the dime and said, "You gave me too much change."

The bus driver replied, "Yes, I gave you a dime too much. I did it on purpose. You see, I heard your short sermon yesterday and watched in my mirror as you counted your change. If you had pocketed the extra I would never have had any confidence in preaching or preachers again."

Think of what had been at stake if this young man had decided the annoyance of his fellow passengers had not been worth a dime's worth of honesty!

All of us need to remember that we can never take a vacation from being honest. We are always on duty to do what we know is right!

There is nothing concealed that will not be disclosed, or hidden that will not be made known (Luke 12:2).

70. THE WORLD'S FUNNIEST JOKE

Don't tell me the Brits have no sense of humor! The British Association of the Advancement of Science recently issued a challenge: "Help us find the world's funniest joke." They got help; more than 10,000 jokes were submitted to their website and more than 100,000 people from 70 countries cast their votes to select the following winner:

> The fictional British detective, Sherlock Holmes and his trusty associate, Dr. Watson, are camping in the woods. They pitch a tent and go to sleep. Later, Holmes abruptly wakes up Watson.
>
> Holmes says, "Watson, look up at the stars and tell me what you deduce."
>
> Watson replies, "I see millions of stars, and if there are millions of stars, and if even a few of those have planets, it is quite likely there are some planets like earth; and if there are a few planets like earth out there, there might also be life."
>
> Holmes, now a bit agitated says, "Watson, you idiot! Somebody stole our tent!"

Okay, if that's the world's funniest joke, we are all in trouble. However, humor is a powerful way to help us cope with life and also helps us keep all the circumstances of our lives in some kind of perspective.

Now a question: Why are many Christians portrayed as people who have no sense of humor? Another question: Do you think God ever laughs? How about this for an answer: "The One enthroned in heaven laughs" (Psalm 2:4). Living a life without humor is sort of like driving a car without a bumper. Besides, the Bible also says, "A merry heart does good, like medicine" (Proverbs 17:22 NKJV).

All the days of the oppressed are wretched,
but the cheerful heart has a continual feast (Proverbs 15:15).

71. LIVING WITH THE CONSEQUENCES

Eighteen-year-old Kyle Todd was shot and killed in the living room of his mother's home in Pascagoula, Mississippi. Why? Todd was a freshman at Louisiana State University and had come home for the weekend so he could study in peace and quiet because of the noise and partying of a Saturday LSU and University of Tennessee football game.

At about 1:00 a.m. on that Saturday night, a bullet smashed through a picture window, striking Todd in the chest. He was killed instantly.

The gunman, Joseph Goff, was apprehended, arrested, and charged with murder. During his trial, Joseph managed to plea-bargain his charge down to manslaughter. The judge then sentenced him to the maximum term of twenty years in prison.

The sentencing judge also added another punishment: Goff must always have an eight- by ten-inch photo of his innocent victim hanging in his cell 24/7. Every day, in his prison cell, Goff was to be reminded of the life he had taken and reminded of how the actions of his life had led to his spending at least twenty years of his life behind bars.[10]

You and I are free to make any kind of life choices we want. What we cannot choose will be the consequences that always follow the choices we make. Yes, we can be forgiven for our sins; you are right about this. However, never forget God may not choose to reverse the impact of these consequences in our lives. Whatever kinds of seeds we sow will eventually grow until there is a harvest. But remember that we will always harvest more than the seed we planted. How about giving some serious thought to the decisions you are making today?

> *Do not be deceived; God cannot be mocked. A man reaps what he sows. The one who sows to please his sinful nature, from that nature will reap destruction; the one who sows to please the Spirit, from the Spirit will reap eternal life* (Galatians 6:7-8).

72. FINDING THE RIGHT BALANCE

College life can be very busy for Tobin Heath. This University of North Carolina senior is the soccer team midfielder and a four-time All-American with the Tar Heels. During her illustrious career she has helped her team win three NCAA titles, including the one in 2009. She also was selected "all-tournament" each of those three times. She ended the 2009 tourney with five goals, ten assists, and twenty points!

Her accomplishments don't stop there. Heath can count a gold medal in the 2008 Olympics as a member of the USA women's national team. As a teen she counts it a privilege to have played with some of the game's legends—-Kristine Lily, Abby Wambach, and Carli Lloyd. She has played for the full national team fourteen times while scoring two goals and numerous appearances with the national youth teams. Quite a resume for a twenty-one year old. She figures to be the face of women's soccer in America for the next decade.

Along with her athletic demands she has spent plenty of hours in the library studying for classes. What an exciting life. Heath says, "For me, soccer is a game that brings me great joy. I am extremely grateful that God has blessed me with the ability to play this awesome game!"

Besides all this she makes family time and says she counts worshiping the Lord as one of the great joys of her life. Despite her athletic accomplishments and busy schedule, one thing comes first for Tobin. "I try to incorporate God into everything I do. I don't find the balance hard because I have given everything to God to take care of."[11]

Now that is a goal worth scoring!

I press on toward the goal to win the prize for which God has called me heavenward in Christ Jesus (Philippians 3:14).

73. ARE YOU A CHEATER?

Andy Stanley says that cheating is a decision "to give up one thing in hopes of gaining something else of greater value." Perhaps the question is not "Do you cheat?" but "Where do you cheat?" What do you do when family, work, play, God, and school all collide? How are you juggling the activities and schedules of your life? You may be thinking, "There are not enough hours in the day to do what I want to do." So, in the end, you cheat; you cheat someone or yourself. Am I right? What can be done to put an end to cheating? How about considering the following tips?

Make up your mind to stop cheating at home. Consider the young man, Daniel, who was exiled a long ways from home in the king's palace in Babylon. Daniel didn't know how things would turn out, but he made up his mind to not eat food offered to idols. Where did he learn this discipline? At home long before the testing took place in a foreign place. Start at home!

Develop a plan. How will you handle the test? Decide now. Maybe the plans you make seem like a long shot, but you will never know what happens unless and until you take an action. Decide what specific steps you will take to stop cheating at home so the same plan will be in place wherever you may be.

Watch for God. If you make the decision not to cheat, you will discover God will give you the grace to pull it off. God cannot or will not make such decisions for you, but if and when you make the decision, you can depend that God will bless your right choices and help you keep them when the big test comes!

Now God had caused the official to show favor and sympathy to Daniel (Daniel 1:9).

74. THE KOREAN GOLFER WHO LOVES TO GIVE

He was born the son of a rice farmer in Wando, South Korea, and didn't become interested in golf until age sixteen. K. J. Choi started out to be a powerlifter but retired when his five-foot, eight-inch frame could not handle powerlifting at the highest levels. He was raised in the Onnuri Community Church in Korea, a church known for its cell groups and their spreading the gospel through discipleship. He met his wife in this church and was discipled by Pastor Yong Jo Ha there.

He began competing in the PGA in 2000 by placing dead last in their qualifying school. He said, "I was overwhelmed."

What was his goal in golf? "I always said to myself I would be the first PGA Tour player out of Korea, and I never deviated from that."

His first PGA Tour victories came in 2002 at tournaments in New Orleans and Tampa, and two years later he came to America to play on his first President's Cup team for the international squad in 2003. He went on from there, and as they say, the rest is history—really "HIS"-story. He has won more than $18 million in prize money, wants his success to motivate other Korean golfers, and uses his "God-given riches to help and bless other Christian causes." After his 2005 victory at the Chrysler Classic, Choi donated $90,000 of his earnings to the Korean Presbyterian Church in Greensboro!

Humbleness keeps his focus on the right path. "When I'm getting mad at golf or getting upset or nervous on the golf course, I just start singing hymns or thinking about Bible verses," he says.

I'd say it's a lesson that comes across in any language!

Be strong and very courageous. Be careful to obey all the law my servant Moses gave you; do not turn from it to the right or to the left, that you may be successful wherever you go (Joshua 1:7).

75. CAN A LIE EVER BE JUSTIFIED?

Is lying ever a good thing? There's a clerk who works in a Canadian Subway fast-food restaurant who might think this is so. Here's the story.

Two men entered the restaurant and ordered Subway sandwiches, but they wanted more than a meal. One of the men pulled a knife on the clerk and demanded cash.

Instead of giving over the cash in the cash register, this quick thinking and acting clerk locked the cash register. Then he came out from behind the counter and disarmed the would-be-robber, who then ran outside where his partner in crime had fled. The clerk ran outside too, caught up with the pair, talked to them, and convinced them that he would give them a free sandwich meal if they would just come back inside.

When he had locked the cash drawer he had also set off the silent alarm that rang in the nearby police station. This lie the clerk had told must have been believable. When the police arrived, both of the would-be-robbers were quietly sitting and waiting for their "free" sandwiches. Police made the arrest before the food was served.

Okay, so how was that for quick thinking? "I know you have just attempted to rob me and my store, but how about a twelve-inch roast beef sub with all the trimmings?" Sure, no robber ever expected to hear an invitation like that.

But was this lie justified? On the positive side, it did lead to the arrest of two thieves, but does the lie ever justify the end result? Why do people tell lies? Why do you tell lies? What does God think about lies?

Save me, O Lord, from lying lips and from deceitful tongues (Psalm 120:2).

76. LIFE'S MOST FRAGILE GIFT

Quickly think . . . As a teenager, what is the most fragile gift you have? Give up? It's something that can be lost. It's something that can be taken away. It's something all of us have. Each day it must be used up because it can never be taken back.

Let's look at it this way. Suppose you have just won the lottery. This grand prize is unlimited, but it will be given to you each day at midnight. At 12:01 each morning, $1,440 will be deposited in your bank account. There is one catch—you will be required to spend it all on the next day. This will go on as long as you live! You are not allowed to carry any of it on to the next day; each night at midnight your account must be zeroed. You will need to spend each day's amount wisely.

Every day you are given exactly 1,440 minutes or 86,400 seconds. What a gift you've been given! Each night your account is zeroed and you start over every day with 1,440 minutes. The most fragile gift you have is time. How many of these allotments will you be given? Nobody knows except God.

I want to ask you, are you making good use of all 1,440 minutes in each day? Are you living each day to the fullest? When your account is finished, will you have spent those minutes wisely? You may be thinking, I'm too young to be bothered by this issue, and besides, I have lots of life to live.

Benjamin Franklin said, "Lost time is never found again." So live well because you will never get any of those 1,440 minutes you have lived back again!

It is time to seek the Lord (Hosea 10:12).

77. SOME LAWS OF LIFE FOR TEENS

An interesting book written by teens for teens, *Teen Ink What Matters*, tells it like it really is. The following "Laws of Life" was written or compiled by Jade Lauren Tollis (age eighteen), and I don't think I can improve on them. Here they are:

- Those who live without jealousy and enjoy life are most at peace with those who really are.
- To grow without character and integrity is building the values of life on sand alone.
- The argumentative, hostile, and antagonistic will never find the tranquility of peacefulness.
- Treat your neighbor as your brother; blind your eyes to race, religion, and color.
- It does not matter what is in your bank account; what really matters is what is in your "devotions account."
- To be valued for your honesty is more important than being valued for your valuables.
- To steal what is yours is only cheating your own self-worth.
- Being humble with your accomplishments is an excellence the overly proud never achieve.
- Those with a generous heart will be forever rewarded with life's generous treasures.

The fear of the Lord is the beginning of wisdom; all who follow his precepts have a good understanding (Psalm 111:10).

78. WHAT ARE YOU COLLECTING IN LIFE?

Do you know of any of your friends who happen to be collectors? It could be a collection of bottle caps, DVDs, movie posters, posters of sports heroes—the list is endless.

But I want to challenge you to begin collecting "life principles." You may be thinking, *Life principles? What's that?*

According to Bobb Biehl, "Principles are mini-statements of cause and effect. Collect principles because they help explain why things do or do not work." Interesting! How old you have to be to be a collector of life principles? Never too young or never too old, so teens are included.

How do you get started? It's as simple as a notebook and a pencil. Write down all the principles you already know. This includes what you have learned from parents, friends, relatives, books, professors, TV, and so on. A host of wise things that are out there if you begin to look for them.

Here are some examples of life principles:

- "One of the realities of life is that if you can't trust a person at all points, you can't truly trust him or her at any point" (Cheryl Biehl).
- "Take a shower a day or friends and dates stay away!"
- "Before you trust a man or his message, study his life."

Are you getting the idea? Here's another example from Peter Drucker, "Once the facts are clear, the decisions jump out at you!"

What a fabulous concept for living! I only wish I had come across this idea when I had been a teen. Principles to live by—go for it!

Here is the conclusion of the matter: Fear God and keep his commandments, for this is the whole duty of man (Ecclesiastes 12:13).

79. A SCENE FROM THE PRINCIPAL'S OFFICE

"Chase, come on in." Principal Russo's voice was strong and firm, just like always. Chase, a senior at a high school in Delaware slowly rises to his feet and strolls into the principal's office while being filmed by TruTV's *The Principal's Office.*

Principal Russo began his planned speech by trying to see if Chase will confess to the crime that he committed. But the quick-witted senior was one step ahead and pretended as if he had no idea what this was all about. Not to be outsmarted, the principal lays it out: "You know, think about what will happen if I find out you committed this crime and lied about it to me!"

This changes the situation. Chase immediately comes clean and admits that he is guilty. Nobody likes going to see the principal because it's the place you go when you mess up. Come to think about it, this TV show could be a way to open up a conversation to get people to talk about God.

The Bible makes it perfectly clear that each of us will one day stand before God to give an account of how our lives have been lived. The Bible specifically says, "Each of us will give an account of himself to God" (Romans 14:12). So here's the way to use this TV show by talking about the idea that actions have consequences. When a student goes to the principal's office, the principal determines the punishment. In the same way, when we stand at the judgment seat of God, He will determine our punishment for an eternity. We will get the most amazing reward, eternal life in heaven, or the most unbelievably horrible punishment ever, to spend an eternity in hell!

"As surely as I live," says the Lord, "every knee will bow before me; every tongue will confess to God." So then each of us will give an account of himself to God (Romans 14:11-12).

80. CAN YOU BE FUNNY FOR A REASON?

Little did a fourteen-year-old know when he accepted a dare from a friend to provide some entertainment during a technical glitch at the theater that he would become a full-time standup comedian. He has been on the same stage with such comedic stars as Jerry Seinfeld, George Wallace, Jay Leno, and Chris Rock.

As a young teen and long before he became famous or a Christian, he had made a pact with a friend that the two of them refused to curse or swear because it "wasn't an intelligent way to communicate." If they did, each would be able to hit the other in the stomach, really hard. Capital punishment enforced this pact.

Back to the story of the teenager in the theater. He responded to the dare and made his way to the front. There were four hundred unhappy people, and he quickly had to clean up the only joke he could remember. However, when he told the joke, he says, "Everybody laughed. Seeing their reaction gave me this ultimate high—not that I've done drugs before."

In retrospect, Michael Jr. says, "I could clearly see that this was God saying, 'This is what I have for you to do,' even before I came to Christ."

Before he made his standup debut at age fourteen in that movie theater, this comedian says he's always had a strange ability to take the mundane and ordinary, flip it upside-down and wrong-side out, and etch out life truths.

He also knows the importance of keeping God's Word at the forefront of his life. Michael Jr. has discovered he still needs his Friend with whom he made the pact not to curse when young, along with a spiritual mentor at his home church in California.

How about you? Do you have a mentor with whom you can make a life pact?

As iron sharpens iron,
so one person sharpens another.(Proverbs 27:17).

81. HAVE YOU EVER BEEN LATE FOR WORK?

Do you have a job? If you don't currently have a job, someday you will. But it seems as though many people who have jobs do poorly at them. According to careerbuilder.com, at least a full 15 percent of employed workers admit to showing up to work late at least once a week. Their reason for being late? Check out these excuses that have been given some employers:

- I have transient amnesia and couldn't remember my job.
- I was indicted for securities fraud this morning.
- Someone stole all my daffodils.
- I had to go audition for American Idol.
- I was trying to get my gun back from the police.

The pressures of the workplace seem to bring out all kinds of weirdness and even stupidity in people. Another website, overhearintheoffice.com offers these and other examples:

The boss says, "You make too many mistakes. You're not very consistent."
The cube dweller replies, "Well, you can't be consistent all the time."

The cashier asks, "And what form of payment will you be making today?"
The customer says, "Money!"

The office manager asks, "Where were you yesterday?"
The peon answers, "I was at my cousin's funeral."
And the office manager asks, "Why? Did she die?"

The Bible has a very special word for all of us who are or who will be working for the rest of our lives:

And whatever you do, whether in word or deed, do it all in the name of the Lord Jesus, giving thanks to God the Father (Colossians 3:17).

82. IS THIS ALL THERE IS?

Famous football play Bob Lily tells his story: "In 1972 we beat the Miami Dolphins in Super Bowl VI, 24 to 3. It was very exciting to finally win an NFL Championship. But I'll never forget the morning after the game.

"Football had been eleven years of my life and I had accomplished all of my goals. Winning the Super Bowl was supposed to be the ultimate. But about

6:30 on the morning after, I walked out on the parking lot of our hotel in New Orleans. There were beer bottles, beer cans, and all kinds of trash left from the night before. I remember stumbling around and saying, 'Is this all there is?' This was eleven years of my life and I had accomplished all those goals and yet I was hollow inside. Suddenly, it was over; the elation and joy had burst like a balloon."

Have you ever admired a sports or music hero? Have you thought you would like to have their lifestyle? I have a little secret for you. Even if you become rich and famous and I am not, we are still created the same with an empty hole inside that only God can fill. You can do everything you want to fill that hole, but it's always there and may even get larger and emptier as you live your life. Only a relationship with Jesus Christ can fill that empty void. Take it from Bob Lily.

Yes, to finish this story, Bob Lily did become a Christian and discovered that this emptiness was filled. He says, "In 1981, I rededicated my life to Christ and suddenly the light came back into my life!"

Does your life have an empty hole? You can give Him your life and you too will find the most fulfilling one you could possibly know!

and to know this love that surpasses knowledge—that you may be filled to the measure of all the fullness of God (Ephesians 3:19).

83. GENEROSITY—HAVE YOU EVER TRIED IT?

Generosity can be a simple gesture that makes a difference in somebody else's life. Consider the story of Raymond Chan who was formerly Canada's Secretary of State for Asia. He came to Canada with only twenty dollars in his pocket, so his sister had given him a job in her modest shop in Vancouver. Every day he rode the bus to work.

One rainy day he wore a coat and hat not typical in Canada; it was what you would wear on a rainy day in Hong Kong. He realized he would be recognized as a foreigner, especially if he spoke since his English was still not very good. He was not sure how people would respond to him.

When he arrived at the bus stop, two quite tall Canadian ladies were in serious conversation, and Raymond hoped against hope they would not notice him. But to his dismay, one turned and addressed him, "Young man, where are you from?"

In his very poor English, Raymond managed to stammer, "I am from Hong Kong."

Without a moment's hesitation, this striking lady put out her hand, shook his hand, and warmly said, "Welcome to Canada!" Then she made a sweeping gesture with her arm and pointed to the mountains and continued, "Look all around you. This is a big country and we need strong young people like you to help us build it!"

Tears come to his eyes when he relates this story. The woman's encouragement was just three simple sentences. Raymond says, "Her words were a significant factor in my life" on his way to becoming the first ethnic Chinese Canadian to be a member of the Federal Cabinet.

What this unknown lady did was a simple act of kindness based on a wonderful attitude of generosity. How about beginning to be generous with others and encourage them today?

A word aptly spoken is like apples of gold in settings of silver
(Proverbs 25:11).

84. WRONG IS WRONG, RIGHT IS RIGHT

Life is really all about making choices! There are right choices, good choices, wrong choices, lukewarm choices, evil choices—you get the idea. Nobody makes the right choices all the time. There are no perfect teens, no perfect parents, no perfect siblings. And that's okay because we are all human and humans make mistakes. Mistakes are a part of growing up and can be very useful because of the lessons learned. Plus, there is forgiveness!

The older we get, the easier we should be able to see the differences between right and wrong choices that can lead to right or wrong actions. This is more than the simple day-to-day decisions of what to wear to school, what magazine to buy, or what kind of a hamburger to order.

Life is loaded with choices. Am I going to lie to my parents about my activities? Will I cheat on my boyfriend? Will I cheat on my girlfriend? Will I cheat on the next English test? Will I cheat on my entrance exam for college? If or when you make a bad choice and follow it up with a wrong action, you can fool some of your crowd or you might even fool everybody; but you can never fool yourself! And you have to live with yourself the rest of your life.

One of life's greatest lessons to learn is that happiness is all about doing the right thing time after time. There is no such thing as a "kind of" right or a "sort of" wrong. No amount of fun can change a wrong into a right. Only Jesus Christ can forgive a wrong and make right. Wrong is wrong, right is right. Do the right thing!

You shall not give false testimony against your neighbor (Exodus 20:16).

85. DO SOMETHING OUT OF THE ORDINARY!

Do you want to be a movie star, rock star, professional athlete, doctor, or lawyer? Are you aware that you have more than 20,000 other choices of what you could do with your life?

If you live a normal typical life—working forty hours a week until you retire at age sixty-five—you will likely be spending something in the neighborhood of 86,000 hours on the job of your choice. Doesn't it make sense that you should consider all of your options or at least as many as you possibly can before you settle on a life's work?

Chris had always thought it would be cool to be a lawyer. One school break he visited his grandparents, who were very well connected in their community. Arrangements were made so Chris could shadow two different lawyers for four days. One was a criminal defense attorney and the other was a corporate attorney. At the conclusion of a wonderful time of exploring these new mysterious worlds, he had made a choice. Chris said, "Being a lawyer is something I could not do and do not want to do." He changed his college major and now is working on a doctorate degree so he can become an English professor and professional writer.

He considered his options. Of those 20,000 plus possibilities, is there something you'd really like to do the rest of your life? Check it out. Make a satisfying choice. And of course, in the process, have you ever asked the Lord, "What would You have me to do?" While you are making these important decisions, choose wisely and choose the best; reach high and don't settle for second best.

Six days do your work, but on the seventh day do not work (Exodus 23:12).

86. THE POWER OF FORGIVENESS

Leonardo da Vinci had been commissioned to paint his depiction of the Lord's Supper. However, just before he began, he had a violent, bitter quarrel with a fellow artist. Leonardo became so incensed he decided to use the face of his enemy as the model for the face of Judas. He would take revenge by holding up his enemy to scorn.

The face of Judas was the first face completed, and everyone easily recognized the face of the other artist with whom he had quarreled. However, when he began painting the face of Jesus, Leonardo couldn't get it right. Everything he tried didn't seem right to him. Something was holding him back and frustrating his efforts. Finally, he concluded that the problem was because he had painted his enemy as Judas.

When he had painted over the face of his enemy, he tackled the face of

Jesus Christ. This time he was successful, and this famous work of art remains on display in Milan, Italy, more than five centuries later.

You cannot be painting the features of Jesus Christ into your own life and at the same be painting another person with anger, enmity, hatred, and revenge! If you are holding bitterness against another, if you want revenge to be yours, if you are filled with hate, there is really only one real answer: forgiveness.

Your future and your happiness depend on forgiveness. Yes, I know, it's costly! You are slicing away the joy of revenge and letting the person who has offended you go free without any penalties. But it's the only way to deal with a hurtful past. And remember, when you forgive, you will also be forgiven.

> *For if you forgive men when they sin against you, your heavenly Father will also forgive you. But if you do not forgive men their sins, your Father will not forgive you your sins* (Matthew 6:14-15).

87. I ONLY HAVE TO GO

Marcie had just graduated from Bible College. She was visiting with her parents and went to her home church on Wednesday night. The pastor gave an altar call and she responded. At the altar she motioned for her pastor, "Pastor I have surrendered my life to go to the mission field, and I would like you to pray and bless me."

"Marcie, that's wonderful! Where are you going?"

She replied, "To Malaysia, to the tribes of head hunters because for eleven years they have had no missionaries. Even the oil companies have recalled their workers."

He replied, "Marcie, you?" (She's tiny, petite, about 105 pounds at most.) The pastor thought, *Even I'm not going to Malaysia. She will be eaten. God, spare her life. I'm praying a death sentence over her.* Her parents pled with the pastor, "Talk some sense into her head."

Nobody would go with her. The location was so remote that a helicopter was the only way in. She was flown by a chopper that couldn't land because the natives had discovered how to disable the chopper with their spears and eat the crew. She had to repel 150 feet down a rope. They threw two duffel bags down and she followed. The plan was to leave her for sixty days and return for her.

The chopper pilot who says he never cries, bawled and pled, "Don't go. I'll be back in sixty days but you won't."

She replied, "You don't understand. I only have to go; I don't have to come back!"

Sixty days later, the chopper returned. There's Marcie, in the clearing, waving, with more than seventy converts! What nobody knew was the head hunters only ate men and had a 200-year-old legend about a "god" who would come from the sky to be worshiped. She said, "I told them 'I am not a god, but I come from God. It was the easiest soul-winning I have ever done!"

Go and make disciples of all nations . . . and surely I am with you always, to the very end of the age (Matthew 28:19-20).

88. WHY WOULD YOU WASTE YOUR TIME?

The following is a question you may never have asked yourself: Why would you waste your life merely doing something great for God? Yes, you read the right words. Why? Lots of people are doing great things in this world without God's help. Read any business journal or any service club's magazine. For example, the world's rotary clubs have wiped out polio in the world.

So why would you want to waste your life merely doing something great for God, when you could be doing the impossible with God's help? If something is impossible, it is impossible for any of us! But if I read my Bible correctly, we serve a God who makes the impossible possible! For example, Jesus fed 5,000 men along with 10,000 to 20,000 women and children with a little boy's lunch. Twelve baskets were left over! Immediately after this miracle Jesus put His disciples into a boat. A storm came up, and Jesus and Peter walked on the water. Both actions are impossible for any of us but not with God!

A family gathers around the supper table and the father announces, "We are going to ask God to do the impossible!" He had their undivided attention. What? "I am asking the Lord to make it possible for us to live on 10 percent of our income and give the other 90 percent to the Lord and His church!" They were stunned. Do the numbers—they can't do this, it's impossible.

The next Sunday, the father wrote a check for 90 percent of his income to the church and has done it every Sunday since. He had begun a small business in his garage and God blessed it. On the 10 percent this family lives on, they are now fully supporting three hundred full-time missionaries.[12] Impossible? Not with God!

Jesus looked at them and said, "With man this is impossible, but with God all things are possible" (Matthew 19:26).

89. HANDS OFF SALLY!

While touring Eagle's Rock African Safari Zoo with friends from Russia, Ronald DeMuth, from Vermont, found himself in a tough situation. They were at the petting part of the zoo and saw a rhino that was one of the animals that was accustomed to being touched and petted by visitors.

DeMuth wanted to show his Russian friends the marvelous American invention called Krazy Glue. So he put about three ounces of this Krazy Glue on the palms of his hands and jokingly placed them on the rump of this petting zoo rhino. In the thirteen years of her life in the zoo, Sally the Rhino had never before felt any of her viewers leave their hands on her for so long until now. And Sally did not like this sensation. The rhino panicked, running around the zoo with DeMuth following closely behind.

DeMuth's misfortune was not yet complete. Sally had not been feeling well and her keepers had just given her a laxative and some antidepressants to relax her bowels when DeMuth played his innocent but stupid prank. Sally destroyed two fences, three pygmy goats, and one duck. During the four hours it took to remove DeMuth's hands from the frightened rhino, the laxatives began to work. Thirty gallons of rhino showers later, DeMuth was freed from Sally's behind! And by the way, DeMuth's Russian friends were quite impressed!

Is there a moral in this story? Yes. You can make any kind of life choices you want; however, you can't choose your consequences!

Do not be deceived: God cannot be mocked. A man reaps what he sows
(Galatians 6:7).

90. WHICH AM I?

Jess Keener is an interesting man with an interesting story. While still a young construction worker, he received an injury that left him paralyzed from the neck down. He's confined to a hospital bed, but that has not stopped him from being a productive human being. He's still able to speak and has turned to writing notes and letters of encouragement to people who might be depressed. Awesome! Among his writings is the following:

I watched them tearing a building down
A gang of men in a busy town,
With ho-heave and a lusty yell
They swung a beam and a side wall fell;
I asked the Foreman, "Are these men skilled
And the men you'd hire if you had to build?"

He gave a laugh and said, "No, indeed!
Just common labor is all I need;
I can easily wreck in a day or two what
Builders have taken a year to do!"
And I thought to myself as I went away
"Which of these roles have I tried to play?"

Am I a builder who works with care, measuring
Life by the rule and square?
Am I shaping my deed to a well made plan,
Patiently doing the best I can?
Or am I a wrecker, who walks the town
Content with the labor of tearing it down?[13]

By the grace God has given me, I laid a foundation as an expert builder, and someone else is building on it. But each one should be careful how he builds (1 Corinthians 3:10).

91. CHECK YOUR FQ

Failure Quotient has been defined as the ability to get up one more time after you have failed or been defeated. For example, take big league baseball players. They wallow through defeat after defeat to come to the dramatic moment of a home run. If they fail three out of four times, their batting average will be .250. If they fail only two out four times, they are batting .500. Do you catch this concept? Let me illustrate with a story.

Frank Budd is his name and he ran the hundred yard dash in 9.2 seconds in the national championships, setting a new world record. Following this feat, he was interviewed by Bob Richards, a former world champion pole-vaulter. He said to Frank, "This is a little different than Rome." Few people remembered what he was talking about.

The previous year in the Rome Olympics, while running in the four-man relays, Frank Budd, running in the number three slot, fumbled the baton and failed to get it to Ray Norton in the exchange area. Because of the bobble, the USA team lost what would have been four gold medals and a new world's record.

Back to the interview. In the roar of the crowd and the excitement of running the world's fastest one hundred, Frank Budd sobered and said, "You've got to go through Rome before you can appreciate a moment like this!" That is profound psychology for a nineteen-year-old.

Now, how about your own FQ? Will you be getting up the next time you are knocked down or defeated or have failed? You can do it!

But we have this treasure in jars of clay to show that this all-surpassing power is from God and not from us. We are hard pressed on every side, but not crushed; perplexed, but not in despair; persecuted, but not abandoned; struck down, but not destroyed (2 Corinthians 4:7-9).

92. YOU BROUGHT WHAT?

The story is told about a particular banker who died and was approaching the Pearly Gates. He was sweating and struggling with a very heavy suitcase. St. Peter greeted him and said, "Set that heavy suitcase down and come on in to heaven."

The banker barked, "No way! I have to bring this in with me!"

"Well, what could possibly be so important that you have to take this into heaven?" St. Peter asked.

The banker opened the suitcase to reveal fifty gold bricks. Peter's jaw drops and said, "Why are you bringing pavement with you?"

Well, what about this? What are you planning to bring with you to heaven? The only thing you can bring to heaven is yourself. However, you can send on ahead any number of things. Perhaps you've heard it said, "There are no U-Haul trailers behind a funeral hearse!" When you die, it's all over, except what happens after death. The Bible is very clear about who goes to heaven and how we can get there. It's the only road map available to tell us such things.

Think with me . . . What can you send on ahead? How about random acts of kindness . . . how about acts of compassion . . . how about providing for people who may be poor . . . how about helping the widows . . . and how about gifts you give to others? The list really is quite long.

You may be thinking, Heaven is a long ways off. I'm too young to be thinking about heaven. How many young people have you heard of lately who have died in car crashes or from some devastating illness? It happens more frequently than we'd like. None of us is too young or too old to think about heaven and eternity.

In my Father's house are many rooms; if it were not so, I would have told you. I am going there to prepare a place for you (John 14:2).

93. ANGEL AT AN ABORTION CLINIC

The Bible tells us that every one of us have been wonderfully made as a testimony to a God that loves every human being. What about the babies who are never born but aborted? Think of the millions of babies that have been aborted, cutting their lives short. Do you think God loves them too?

A few months before Thomas was born, his mother, Cecily, was sitting in a Liberian abortion clinic waiting to abort her unborn child. She was yielding to the demands from her child's father to abort the child.

She was taken into the operating room, waiting for the operation to take place. It was at this point that an anonymous lady walked into this operating room and commanded her, "Get up. You are not going to abort this child!"

This anonymous lady helped Cecily get off the table, picked up her clothes, helped dress her, and walked her outside and sat her down on the curb. When Cecily looked up, this lady who had been so forceful simply disappeared. To this day Cecily is convinced this anonymous visitor was an angel sent from God.

What about the child who almost was aborted? His name is Thomas Tapeh, who at age nine migrated to St. Paul, Minnesota, where he was introduced to the American game of football. Years later, he made the *USA TODAY* second-team All-American honors and was later named Minnesota State Player of the Year. He played football at the University of Minnesota and was selected by the Philadelphia Eagles. Later he played for the Minnesota Vikings.

Have you thanked your mother for giving you life and letting you be born?

Before I formed you in the womb I knew you, before you were born I set you apart (Jeremiah 1:5).

94. A LIGHTNING STRIKE

Anthony Marchese works for Digital Color, Incorporated as a salesman. He lives in Wisconsin and is used to driving in all kinds of weather, good and bad. If you live and work in Wisconsin, snowstorms and rainstorms are normal parts of life.

What is not normal is being struck by lightning. This story was carried in the *Milwaukee Journal Sentinel.* Marchese was on his way to make a sales call on a client when his car was hit by lightning. The rear window was blown out, both rear tires were burned up, the car horn would not stop honking, and the car finally stopped dead.

Later it was determined that the lightning strike had entered by way of the rear car antenna, which was destroyed, and exited by way of the rear tires. Also, a pair of six-inch deep holes were left where the tires had touched the road. Marchese was noticeably shaken but not hurt. His boss came to his rescue so he could make the sales call, and he returned to work for the rest of the day.

Have you ever had a second chance in life? If so, how did you feel after your experience? For sure, Marchese had a second chance, even getting a real break. A stroke of luck like this could be called God's mercy or God's grace in action. Did Marchese express thanks for his escape? We don't know. But what about you? Have you been grateful after a second-chance opportunity?

Or let's take it another step. Have you ever offered a second chance to somebody who may not have deserved it?

But because of his great love for us, God, who is rich in mercy, made us alive with Christ even when we were dead in transgressions—it is by grace you have been saved (Ephesians 2:4-5).

95. WHAT DOES THIS WORLD NEED?

This world needs teens
Who cannot be bought
Whose word is their bond
Who will put character above gaining wealth
Who possess strong opinions and a strong will
Who are larger than their chosen vocations
Who do not hesitate to take chances
Who will not lose their individuality while in a crowd
Who will be as honest in the little things as in the great things
Who will not make compromises with what is wrong
Whose ambitions are to be confined to only their own selfish desires
Who will not say they are doing it "because everybody else is doing it"
Who are true to their friends through good and bad, in another's adversity as
well as when they prosper
Who do not believe that shrewdness, cunning, cheating, compromise, or hard-
headedness are the best life qualities for becoming successful
Who are not ashamed or afraid to stand for the truth even when it is unpopular
Who will say no and mean it when the rest of the world is saying yes![14]

The quiet words of the wise are more to be heeded than the shouts of a ruler of fools. Wisdom is better than weapons of war (Ecclesiastes 9:17-18).

96. CONSIDER THE CHINESE BAMBOO

Most teenagers have a deadly problem, and it may be due completely to being young and lacking in life experiences. What is it? Too many teens think only in the short-term, thinking of the present with no thought about consequences down the road, either positive or negative. Any teen who doesn't begin thinking in the long-term will eventually be doomed to failure.

So let's consider the Chinese bamboo. This particular species of bamboo has a seed that is in reality a nut with a very tough outer skin. After it has been planted, it must be watered regularly and fertilized. But the first year nothing happens.

There's more watering and fertilizing the second year and nothing—no plant emerges from the soil. The same process is repeated during the third and fourth year and still nothing happens. Then in the fifth year the stalk bursts through the ground, and in a period of only six weeks this Chinese bamboo grows to some ninety feet tall.

So now the question: Did the bamboo grow ninety feet in six weeks or ninety feet in five years? What do you think?

When looking at life from your perspective, it may be a very narrow view that includes only today and tomorrow. Ever hear of "delayed gratification?" This means you are willing to take the longer look and delay your instant gratification. Any actions you take in the present will have consequences in the future. When you plant positive seeds in making life preparations, you can expect a positive harvest down the road. In other words, be prepared, even if it takes years, for an exciting life goal.

Trust in the Lord with all your heart and lean not on your own understanding; in all your ways acknowledge him, and he will make your paths straight (Proverbs 3:5-6).

97. WHAT HANDICAP?

Jeff Resler, a six-foot, two-inch, 260-pound left guard for the University of Oklahoma football team, has not had the use of his left hand since birth. After being born with a malformed and diseased left hand, he had to have it amputated when he was just seven days old to avoid infection.

As the years went on, he considered it more of an inconvenience than a handicap. Take golfing, for instance. He beats his dad with the help of his 280-yard drives. Want to talk about baseball? He played on a Little League team until junior high. How about team wrestling? He made the varsity team in his sophomore year. Do you think he could compete in the shot put event in track? He became the state high school champion with a throw of 59 feet 6 inches. What about football? In high school and college he was named second-team in the All-Big Eight conference.

All of us have some challenges in our lives that need to be dealt with. How will you handle yours? They likely will be as big as you make them. We all must overcome obstacles and deal with difficulties in order to achieve success. We need to pray for strength as we confront our problems so we won't be defeated before we even begin.

When Jeff Resler looks back on his life and what he has accomplished, he says, "It never occurred to me that I couldn't!"[15]

I can do everything through him who gives me strength (Philippians 4:13).

98. YOU ARE A MARVEL

Pablo Casals, one of the greatest cellists of all time wrote, "Each second we live is a new and unique moment of the universe, a moment that will never be again . . . And what do we teach our children? We teach them that two and two make four, and that Paris is the capital of France."

That sounds simple enough, but how will we teach you to become what you are and should become? Every child and teen should know something very special about themselves. Do you really know who and what you are? You are a marvel of God's creation! You are special because you are one of a kind. Nobody else in this world has your combination of gifts. You are unique. From the moment when time began, there has never been a person exactly like you! Everything about you is rare, the rarest of the rare. You are priceless!

Think of how you were put together: your legs, your arms, your fabulous hands, the way you move, the way you talk, the way you think! You are something very valuable and very precious, especially to your Creator and we hope to yourself as well.

In today's world there are more than twenty thousand plus possibilities of a vocation. But even more importantly, what will *you* become? You could become another Shakespeare, a Michelangelo, a Beethoven, an apostle Paul, a Bill Gates, a Mother Teresa, a president of your country, an Albert Einstein, or even another Martin Luther King who said, "Everybody can be great because anybody can serve. You don't have to make your subject and verb agree to serve. You only need a heart full of grace, a soul generated by love."

When the righteous thrive, the people rejoice; when the wicked rule, the people groan (Proverbs 29:2).

99. TRUE GRIT

The Munich Olympics is most remembered by the amazing feat of Mark Spitz, who won a record-setting eight gold medals. However, there is another exciting story about Steve Genter of Lakewood, California. He is a competitive swimmer too, but his story was mostly lost or overlooked.

Less than a week before the competition was to begin, one of his lungs collapsed while he was in training! The doctors made an incision, repaired the lung, put the stitches in, and taped him up. The consensus was "Too bad, this poor kid is out of the competition." They didn't know Steve Genter very well.

At the beginning of his event when his name was called, Steve Genter stepped to the starting block. Now, athletes can't compete with any kind of drugs, including painkillers, in their system, so he was standing on the blocks probably in much pain. This was the 200 meter freestyle event. The gun sounded and off he went with the rest of the field. At the 100 meter turn, in a dead heat with Mark Spitz, he hit the wall and made his turn, tearing the stitches loose! This threw his timing off but he continued swimming. Spitz beat him by less than 1/10 of a second, and Genter won the silver medal. Genter continued to compete and went on to also win one gold and one bronze medal. Success can come out of what looks like a defeat or a setback.

What happens to you when things go wrong? Are you ready to quit or compete through the pain? Do you surrender to circumstances or do you never give up? If you have made up your mind you can do something, you're right! If you think it can't be done, you're also absolutely right!

One thing I do: Forgetting what is behind and straining toward what is ahead, I press on toward the goal (Philippians 3:13-14).

100. GOALS

Statistics and surveys tell me that if I were to ask each of you what your goals are, less than 5 percent of you could do it. These same surveys tell me that 95 out of every 100 people have no idea where are they are going or what they want to do with the rest of their lives. We can conclude that the vast majority of people are simply moving with the tides of life and chance.

But not one eight-year-old boy! He told his mother and everyone who would listen to him, "I am going to be the greatest baseball catcher that ever lived!" People laughed at him. His mother told him he was too little to be thinking about such things, saying, "This is an impossible dream."

When he walked across the platform to receive his diploma at his high school graduation, the school superintendent stopped him and said, "Johnny, tell us what you want to be."

The young man stopped, squared his shoulders and said, "I am going to be the greatest baseball catcher that ever lived!" And you could hear the laughs and snickers across this crowd.

But history, the record books, and the National Baseball Hall of Fame tell the story and confirm that sure enough, Johnny Bench went on to become one fine baseball catcher. According to Yankees manager, Casey Stengel, "Johnny Bench became the greatest baseball catcher who ever played the game!"

So, my young friends, what is your goal in life? Real leaders and real winners are very ordinary people with extraordinary determination!

Cast your bread upon the waters, for after many days you will find it again (Ecclesiastes 11:1).

101. CONVICTIONS

What single life attitude could change your life around? What is the attitude that really stands behind the reality of progress? Ari Davis of Boston, who owned a factory that manufactured tools and instruments, said, "Why are you bothering yourself with a knitting machine? Why don't you make a sewing machine?" That question was overheard by the nineteen-year-old Elias Howe, who accepted the challenge.

No one else took this challenge seriously except the young Howe. This question haunted him day and night until he resolved he would be the one to invent a sewing machine.

He had an almost insane conviction that this achievement was possible and he would be the one to do it. He nearly starved in the process of designing, experimenting, and building the machine. In fact, he may have starved had it not been for some friends who came to his rescue to help with his living expenses.

Finally in July of 1845, the sewing machine was completed and proved its practicality by sewing the seams of two men's wool suits. It could sew three hundred perfectly matched stitches a minute. The mechanism he invented was nearly perfect and is still today the way sewing machines are built. It happened all because one young man had the conviction it could be done and he could do it!

The apostle Paul lived with this same kind of conviction. He even wrote it down for us to read, "[This] one thing I do" (Philippians 3:13). Today's world is filled with people who are wimps without convictions! What do you have strong convictions about?

We continually remember before our God and Father your work produced by faith, your labor prompted by love, and your endurance inspired by hope in our Lord Jesus Christ (1 Thessalonians 1:3).

102. CHANGE IT OR LIVE IT

Alexander the Great had a soldier in his army who happened to have the same name as the great commander. But it had come to his attention that the man was a coward when it came time to do battle. This man would run away or find some excuse for not going into the battle. Word finally leaked up through the ranks to Alexander that the man was a coward, and so he sent for the man.

This soldier stood before his commander with fear and trembling. What was going to happen to him? Alexander simply said to him, "You will either change your name or you will change your conduct!"

The same goes for the whole lot of us. If you name it, you better live it!

When you call yourself a Christian, you must also conduct all your lifestyle like a Christian. When you are at school, if you have a job, when you are at play, when you compete, and how you treat others are always important. If you name it, you had better live it!

Life has a way of testing all of us. Therefore, our life actions need to reflect who and what we really are—when people can watch us or when nobody is around. This world is tired of hypocrites and is looking for a Jesus Christ that can be worshiped and followed. This world wants to see Jesus Christ living in blue jeans! They want to see a believable lifestyle. They are hungry to see the real Christian, the kind of Christian who can be trusted, who has integrity, who lives out the concepts of a loving, compassionate, caring God. It's time . . . let's live it!

Now when Daniel learned that the decree had been published, he went home to his upstairs room where the windows opened toward Jerusalem. Three times a day he got down on his knees and prayed, giving thanks to his God, just as he had done before (Daniel 6:10).

103. THE SCREAM

Samantha "Sami" Jones named her Soap Box Derby racecar "Singin' Sami." She was thirteen years old and had just won the Master's Division on Saturday, August 11, 1990. This was the fifty-third running of the All-American Soap Box Derby in Akron, Ohio.

Singin' Sami had suffered some cracks and scrapes in the competitions to win the way to the derby. Sami merely taped them up with duct tape. And her handiwork was quite evident alongside some of those other "perfect" racers. Because of her handiwork she said, "People are going to wonder how I could win with such a beat-up car."

She made it down the 975-foot-long Derby Downs hill in the fastest time of 28.04 seconds. She represented her home town of Salem, Oregon, and was only the eighth girl to win this title since girls were allowed to compete beginning in 1971. This running of the event had drawn 153 other area champions from across America. She walked off with the first prize trophy and a five thousand dollar college scholarship.

But why the name Singin' Sami for a Soap Box Derby Racer? She explained, "I scream as loud as I can when I'm going down the hill. It makes the car vibrate and makes the car go faster." Pretty clever girl! Whatever it takes, I say.

What does it take to put your life in the winner's circle? You may be thinking, *I could never do that.* Why not? Failure is not the worst thing in the world. The worst thing is not even to give it a try!

104. STAYING FOCUSED

F lorence Chadwick, the world famous San Diego distance swimmer failed in her first attempt to swim the English Channel just a mere three miles short of the French coast. Why? The day was cloudy, foggy, and overcast. She explains, "I failed in this attempt because I could not see my goal, the coast of France."

She tried again and attempted the crossing from France to England. This time the day was bright and sunny, and she made it! She explained her successful second attempt like this, "The day was clear and I could always see the coast of England, my goal."

Chris Hagarty, a management consultant from Tiburon, California, cites a study done by Yale University of their graduates who have been out of the university for twenty years. They found that only three percent of the grads had written down their specific life and work goals. Ten percent had talked in broad terms about what they would like to do with their life. Eighty-seven percent had not bothered to write anything down or even discuss their goals.

The results? According to this study, the results showed that the three percent who had written out their specific goals had achieved more success, more recognition, and had earned more money than the other ninety-seven percent combined!

Awesome! Benjamin Franklin wrote, "Living without a goal is like shooting without a target."

This object lesson is very clear. Think about, pray about, and write down your life goals. Yes, you can! You live better and you will achieve more when you can see your goals clearly defined and written down.

I want to know Christ and the power of His resurrection and the fellowship
of sharing in his sufferings, becoming like him in his death, and so, somehow,
to attain to the resurrection from the dead (Philippians 3:10-11).

105. ENTHUSIASM

E nthusiasm is one life quality that most people applaud. Perhaps it is also one of the most fascinating and misunderstood qualities of life.

One example of how enthusiasm for a product has skyrocketed the demand is seen in the hen—yes, the lowly chicken hen. When a hen lays an egg, it's usually an all day job. When finished, she cackles excitedly as she announces her latest egg to all who might be within hearing. On the other hand, a duck hen, or a turkey hen, or a goose hen lays her egg and is passive about the whole thing. All of us know that the demand for chicken eggs over duck eggs or turkey eggs is much greater, even though a duck or turkey egg is two to three times larger than that of a chicken leg.

Let's take a closer look at the word enthusiasm. It's one of those really interesting words when we consider its meaning and origin. This word originated with the Greeks. It is really two Greek words: *En* and *Theos*. Put them together and you have En-Theos. When it's broken down, En means something within a person and Theos is a word for God. Therefore, it means that enthusiasm is the quality of life you have. En-Theos literally means, "God is within you!"

To become enthusiastic is never an accident; it is always the result of high intention, sincere effort, intelligent direction, and skillful execution; it represents the wise life choice. And this is a life quality worth catching! Say this out loud now, "I am enthused!" Begin each day by repeating this little sentence three times. You can become an enthusiastic person with God's help.

The Lord your God is with you, he is mighty to save. He will take great delight in you, he will quiet you with his love, he will rejoice over you with singing (Zephaniah 3:17).

106. THE TOUCHSTONE

There's an old legend that I believe originated in South Africa. Folklore has it that one day a traveler stopped at a happy farmer's home and talked at length about life beyond the farm and how beautiful other foreign lands were. Then he regaled the farmer about the touchstone. It could only be found on the shores of the beautiful Black Sea. It had special powers; anything it touched would be turned to gold, and the owner of this stone would become rich beyond this person's wildest dreams. The traveler went on and said the touchstone could be identified by the feel of it; it would be much warmer and smoother than the other stones.

This farmer was so fascinated by this story and wanted the stone. So to finance his journey to the Black Sea, he sold his farm and placed his family with neighbors who would care for them until he returned. He set off in search of the touchstone. On the shores of the Black Sea, he picked up a stone, felt it, found it to be cool, and dropped it back on the shore. Quickly he knew he would have to devise a plan or he could pick up the same stone many times. Here was the plan: he would pick up a stone and feel it; if it was cool or rough, he would throw it into the sea. Day after day, week after week, and soon it was year after year.

One day he picked up a stone, smooth and warm to the touch. It was the touchstone, and he threw it into the Black Sea! Why? His habit had been so strong that when he found it, he couldn't break the habit so he threw it away!

What's your life touchstone? It's called choice! Freedom to choose. Exercise it wisely and value it highly.

But if serving the Lord seems undesirable to you, then choose for yourselves this day whom you will serve (Joshua 24:15).

107. LIVING BENEATH YOUR PRIVILEGES

What would you think of a person who lived in absolute poverty, who also had a modest fortune available to them of more than a quarter of a million dollars? Most of this money was in ready cash! What would you think of this same person living in a house badly in need of paint, no electricity, no bathroom, no running water, no modern conveniences, and this same person made a daily trip to a nearby service station for water after it had closed at midnight? Okay, what do you think?

This is the story of a real lady who lived in Wyandotte County in Missouri and was brought to the attention of the county authorities who began an investigation. They discovered she had hidden away the sum of $265,781.60 in her house! More than half of that was in cash and the rest in securities. The judge declared this lady to be incompetent to handle her own affairs. He also stated that in America no one should live life like that, and so he made her a ward of the state. She was sent to a nursing home for care.

The judge is right; no one should live like that if at all possible. However, too many of us are doing just that! We live beneath our privileges, especially if we are not Christians or if we read God's Word and don't believe when the Bible tells us we can live like children of the heavenly Father. The Bible tells us that when we become Christians we are part of the family of God and a joint heir with Jesus Christ. Now that's living with privileges!

Margaret Thatcher, former Prime Minister of Great Britain, said, "I stand before you tonight in my green chiffon evening gown . . . the iron lady of the Western world? Me? A cold warrior? Well, yes . . . if that is how they wish to interpret my defense of the values and freedom fundamental to our way of life."

Then Peter said, "Silver or gold I do not have, but what I have I give you. In the name of Jesus Christ of Nazareth, walk" (Acts 3:6).

108. BE DECISIVE

This world seems to be made up of at least three classes of people: those who make things happen; those who watch things happen; and those who don't know that something has happened.

There's an interesting anecdote from the dramatic story of General Curtis LeMay. The story goes that the general was making an inspection in the old plane described as "the flying boxcar." Making his way through the plane, he was carelessly puffing on his ever present cigar.

A young officer, a lieutenant who was freshly out of flying school, angrily approached another officer to complain bitterly, "What's the matter with that old fool? Doesn't he know this aircraft is a firetrap? It could blow up!"

To which the other more mature officer calmly replied, "It wouldn't dare!"

Have you noticed in our world we have too many weak-willed, wimpy, spineless people? Really it's quite refreshing to find people with a strong will, people who are decisive, people who are determined!

People who can make intelligent decisions are the ones who also can make good, positive things happen. I believe this is one ingredient of the people who make this world go round. It's a common trait.

How do you make good decisions? By first making bad decisions. Life can teach us how by a tough process of trial and error. But don't let the mistakes overwhelm you. Try again, only this time try harder! Our world is looking for many more decisive young people. Be one of them!

"Simply let your 'Yes' be 'Yes,' and your 'No,' 'No'; anything beyond this comes from the evil one" (Matthew 5:37).

109. WHO DID YOU SAY?

Many people have painted the face of history with their dramatic life styles; however, some individuals change the direction of history through their quiet but powerful influence. Felix Kersten is just such a person.

We go back in history to World War II to share his story. During the years between 1940 and 1945 the world had been plunged in a bloodbath that nearly totally destroyed Europe and especially Germany. Names like Hitler, Himmler, and Goering struck terror to the world. During this time, Dr. Kersten rescued thousands of Jews from a certain death in concentration camps. He was the personal physician and manual physical therapist to Heinrich Himmler, and in this trusted position had an amazing power over Germany's number two man. Dr. Kersten used his influence to keep many people from becoming victims. Week after week, he was able to snatch Himmler's victims from concentration camps and gas chambers.

The World Jewish Council credits Dr. Kersten with saving at least sixty thousand Jews. He was able to save thousands of Dutch, Polish, Finns, and Norwegians. You can read this amazing story and how he was able to save so many lives in the book called *The Man With the Miraculous Hands.*

Albert Einstein wrote, "Try not to become a person of success but rather try to become a person of value."

All of us have the possibility of making a difference for someone else! Let's make that more personal. You can make a difference for someone. I can make a difference for someone. But the question is, will we?

> *For if you remain silent at this time, relief and deliverance for the Jews will arise from another place, but you and your father's family will perish. And who knows but that you have come to royal position for such a time as this?*
> (Esther 4:14).

110. THE PILTDOWN MAN HOAX

According to anthropologists, the Piltdown Man was an honored member of the society of earliest humans for more than forty years. Then a startling discovery proved this "discovery" to be an enormous fraud foisted on a trusting evolutionary world! The complete story has been told in the book, *The Piltdown Forgery,* written by anthropologist J. S. Weiner.

In early 1912, fossil hunter Charles Dawson brought the first finds of the Piltdown Man to the British Museum. Immediately the finder became world famous and soon other fragments of this missing link came from Dawson. This find was named "Eoanthropus Dawson" or in other words, "Dawson's Dawn Man."

However, some forty years later, scientists found that Dawson had deceived them all. The jaw had come from a modern day ape, which the faker had "fossilized" by staining it a mahogany color by using iron salt and bichromate. Then an oil paint, probably red sienna, he used to stain the chewing surfaces of his teeth. Further tests revealed that every fragment of the Piltdown Man was a forgery, a fake that had been foisted on the scientific community. It had once been touted as the "missing link" in evolution. It was one of the greatest hoaxes ever perpetrated!

The true story of man is recorded in the Bible in the book of Genesis. There is no missing link. God created a man and a woman! He named them Adam and Eve. No evolutionary process here! It's the story of our beginning. You just can't believe everything you hear in this world. Put what you hear through the absolute truth test. Measure it against the Word of God.

He who works his land will have abundant food, but the one who chases fantasies will have his fill of poverty (Proverbs 28:19).

111. WHAT ARE YOU WILLING TO RISK?

Webster's New College Dictionary defines risk as "the chance of injury, damage, or loss." Taking a risk could be costly, but without risk no progress can be made in life's journey. To not take a risk may be even more costly than risking something to help others. Let's think about the following:

- To laugh is to RISK appearing the fool.
- To be joyful is to RISK being a bigger fool.
- To cry is to RISK appearing too sentimental, too weak.
- To reach out to help another person is to RISK involvement in another's life.
- To place your ideas and your dreams before the crowd is to RISK their loss.
- To live with adventure is to RISK dying.
- To hope is to RISK despair.
- To love is to RISK rejection.
- To attempt something new is to RISK failure.
- To ask boldly is to RISK receiving a no reply.
- To build is to RISK collapse.
- To save and invest is to RISK losing.
- To compete is to RISK another beating you to the finish line.
- But RISKS must be taken because the greatest hazard in life is to RISK nothing.
- The person who RISKS nothing does nothing, has nothing, and is nothing.
- Only the person who RISKS is free!
- To invite Jesus Christ to be the Lord of your life is RISKING nothing and gaining everything, including eternal life!

Listen . . . accept what I say, and the years of your life will be many. Hold on to instruction, do not let it go; guard it well, for it is your life (Proverbs 4:10, 13).

112. WHAT ABOUT TAKING REVENGE?

Much speculation surrounds the origin of the Mafia. It's a fascinating story. Most historians agree that on a Monday, sometime in the year of 1242, a

French soldier viciously attacked a young Palermo Italian maid at her wedding. As the word spread about the attack, a band of Sicilians retaliated by destroying this French troop.

The Mafia is theorized to have begun at this point by taking revenge. They adopted the name from the anguished cry of the girl's mother, who ran through the streets of Palermo shouting, "Ma-fia, Ma . . . fia," which is translated to read, "My daughter, My . . . daughter!"

The French retaliated; the Sicilians sought more revenge, and on and on it went. What started as an attempt to right a wrong has evolved into a loathsome parasite on society. How do you settle a wrong? The Mafia—a perpetual scourge on the people— has plagued society with their actions of dealing in extortion, murder, kidnapping, drugs, pornography, prostitution, gambling, and more.

Taking revenge—getting even—starts the circle of revenge, which keeps on enlarging until all involved people are destroyed. There is absolutely no passion that is released into the human heart that promises so much satisfaction and pays off so little as the action of taking revenge. Taking revenge is volatile! When have you taken enough revenge? Can a put-down be fixed by doing two put-downs to the perpetrator? Revenge is such a raging passion that God says He is the only One who settles the wrongs in this world. Revenge is an action for fools! Don't get caught in the downward spiral of human actions.

For we know him who said, "It is mine to avenge; I will repay," and again, "The Lord will judge his people." It is a dreadful thing to fall into the hands of the living God (Hebrews 10:30-31).

113. DON'T BE AFRAID TO FAIL

Are you afraid to fail? Has fear of being made a fool kept you from attempting something new? The Bible tells us that fear is tormenting, fear can paralyze you, and fear will keep you safe in the boat but out of reach of the treasure. And a study taken of teenagers stated that public speaking is their number one fear. The second most fearful thing for teens is being different from their peers who might make fun of them. Carefully read the following:

- You've failed many times already, although you may not have remembered.
- You fell down the first time you tried to walk.
- You almost drowned the first time you tried to swim, didn't you?
- Did you hit the ball the first time you swung a bat?
- Heavy hitters, the ones who hit the most home runs, also strike out a lot.

- R. H. Macy failed seven times before his store in New York caught on.
- English novelist John Creasey received 753 rejection slips before he was published.
- Babe Ruth struck out 1,330 times, but he also hit 714 home runs.
- Don't worry about failure.
- Worry about the chances you miss when you don't even try![16]

I like that line, "Don't worry about failure." It's a great life concept! Yes, you might fail, but if you don't try you might not succeed either. The person who becomes a success in life is the person who does more than is necessary to get by, and keeps on doing it!

The Lord will make you the head, not the tail. If you pay attention to the commands of the Lord your God that I give you and carefully follow them, you will always be at the top, never at the bottom (Deuteronomy 28:13).

114. THE HIGHLY VALUED BOOK

A man who was an antique dealer and specialized in rare books saw this very un-bookish man who was browsing through his store. Somehow the subject of old books came up, and this un-bookish guy said that he had just thrown away an old book that was just taking up room in the family attic. He added, "It had been packed away for generations in the attic, and we needed to clean it out."

Then he added, "Somebody named 'Guten' something or other had printed it."

The book lover gasped, "Not Gutenberg?"

"Yes, I believe it was Gutenberg," the very un-bookish man replied.

The antique dealer said, "You may just have thrown away one of the first books ever printed. One copy of the Bible recently sold at Christie's at auction for more than $600,000!"

The other man, still unmoved replied, "Oh, yes, but my copy wouldn't have brought a dime because some guy by the name of Martin Luther had scribbled notes all over it."

Okay, so your Bible may not be worth that much. In reality it may be worth more than the rare copy of the Bible we just talked about because of the wisdom for life and living it contains! By the way, when was the last time you read or studied your Bible? This is my challenge to you: will you read your Bible every day? How about intentionally reading your Bible completely through this year? The study of the Bible is a post-graduate course based on the richest library of human experience!

Do your best to present yourself to God as one approved, a workman who does not need to be ashamed and who correctly handles the word of truth (2 Timothy 2:15).

115. AN INSIDE JOB

In a Southern California University an interesting experiment is repeated on an annual basis for each class of new students by the same physics professor. The scientist/professor takes a one-quart glass beaker. You've seen them in science class; it has a narrow neck and a flat bottom that is used in experiments. The fragile looking beaker is then especially treated and tempered. The demonstrator then uses it as a hammer to drive a spike into a wooden plank. It's so well-tempered it doesn't break!

Then the professor takes a small steel ball bearing, about the size of a pea, and drops it inside the beaker while holding it by the neck. When the small ball bearing hits the bottom of the beaker, the glass shatters in a spectacular crash. The beaker is broken from a simple blow from the inside.

This is much like real life. It's not the blows from the outside that break us, it's the little things from the inside that do the real damage! In reality, life consists of 10 percent of the things that happen to us on the outside and 90 percent of what happens on the inside in how we react to what has happened to us.

Og Mandino, who is one of the greatest motivational writers of our day, wrote the following in his book *The Greatest Salesman in the World:* "I was not delivered into this world in defeat, nor does failure course in my veins. I am not a sheep waiting to be prodded by my shepherd. I am a lion and I refuse to talk, to walk, to sleep with the sheep!" Incidentally, this is a book I recommend for all teens to read. You will especially enjoy the conclusion.

Do not pay attention to every word people say (Ecclesiastes 7:21).

116. THE FLYING TEAKETTLE

A car wreck in 1907 changed the face of the automobile industry and at the same time could well have been responsible for much of the air pollution on the face of our planet today. At that time the auto industry was in the throes of indecision with two major choices: Should cars be steam driven or gas powered? Steam driven seemed to be the best choice—until the annual auto races in Ormond, Florida.

At this race, several gas powered and a few electric powered cars attempted to break the hundred-mile-per-hour barrier. None were successful until the Stanley Steamer, nicknamed the "Flying Teakettle" took the track.

Let's let Fred Marriott, the driver, explain what happened: "I quickly got up to 197 miles per hour, and the speed was still rising fast when the car hit a bump. I felt it twist a little in the air, it rose off the beach and traveled about a hundred feet through the air before it struck. I was thrown clear. The machine broke to pieces with the boiler rolling and blowing steam like a meteor for a mile down the beach."

John Carlova, auto expert, said, "This was the turning point, so gas became the choice." Think of the consequences of this choice; we could all be driving steam cars with no pollution! No more low-hanging smog over the world's cities. The only gas to escape would have been steam vapor, non-polluting water. Perhaps there's a bright young engineer out there who will rediscover steam power and how to harness it safely for the next generation of cars.

Think with me how decisions can easily set a lifetime of directions. So when you make your life decisions, choose wisely because you may set something into motion that will be with you your entire life!

The wise heart will know the proper time and procedure. For there is a proper time and procedure for every matter (Ecclesiastes 8:5-6).

117. BLACK BART

A handkerchief that happened to be dropped brought an end to the career of California's most colorful stagecoach robber. Black Bart had terrorized stage coaches for six years by committing 28 robberies between 1877 and 1883 in the rugged foothills of the Sierra Mountains. He dressed in a long black linen duster with a flour sack over his head. He would hold his shotgun on the driver and demand, "Will you please throw down your treasure box, sir?" The treasure box was usually filled with a gold shipment.

Finally, near Copperopolis, Bart was wounded while escaping a holdup and dropped a handkerchief with the laundry mark "FX07." This was traced to San Francisco where police made one of the most surprising arrests in the city's colorful history. Black Bart the stagecoach robber turned out to be Charles E. Bolton, one of the city's leading citizens. He had a reputation as a non-smoking, non-drinking, God-fearing man with big business interests in gold mines and local banks. Under interrogation, he finally confessed to his crimes when confronted with the hankie and a positive identification. He was sentenced to make restitution and to serve six years in San Quentin.

Black Bart was not the first nor will he be the last person to live a lie. In our day, the media is filled with a long parade of people who are finally caught in their lies. When revealed for what they are, disgrace follows, the family is embarrassed, and their organizations are no longer trusted. Even more than this, God will also be judging such people! Deception is a lousy way to live.

83

Blessed are those who wash their robes, that they might have the right to the
tree of life and may go through the gates into the city. Outside are the dogs,
those who practice magic arts, the sexually immoral, the murders, the idol-
aters and everyone who loves and practices falsehood
(Revelation 22:14-15).

118. JUST A SIMPLE DOT

Roger van Oech, author of *A Whack on the Side of the Head*, tells the following story:

> When I was a sophomore in high school, my English teacher put a small chalk dot on the blackboard. Then he asked the class, "What is this?"
> Time passed. After a couple of minutes, finally someone timidly offered this answer: "A chalk dot on the blackboard?" Then the rest of the class seemed relieved that the obvious had been stated.
> "I'm surprised at you," the teacher told the class. "Yesterday I did the same exercise with a group of kindergarteners, and they thought of more than fifty different things. They said the chalk mark could be the eye of an owl, a cigar butt, the top of a telephone pole, a star, a round pebble, a button, a rotten egg, a chalk circle, a dot, a period, a pearl, the moon, and a whole lot more."

What has happened in the ten year period between kindergarten and high school? Not only have we learned the supposedly correct or right answers, we have also lost the ability to take the long look or the big picture look or the look outside of the box of conventional thinking! We have also lost the ability to look for more than one right answer. We might have learned how to be specific, but we have also lost much of our imaginative power!

The power to think with God given imagination is a wonderful gift. Let's once again learn how to use our imagination. It's too bad that children enter school as question marks but too often leave as periods!

But the one who received the seed that fell on good soil is the person who
hears the word and understands it. He produces a crop, yielding a hundred,
sixty or thirty times what was sown (Matthew 13:23).

119. IS THE GLASS HALF FULL OR HALF EMPTY?

Two teens happened to be leaning over the guardrail of a fifty-story sky-scraper when the rail broke and both teens fell. As they passed the fifteenth floor, the pessimist of the two was heard to yell, "Helppppppp!"

The other, an optimistic teen, shouted, "So far, so gooooood!"

Your viewpoint, your attitude, your perspective is important in regards to how you are living and will be living your life! Is the glass half empty or half full? Is it a stoplight or a go light? Is the day partly cloudy or partly sunny? Is life boring or exciting? Now you may be thinking, *What's the big deal?* Your attitude may not change the reality of a situation, but your attitude affects you as well as all the people around you.

Two salespersons were sent to an emerging country to sell shoes. One sent a fax back to the home office: "Send me a ticket home. Nobody here wears shoes!"

The other, more optimistic, sent this fax to the home office: "Nobody wears shoes over here. Everybody is a prospect for our products! Send me more shoes, more samples, more order blanks, and some more help!"

Okay, now it's your turn! Are you looking at obstacles or opportunities? Is your life half full or half empty? Are you an optimist or a pessimist? Are you joyful or unhappy? Do you need help to improve your attitude?

If so, the Bible is the best place to start! The Bible is a happy book. The word joy in any number of forms appears more than five hundred times in the Bible. Most people sort of hope for the best, but the Bible-based, born-again Christian has faith that it will actually happen!

Dear friends, build yourselves up in your most holy faith and pray in the Holy Spirit. Keep yourselves in God's love as you wait for the mercy of our Lord Jesus Christ to bring you to eternal life (Jude 20-21).

120. HOW DO YOU KNOW IF YOU'RE SUCCESSFUL?

That person is successful who has lived well and laughed often.
Who has loved much.
Who has gained the respect of intelligent people.
Who has been loved by little children.
Who has found and filled a very special niche in life,
And who has learned how to finish every job attempted.
Who has left this world a much better place than he or she found it.
It could be done by developing an improved flower or veggie.
It could be done by writing an uplifting story or happy poem.
It could be done by helping those who are in poverty or are broken in life,

Or by having rescued somebody who has fallen.

Who has never lacked an appreciation for the earth's beauty.

Who has loved God's creations and learned how to express this love.

Who has looked for the best in others and has given their best to others.

Whose life became an inspiration and encouragement to others.

Who has served God well.

Who has served others often and well.

Whose memory will be cherished fondly.

Who has a relationship with God so eternity will be spent in His heaven.

Jesus replied, "'Love the Lord your God with all your heart and with all your soul and with all your mind.' This is the first and greatest commandment. And the second is like it: 'Love your neighbor as yourself.' All the law and the Prophets hang on these two commandments" (Matthew 22:37-40).

121. BEHIND THE GOLDEN ARCHES

Ray Kroc, the founder of McDonald's, is an example of one man who had a dream and never gave up on it. But he didn't really hit his stride and become a success until he was fifty-two years old. He began his colorful career by selling paper cups for seventeen years. Then he gave it up.

He started over again, and this time he began selling milkshake machines. He had heard about the McDonald brothers in San Bernardino who had a drive-in fast-food restaurant. They were so successful that they were turning out forty milkshakes at a time on eight of his multi-mixer machines. He was curious about how his best customer was doing this kind of business. After looking at the operation, he asked the McDonald brothers, "Why don't you open other restaurants just like this one?"

They replied, "It would be a lot of trouble, and we don't know who we would get to open them."

Ray Kroc responded that he had such a person in mind.

"Who," they asked, "would that be?"

Kroc replied, "Me!" And he bought them out and began this new business at the age of fifty-two. He took the McDonald concept and built it into a billion dollar business in twenty-two years! That was no easy accomplishment. It took IBM forty-six years and Xerox sixty-three years to reach the same billion dollar level in sales revenue.

How did Ray Kroc do it? He said, "The key is perseverance and paying your dues!"

So my teen friend, do you have a dream for your life? If you have a dream, what are you willing to do to make it a reality?

Blessed is the one who perseveres under trial because, having stood the test, that person will receive the crown of life that the Lord has promised to those who love him (James 1:12).

122. I'D RATHER WATCH A WINNER

I'd rather watch a winner, than hear one any day.
I'd rather have one walk with me than merely show me the way.
The eye is a better pupil and more willing to learn than the ear.
Fine counsel is confusing but an example is always very clear.
And the best of all the coaches are the ones who live out their principles.
For to be able to see the good in action is what everybody needs.
I can soon learn how to do it if you will show me how it is done.
I can watch your hands in action but your tongue is too fast to follow.
And the lectures you deliver may be very wise and true,
But I'd rather get my lessons by observing what you do.
For I may misunderstand you and the high, wonderful advice you give,
But there's no misunderstanding how you act and how you live.
I'd rather watch a winner, than hear one any day!

Edgar A. Guest expressed it so well for all of us. A good example is much better than a good sermon! Perhaps you have discovered that it's easier for others to tell you how to live than it is to see somebody live out in real life the advice they give you. As for me, I am not interested in people who deal in theory. I want to hear and listen and follow the example of a practitioner. I want to follow a good example. I want to follow a real winner! How about you? Paul the apostle told the young man Timothy to "be an example" so others can see how a Christian is to live, act, and become.

Now all has been heard; here is the conclusion of the matter: Fear God and keep His commandments, for this is the whole duty of all mankind (Ecclesiastes 12:13).

123. FAITHFULNESS

Gene Stallings, a former football coach, tells of an incident when he was the defensive backfield coach for the Dallas Cowboys of the National Football League. Two All-Pro players who are now retired, Charlie Waters and Cliff Harris, were sitting in front of their lockers after playing a really tough game against their archrivals, the Washington Redskins. It had been a hard fought game, one that had gone right down to the final gun to determine the winner.

Both players were still in their pads and uniforms, sitting with their heads bowed in utter exhaustion, too tired to move. Charlie Waters turned to Cliff Harris and asked, "By the way, Cliff, just what was the final score and who won?"

In our rough and tumble competitive world and society, we sometimes fail to remember that excellence isn't always determined by comparing our score to someone else's. Excellence comes from excellent preparation, giving one's best, having the best game plan, playing to exhaustion if needed, and holding nothing back—no matter what the final score might be!

Calvin Coolidge, former President said, "Press on; nothing in the world can take the place of persistence, talent will not; nothing is more common than unsuccessful individuals with talent. Genius will not; unrewarded genius is a proverb. Education will not; the world is full of educated derelicts. Persistence and determination alone are omnipotent!"

Two things I ask of you, O Lord; do not refuse me before I die. Keep falsehood and lies far from me; give me neither poverty nor riches, but give me only my daily bread. Otherwise, I may have too much and disown you and say, 'Who is the Lord?' Or I may become poor and steal, and so dishonor the name of my God (Proverbs 30:7-9).

124. THE BIG BANG

One of America's major symphony orchestras gave a rousing and stirring performance of Tchaikovsky's 1812 Overture, complete with sixteen cannons for extra effect. (Of course, they were shooting blanks and not real cannon balls.)

At the dramatic moment, however, a problem occurred in the electrical firing system, and all sixteen fired off at the same time! The sound was deafening. The smoke hung heavily in the auditorium. It was much more rousing than usual! This malfunction triggered the smoke alarms in the building. This finale featured the fire alarms, fire bells, claxon horns, a shower of water from the sprinkler system, and a blanket of safety foam from the backup system all combined with the sirens of six fire engines as the building was being evacuated. The audience had been treated to a finale of all finales, including a bath in foam and water. What a way to go!

I don't know about you, but I love exciting endings—graduations, weddings, crownings, Olympic gold medal ceremonies, and more wonderful endings. There's something to be said for saving the best till last. How about you?

I know you might be too young to think about how your life might end, but do it! Will your grand finale be a glorious home going to heaven or end with a sizzle in a very hot place? How you choose to live determines how it will end. It's not too soon to be thinking about how you will end. As for me, I'm planning on making heaven my home!

> *. . . the faith and love that spring from the hope stored up for you in heaven and about which you have already heard in the true message of the gospel* (Colossians 1:5).

125. KING GILLETTE

How would you like to make your name a household word? Eventually guys as well as girls begin the habit of shaving, so sometime in your future you might also give thought to the products offered under the name of "Gillette." Here's the story:

William Painter is the name of the man who invented the common bottle cap and he had a friend, King G. Gillette, who was a traveling salesman. Painter became a rich man and talked often to his friend Gillette about inventing something that people could use more than once but eventually would throw away so they could buy more.

In 1895, while exasperated with his dull razor, Gillette had the bright idea that disposable razor blades would be this perfect invention. He quickly discovered that devising a thin steel blade was the problem. After 700 different blade failures and 51 razor blade holders failed, he finally got it right in 1903! In about three years he was selling more than half a million razors annually. And as they say, the rest is history!

So what will it take for you to do likewise? The starting point or "seed" idea is to find a need and fill it. Follow that with innovation, attention to every detail, persistence, and add to that a little bit of acquired know-how on the subject and presto, some salesmanship and your name could be the next household name! The formula is quite simple even though it may not be that easy. Oh, yes, don't forget to bring God into the equation. After all, He is the ultimate source of wisdom and new concepts. Make Him your partner!

> *Blessed are those who find wisdom, those who gain understanding, for she is more profitable than silver and yields better returns than gold. She is more precious than rubies; nothing you desire can compare with her* (Proverbs 3:13-15).

126. EXCELLENCE

"The quality of a person's life is in direct proportion to their commitment to excellence regardless of their chosen field of endeavor," stated the late Vincent T. Lombardi, one of the most legendary football coaches to ever participate in the game.

So what is excellence? How can excellence in your life be attained? Read carefully:

Excellence can be attained if you . . .

CARE more than other are willing to care, even more than others think is wise or prudent.

RISK more than others are willing to risk, even if others think it might not be safe.

DREAM more than others think is practical.

EXPECT more than others think is possible.

PREPARE more than others are willing to sacrifice in preparation.

LEARN your entire life, not only book learning, but life wisdom.

LOVE more because love is the very foundational element of God.

GIVE more than is expected of you in school, work, worship, and play.

PRAY more because the prayers of persistent people will be answered.

Willa A. Foster wrote, "Excellence is never an accident; it is always the result of high intention, sincere effort, intelligent direction, and skillful execution; it represents the wise choice of many alternatives."

Again, here's one more lifestyle decision you must make. Will I settle for a mediocre life or a life of excellence?

Dear Friend, I pray that you may enjoy good health and that all may go well with you, even as your soul is getting along well (3 John 2).

127. HAVE YOU EVER BEEN BORED?

If my observations are correct, a whole bunch of teens are living a "bored" kind of life. You've heard it and you may have said it, "I'm bored" or "This is boring." If this is your problem, if you're bored, it's time to do something about it!

A teenager, who will be named later, complained to his dad that most of the church songs or hymns were boring, too long, too far behind the times, boring tunes, and meaningless old words. His dad put an end to the conversations that had often been expressed by saying, "If you think you can write better songs, then why don't you do it?"

This teen finally went to his room and began to write and compose. He wrote his first hymn at age sixteen! And he continued to write. In fact, he wrote 349 more! The year was 1690 and if you have been to church lately, most likely you have sung one or more of his hymns. Among the 350 he wrote are such classics as "When I Survey the Wondrous Cross" and the Christmas favorite, "Joy to the World."

Are you feeling bored with this world, with your church, with your school, with your parents, with the music, with the movies, or more? Then do something about! Write something, discover something, create new concepts, invent something better, develop new methods. But no more being bored with life! Life is too precious to waste it on boredom! No more complaining; find a better way or volunteer your time to make life better for someone else. The possibilities are endless, and it's time to do something about it! You can do something about your boredom!

Do something that will let the world remember your name 300 years from now! Oh, yes, the sixteen-year-old teen who wrote his first hymn was Isaac Watts.

For there is a proper time and procedure for every matter (Ecclesiastes 8:6).

128. THE RICH YOUNG RULER

William Boice of Phoenix has written the following observation:

"Dear Lord, I have been rereading the record of the 'rich young ruler' and his obviously wrong choice. But it has set me to thinking. No matter how much wealth he had in his day, he could not ride in a car, have any surgery, turn on a light, buy penicillin, watch TV, wash dishes in hot running water, mow a lawn, fly in an airplane, sleep on an innerspring mattress, or talk on the phone. If he was rich, then what am I?"

I don't know exactly when Bill Boice wrote that, but think of things to add to the list that the rich young ruler could not do: email, blog, twitter, record tunes on an iPod, watch a Blu-ray disc, or have a computer.

Who really is rich? The rich young ruler who came to Jesus, or you and me in today's high-tech world? Something to think about for the rest of the day. This information confronts all of us with some sort of an inventory check. Just what are and what will be the priorities in our living? Who and what will we serve with our investment of time, talent, and resources?

This brings us to an even bigger question: What will we do with what we have? There is this matter of sharing with others who have not been so blessed as we may be. Then there is the issue of gratitude . . . are we grateful and thankful for what we have, whether it is much or little? We could be reduced to nothing.

In this story all kinds of questions are begging for answers—yours and mine. The really huge question: Are we willing to leave all and follow Jesus or continue in our pursuits of gaining more and more material things?

> *When Jesus heard this, he said to him, "You still lack one thing. Sell every-thing you have and give to the poor, and you will have treasure in heaven. Then come, follow me." When he heard this, he became very sad, because he was a man of great wealth"* (Luke 18:22-23).

129. PREMATURE DEATH

You probably never think of dying. Am I right? When we think of dying, it's always old people who die, never young and healthy and strong people like us. Well, let's just visit the subject of dying for a bit.

Consider with me some of these world famous people who died quite young. Let's start with Anne Frank, the young German Jewess who kept that most famous diary out of World War II, which became a best-selling book; she died at age fifteen.

Thomas Chatterton, the very well-known English poet died at seventeen.

King Tut, probably the most famous of Egyptian Pharaohs, had his tomb uncovered by Howard Carter and his exhibits now travel worldwide; he died at age eighteen.

Joan of Arc, the French heroine, is remembered in history because of the way she fought and became a martyr at age nineteen.

Nathan Hale, who is remembered in the USA Revolutionary War as one of the most notable heroes, died at age twenty-one.

James Dean, a Hollywood actor, is remembered by his spectacular death at age twenty-four.

Nero, the infamous Roman Emperor who supposedly fiddled while Rome burned, died at age thirty-one.

Death is not a popular subject but we must remember that it has no age limits. It can happen to anybody at any time, at any age. The life lesson? Any preparations you plan to make for eternal life after your death must be made in advance!

> *There on the mountain that you have climbed you will die and be gathered to your people, just as your brother Aaron died on Mount Hor and was gath-ered to his people* (Deuteronomy 32:50).

130. WHAT IS LEADERSHIP?

Lots of people talk about it, but few really understand it! Most people want it, but very few really achieve it! So what is this illusive thing called leadership?

Boiled down, leadership is influence. Nothing more, nothing less. Leadership is influence; influence is leadership.

James C. Georges said, "What is leadership? Remove for a moment the moral issues behind it, and there is only one definition, leadership is the ability to obtain followers.

So let's reserve our moral judgments and look at some world leaders: Hitler was a leader, Stalin was a leader, Lenin was a leader, Pol Pot was a leader; but all these leaders led their followers into bondage and death. So let's look at leaders who had a positive influence on their followers: George Washington, Abraham Lincoln, Martin Luther King Jr., Margaret Thatcher, and Winston Churchill. Taken from history we know their value systems were different, but they all had followers.

Who today would you consider as leaders? Sports heroes? Political figures? Hollywood stars? Military commanders? High profile religious leaders? What about you? Are you leadership material?

My choice for the world's greatest leader in history? Jesus Christ, the Son of the living God is the greatest leader who has ever lived, and His followers today are numbered in the billions and are growing every day! The best advice I can give you is to become a follower of Jesus Christ before you can become a real leader.

As Jesus went on from there, he saw a man named Matthew sitting at the tax collector's booth. "Follow me," he told him, and Matthew got up and fol-lowed him" (Matthew 9:9).

131. A LITTLE KNOWN OLYMPIAN

Who would you say was or is the world's greatest all-around female athlete in history? This takes in a lot of history and a whole lot of years. Think hard. If you happened to nominate Fanny Blankers-Koen of the Netherlands, you would be right! About now you may be thinking, *I have never heard of this woman; what's so great about her?* Okay, let's take a closer look at her record.

Following the 1936 Olympics, she emerged as the world's greatest female sprinter, but the next two Olympic Games in 1940 and 1944 were canceled due to World War II. We can only imagine what the record books would have said about her had she been able to compete.

Following the '36 Olympics, Fanny married, gave birth to a son and daughter, and again at the age of thirty competed in the 1948 Olympics in

London. She won the 100 meter dash, the 80 meter hurdles, the 200 meter dash, and the 4 by 100 meter relay. She is the only woman in history to have won four track and field gold medals in the same Olympiad. Not only that, during this time, Fanny was also the world's record holder in the long jump and high jump but elected not to compete in these additional events.

Now, do you have a favorite nominee? This is a pretty awesome record by somebody who has been long lost in the dust of history.

What is to be learned from such a woman and her record achievements? Following her record setting competition in the 1948 Olympics, a reporter asked Fanny what was the secret of her success. Her simple reply was, "Continual training and perseverance." With that simple formula you could be the next winner!

I do not consider myself yet to have taken hold of it. But one thing I do: Forgetting what is behind and straining toward what is ahead, I press on toward the goal to win the prize for which God has called me
(Philippians 3:13-14).

132. TABLE MANNERS

How would you like to be invited to the White House in Washington for one of their famed state dinners? Very few of us have been invited, and I don't think too many of us common folks will be invited in the future. But think if it did happen!

It would be a very formal event with white tablecloths, crystal, candles, fancy china, real silverware, and more. This would be the time to really mind your manners. This same kind of thinking must go through the minds of all who are invited. Let's drop in on one of those past White House dinners.

Several friends of President Calvin Coolidge from Vermont had been invited to dine with him. The dinner passed uneventfully; the right spoons and forks had been used at the correct times, and all courses had been served.

All went well until it was time for the coffee to be served. The President poured his coffee into a saucer. Eager to please, these guests all did the same. Then Coolidge added cream and sugar. The visitors all did the same thing. Then the President leaned over and gave his saucer of coffee to his cat!

I love it! My only regret was that I wasn't there to observe it. So, is there a moral to this story? Let's be reminded once more of the power of peer pressure! This is an awesome power. While good friends can be good for us; bad friends can be very bad for us. Mature teens are people who are careful of the friends they make. Teens should be looking for friends and others who can challenge them, lift their sights higher, pull up their expectations, mentor them, and be good examples. Mature teens are not blind followers of the blind!

Two are better than one, because they have a good return for their work: If one falls down, his friend can help him up. But pity the man who falls and has no one to help him up! (Ecclesiastes 4:9-10).

133. FINISH YOUR RACE

At 7:00 p.m., October 20, 1968, just a few thousand spectators remained in the Mexico City Olympic Stadium. More than an hour earlier, Mamo Wolde of Ethiopia had won the marathon.

Then the remaining spectators were startled by sirens and looked toward the marathon gate where a lone figure, nineteen-year-old John Stephen Akhwari of Tanzania appeared through the gate as the last marathon competitor in this race.

One of his legs was bloodied and bandaged. He limped and grimaced with each step. He had injured it in a painful fall earlier in the race. Each marathoner completed his race by a final lap around the Olympic track. It was excruciating to watch his last lap. Each step was an effort—he was limping, stumbling, and hobbling. In a final push he finally crossed the finish line. Spectators were on their feet, silently watching the drama unfold before them. When he crossed the finish line, they burst into cheers!

A reporter described it like this, "Today we have seen a young African runner who symbolizes the finest in the human spirit finish his race."

Akhwari was asked why he hadn't quit after being injured. He quietly replied, "My country did not send me to start this race; they sent me seven thousand miles to finish the race!"

Vince Lombardi said, "The difference between a successful person and others is not a lack of strength, not a lack of knowledge, but rather in a lack of will."

I have fought the good fight, I have finished the race, I have kept the faith (2 Timothy 4:7).

134. LET'S KEEP OUR FOCUS

Maybe you remember the tragedy of the Eastern Airlines jumbo jet that crashed in the Florida Everglades. After all the investigations have been finished and black box information examined, officials were able to piece together the story behind the crash.

The plane was the now infamous Flight 401. It was bound from New York to Miami with a heavy load of holiday passengers on their way home to celebrate with families. As the plane approached the Miami airport for the landing, the light that indicates the proper deployment of the landing gear failed to light. The autopilot was disengaged and the plane then flew in a large, looping circle over the swamps of the Everglades while the cockpit crew checked to see if the gear had deployed or if the bulb happened to be defective or had burned out.

When the flight engineer attempted to remove the light bulb, it wouldn't budge. The other members of the flight crew tried to help. As they were struggling with the light bulb, none of the crew noticed that the aircraft was losing altitude until the plane flew right into the swamp!

Dozens of people lost their lives while an experienced crew of high-priced pilots fiddled with a seventy-five-cent light bulb! It's easy to lose focus, to lose our priorities. Too often, it's the little things that can trip us up.

Winston Churchill said, "The price of greatness is responsibility."

Keep focused. Don't forget what life is really all about. Keep doing what's right!

What does the Lord your God ask of you but to fear the Lord your God, to walk in all his ways, to love him, to serve the Lord your God with all your heart and with all your soul? (Deuteronomy 10:12).

135. CHOOSE TO DIE OR CHOOSE TO CHANGE

It's a well-known fact that may have escaped today's modern teen. During the early twentieth century, from the 1920s through the 1950s, the Swiss made watch was the most prestigious and best quality watch or clock you could buy in the world. As a result, about 80 percent of the watches sold in the world were made in Switzerland. It was a proud industry with a wonderful product—precision made and hand wound.

Then something came on the scene that would change the watch manufacturing industry forever. In the late 1950s the digital watch was presented to the leaders of the Swiss watch companies. They soundly rejected the idea because they knew they already had the best watches and the best watchmakers in the world. The man who had invented and developed the digital, battery run watch finally sold the concept to the Seiko company of Japan.

In the 1940s, Swiss watch companies employed more than 80,000 people. Today, that number is less than 18,000. In the 1940s, I remind you, more than 80 percent of the watches were Swiss made. Today 80 percent of the watches sold are digital.

This true story, a little tragic, represents what happens too frequently to people and organizations when they refuse to change.

The youth of today are living in a fantastic time; change is everywhere! Just take a quick look at our technology and how quickly change happens. The cell phone has just about replaced the land line phone. The choice is yours . . . change or get left behind!

And no one pours new wine into old wineskins. If he does, the wine will burst the skins, and both the wine and the wineskins will be ruined (Mark 2:22).

136. JUST ONE LITTLE PROBLEM

At the annual gathering of a dog food company, all the salespeople were required to be present. The sales manager asked, "How do you like the company's new advertising campaign on television?"

"Great! The best in the business," they replied with enthusiasm.

"How do you like our new labeling and packaging?" asked the sales manager.

"Wonderful! Exciting! Again, it's the best in the business," was the reply.

"How do you like being part of our sales force? Do we pay you well? Are you being rewarded?" demanded the sales manager.

They admitted they were the best sales force in the dog food business.

"Okay, then" said the manager, "so if we've got the best labels, the best packaging, the best advertising program being sold by the best sales force in this business, tell me why we are in fifteenth place in sales in the dog food business!"

A long and unhappy silence followed. Finally, one salesman from the back of the room shouted, "It's those lousy dogs! They won't eat the stuff!"

Do they have a problem? Yes, they have a problem! If they had started with the basics, the foundation on which they hoped to build a prosperous business and created a product dogs loved, their problem would be over.

So my young friend, begin building the foundation of your life on something solid, something that works for your lifetime. Get the foundation right. Build on your firm relationship with Jesus Christ and the rest of life will fall into place.

By their fruit you will recognize them. Do people pick grapes from thornbushes, or figs from thistles? Likewise every good tree bears good fruit, but a bad tree bears bad fruit (Matthew 7:16-17).

137. IS THERE ANYBODY ELSE?

A man named Homer Anderson went off alone one day to climb the steepest face of the well-known Mount Hood. Everything went well until he had dug his crampons onto a ledge that gave way and Homer fell. Fortunately, by some kind of a miracle, he managed to grab onto a small tree growing out from a crevice. He held on for dear life and looked down, hundreds of feet to the next ledge. He was swinging back and forth. He looked up, but it was not possible to climb back up. He looked sideways and saw nothing more to grab on to. He saw only one solution.

Homer began desperately praying, then shouting, "Is anyone up there? Please help me!" He did it over and over until at last an immense voice from above said, "My son, Homer, did you call?"

"Oh yes, yes!" responded Homer, "Please help me!"

The voice replied, "Do you know who I am?"

Homer shouts back, "It's you, Lord, help me!"

The voice again said, "Homer, do you completely trust in Me?"

"Yes, yes, oh Lord. Yes, yes, I do trust You," he replied.

The voice then said, "Okay then, Homer, son, let go of the branch!"

After a really long pause, Homer shouts, "Excuse me, please, but is there anybody else up there?"

Okay, it's an old story but I still want to ask you the question: "When problems and pain come to you: "In whom or what will you be trusting?"

"Come, follow me," Jesus said, "and I will make you . . ." (Matthew 4:19).

138. THREE DOLLAR'S WORTH

Here's a little tidbit of writing by an unknown source that really bothers me, and I would hope it also bothers you.

I would like to buy three dollars worth of God, please. I would like just a little. Not enough to explode my soul or disturb my sleep. Not enough to take control of my life. I'd like just enough to equal a cup of warm milk, just enough to ease some of the pain of my guilt.

I would like to buy three dollars worth of God. I don't want enough of Him to make me pick beets with a migrant. I want ecstasy but not transformation. I just want the warmth of the womb but not a new birth. Not enough to impose responsibility myself. But just enough to make church folks think I'm okay. I want a pound of the eternal in a paper sack. I would like to buy only three dollars worth of God, please!

Wow, that is really disturbing! Something to really think about because we live in a day and time when total commitment is not the "in" thing to do. Sure, this kind of living is politically correct: we're all okay, do your own thing, be your own god, everybody is good, God is good, and all we want is a sort of eternal kind of life insurance. Come to think of it, a whole lot of us are really willing and want to serve God but only on our terms as His consultant!

God is God and we need to serve Him on His terms—total commitment. He makes it very clear, you are for Him or against Him! There is no middle ground, no compromise.

The Lord our God, the Lord is one. Love the Lord your God with all your heart and with all your soul and with all your strength (Deuteronomy 6:4-5).

139. WHEN DO YOU ASK FOR GOD'S HELP?

Mr. Rosten, age seventy-four, was taking his first trip by air to Israel via Amsterdam from New York. As luck would have it, he was assigned a seat next to an Arab who was wearing a turban and a long white flowing robe. The Arab buckled in, stared at the aged Jew, and spat on Mr. Rosten's shoes!

The Boeing 777 took off, leveled at 35,000 feet elevation for the trans-Atlantic flight. Then the Arab fell sound asleep, and they flew into violent turbulence. Poor Mr. Rosten. He grabbed for the airsickness bag too late. He missed and sent a projectile all over the Arab's clean white robe.

The old man, fearfully, closed his eyes and began to pray. "Oh, Lord, please help me when this crazy Arab man awakens and sees and smells his robe, or he will kill me with his dagger! Oh, Lord, you just have to help me. Please!"

After a while, the Arab awakened, stretched, and opened his eyes. Then an inspired Mr. Rosten leaned over, politely smiled, and said, "So, Mister from Arabia, are you feeling better now?"

Why can't we in this diverse world get along with everybody? When will we really see peace? The Bible commands us to all live at peace with all people. So why is that such a difficult thing to do? Living peacefully really begins with you and me living like neighbors need to live. The Bible also says that no peace will be among the nations until Jesus Christ, the Prince of Peace comes to bring peace.

Perhaps the Lord allows some of us to get into trouble because that is the only time we ever think of asking for His help. Own up, is that your truth?

God is our refuge and strength, an ever-present help in trouble (Psalm 46:1)

140. TARGET SHOOTING

A captain in the U.S. cavalry, following the Civil War, was riding through a small town in Oklahoma and stopped his horse to admire and be astonished at what he saw. On the side of a barn he saw about a hundred different chalked bull's-eye circles. In the center of each was a perfectly centered round bullet hole!

The captain stopped the first man he met. "What fabulous shooting! I've never seen such a display of marksmanship. Who is this marksman?"

The passerby slowed, sighed and said, "That's Tim Decker's son. He's a bit strange . . ."

"I don't care what he is," said the captain. "The cavalry needs anyone who can shoot that well."

"Ahhh," said the pedestrian, "You don't understand, captain. You see, first Timmy shoots and then he draws them circles!"

Anybody can be a sure shot in life if he or she shoots first, then draws the circles. But a real marksman learns how to center the bull's-eye by diligent and consistent practice.

And so it seems that each of these devotions eventually gets down to you with questions about your life and living. Yes, each one tells a story, shares a truth, gives us something on which to hook that truth. A story like this is Velcro in the mind. You remember the story, and when you do, the truth also sticks!

So, let me put this truth like this to you. One real danger in life is not that our aim is too high and we miss it, but that our goal is too low and we hit it!

Set your hearts on things above, where Christ is seated at the right hand of God. Set your minds on things above, not on earthly things
(Colossians 3:1-2).

141. SHIPWRECKS

It's a moonless, dark and stormy night, more than two hundred years ago. Four men are standing on a grassy knoll overlooking the North Atlantic Ocean. They are looking through spy glasses pointed out to sea for a glimpse of a ship's light glowing through the darkness. One of these men is pacing back and forth, leading a horse with a lighted lantern tied to its chin that is bobbing up and down as he walks. What are they doing? Attempting to convince the ship at sea that the light on their horse is another ship sailing nearby and that it is safe to sail toward them.

Soon the ship at sea sees the light and assumes it to be another ship. It turns in that direction only to run aground and become another shipwreck. The sand, sea, and the wind would eventually hide the wreck, but not before everything of value had been taken by these four pirates who made their living by deception, treachery, murder, and thievery.

This describes one of many such instances that took place at Cape Hatteras in North Carolina. In fact, more than 2,300 ships met their death here—some by accident but many more by the treachery of pirates!

It's sad to say, but many forces in our world are out to destroy, kill, or steal from you with all kinds of treachery. The Bible tells us that there is a thief roaming out there with the stated purpose of doing everything he can to steal from you, kill you, and destroy you. His name is the devil or Satan or the evil one or Beelzebub. How do you defend yourself? By your relationship with Jesus Christ and using the sword called the Word of God!

Your enemy the devil prowls around like a roaring lion looking for someone to devour. Resist him, standing firm in the faith (1 Peter 5:8-9).

142. A LITTLE BIT ABOUT GOALS

You have probably heard all you care to hear about goals. Yes, goals are important in life and living, but let's take a closer look.

Goals must be something over which you have control. You need targets and directions upon which to focus your efforts. Make sure you control them!

Winning is one of those wrong kinds of targets I've been referring to. Winning is a target; however, it is an impractical one. Why? Winning is something that is not totally under our control. Instead of setting goals based on outcomes, we should set goals that focus on our performance. There's a difference. For example, if you are a golfer, set a goal such as hitting 80 percent of your drives on the fairway; when attained, raise the goal.

By setting our goals on things that we control, we will not be influenced by such factors as what our opponent will be doing, the weather, the problems we might be having in home or school, or even that thing called luck.

We are also much better off if we can break down our goals into smaller, more manageable steps. We need to start with smaller goals. After we complete one goal, then we can move on to larger goals. But we need to always set goals in things within our control.

An African proverb states it like this: "The best way to eat the elephant standing in your path is to cut it up into little pieces."

Laurence J. Peter cautions us, "If you don't know where you are going, you will probably wind up somewhere else."

Humility and the fear of the Lord bring wealth and honor and life
(Proverbs 22:4).

143. HOW TO LOSE YOUR VISION

Here's another story right out of our history books. What happens when leadership or followers lose sight of their vision? The following is an example that may or may not be familiar to all of us.

It started with the Pilgrims who came to America about four hundred years ago to build a new community and to get away from the religious persecution of the old world. They came to this unsettled land with a great vision and the courage to tame and settle in this new land.

In the first year they established a new town, planned it, and did it.

In the second year they elected a town council to give them leadership.

In the third year their town council government proposed building a new road five miles westward deeper into the wilderness.

But in the fourth year these people attempted to impeach their town council because the people thought a road into the forest would be a complete waste of their public funds.

How is it that these courageous, forward thinking, brave acting people had lost their vision? Five years previously they had been able to see across the unknown ocean with enough faith in themselves and their God to take a step of faith into the unknown. But only five years later they could not look only five miles farther into the wilderness!

Never underestimate the power of your vision. But also never underestimate what time and disappointment and weariness can do to your present vision! Keep it alive, keep it moving, keep out of the rut of comfort. Keep renewing your vision!

Where there is no vision, the people are unrestrained
(Proverbs 29:18 NASB).

144. BORN TO LOSE

A man was visiting the Far East and walks through some of the twisted little streets of Kowloon in Hong Kong, enjoying being a tourist. He came upon a little tattoo studio tucked between two stores. In the window were displayed samples of the tattoos available. There were all kinds of anchors, flags, mermaids, animals, and more available for chests, arms, or ankles.

But what struck this tourist the most was the tattoo displayed in the center with three words, large and colorful, that couldn't be missed: BORN TO LOSE!

Out of curiosity he entered the shop and was greeted by a smiling Chinese tattoo artist who asked, "May I help you?"

The tourist pointed to the prominent display and asked, "Does anyone really have this terrible phrase, BORN TO LOSE, tattooed on their body?"

He replied, "It's quite popular."

"But," the dumbfounded tourist said, "I just can't seem to believe that anybody in his right mind would do that."

The artist simply tapped his forehead and in broken English said, "Before tattoo is on body, tattoo is on mind."

The Bible is still correct when it states that whatever a person thinks about in his or her mind will eventually be the kind of person he or she becomes. Think like a loser and soon you will be a loser! Think like a winner and soon you will be a winner! Think negative thoughts and you become a negative person. Think positive thoughts and you soon become a positive, happy, joyful, fulfilled person! Yes, whether you believe it or not, your mind is that powerful!

Above all else, guard your heart, for it is the wellspring of life
(Proverbs 4:23).

145. A LITTLE BIT ABOUT ANGELS

Practically everybody today knows something about angels, at least on some level. There's lots of talk about angels today. You can find angel stories, poetry written about them, songs about them, and lots and lots of books about angels. Why? I think there is a deep, underlying need for all of us to have a look into the spirit world all about us. We are curious to know more.

But there are a couple of things to know about angels:

1) We are never commanded to worship angels! The Bible is clear, only God is to be worshiped.

2) We are not told to pray to angels. It's okay to ask God for help, but not angels. God may send an angel to help you in answer to your prayer. Keep a healthy balance in regards to angels.

How about an angel story? Author Elisabeth Elliot wrote this story about her father. "My father, when he was a boy, was climbing on an upper story of a house that was being built. He walked to the end of a board that was not nailed at the other end and it slowly began to tip! He knew he was doomed! But inexplicably, the board began to tip the other way, as though a hand had pushed it down again. He always wondered if it was an angel's hand."

Just what do angels do and how do they work? It's a mystery, but so many stories and human encounters give us some small clues. Are they always there in an emergency? Does each of us have a guardian angel?

John Milton, the blind poet, wrote: "Millions of spiritual creatures walk the earth unseen, both when we sleep and when we awake."

See that you do not look down on one of these little ones. For I tell you that
their angels in heaven always see the face of my Father in heaven
(Matthew 18:10).

146. WHAT YOU ARE

It was a sunny, warm Saturday afternoon. A happy young father, Jim McGuire, was taking his two boys to play miniature golf. They approached the counter and Jim asked, "How much is it to play a round?"

The nineteen-year-old attendant said, "Four dollars for you and four dollars for any kid who is eight or older than eight. They get in free if they are under eight. How old are they?"

Jim answered, "The football player's five and the baseball player is eight, so I guess I owe you eight dollars, right?"

The young man at the counter said, "Hey, mister, you could have saved yourself some money. You could have told me the older one is seven and I wouldn't have known the difference."

Jim replied, "Yes, that could be true, but the kids would have known the difference."

What do you think? Is it okay to lie if you can save yourself some money? Let's go a step further. Is it ever okay to tell a lie? We live in a world with no strong feelings about right or wrong. They're telling us, "If it feels good, do it" and "Everything is relative." People say situation ethics are the way to get ahead in this world, and that it's old fashioned to believe in absolute truth.

Where do we get our moral compass for living in a compromising and compromised world? There *is* absolute truth whether you believe it or not. A bedrock foundation on which a better society can be built begins with truth! One of the Ten Commandments clearly states, "You shall not lie!" That's under or in any situation of life you are facing or will ever face. Truth begins with God.

I have set you an example that you should do as I have done for you
(John 13:15).

147. WHAT DO YOU THINK ABOUT YOUR DAD?

When it comes to dear old Dad, it comes down to something like this:

At age 4: "My daddy can do anything!"

At age 5: "My daddy is the best dad in the whole wide world."

At age 7: "My dad sure knows a lot, a whole lot!"

At age 12: "Oh, well, naturally, my dad doesn't know that, either."

At age 14: "Oh Dad? He's just out of date, he's old-fashioned."

At age 18: "My dad just doesn't get it, he doesn't understand me."

At age 21: "Oh that man, he's sure not with it."

At age 25: "Dad? Well, he might know something about it."

At age 35: "Before we decide what to do, we'll talk it over with Dad and get his input."

At age 50: "I wonder what Dad would have thought about that?"

At age 60: "You know when I think back, my dad knew something about everything!"

At age 65: "I really wish I could talk it over with Dad just once more!"

How many sixteen-year-old teens do you know who can't possibly believe that someday they will be as dumb as their dad? Your dad may not be appreciated until it's too late. Right here, in your relationship with your dad, is a secret to having a long and fruitful life. The Bible says we should honor our fathers and our mothers so our days would be long on this earth! This is a biblical promise that pays off—honor your dad and God will honor you with a longer life! Pretty cool, huh?

Whoever loves discipline loves knowledge, but he who hates correction is stupid (Proverbs 12:1).

148. A LOT TO GIVE

The newly appointed missionary had been assigned to teach in a school in Tanzania, africa. One of the first concepts she was attempting ot impart to her students was the value of giving. she based her lessons on the lifestyle of Jesus Christ whose entire life was devoted to giving. It proved to be a new concept for her students, but she helped them understand it by using plenty of examples. And she especially emphasized the importance of generosity, the idea of sacrifice, and the value of the recipient. Following this teaching section, there was a long weekend break from school.

On the second day of the break, there was a knock on the missionary's door. As she opened it, there stood one of her students, with his clothing wet with sweat from the intense African heat. He shyly handed her a beautiful seashell. She exclaimed how beautiful it was, knowing full well it must have come from quite a distance since their village was located far from the ocean.

He said, "This is for you, my teacher, in thanks for your teaching."

Thinking of the cost involved in purchasing such an item and knowing his poverty, she asked him, "Where did you get this?"

He said, "From the ocean. I picked it for you myself."

Astonished, she replied, "What a long walk that was!"

He brightened, smiled, and said, "Long walk is a part of the gift."

This student learned his lesson well. What a powerful impact that kind of gift has on the receiver! When we do not have money to share, we can give courage, love, hope, consideration, respect, and even our time to others as the student in our story did in his long walk to the ocean.

There is a deep joy in giving, and through it we can be a powerful avenue of blessing to others. What we have we can give. And when we stop to think about it, all of us have a lot to give.

Silver or gold I do not have, but what I have I give you! (Acts 3:6)

149. THE ONE ARMED SOLDIER

Napoleon Bonaparte of France is one of those towering figures in history. What may not be so well known about him was that he was a powerful motivator, a leader who was able to inspire men to be willing to die on the battlefield for the cause of France and their glorious leader. In order to arouse patriotism, he loved to tell the following story:

Once while visiting a province in France he came on an old soldier with one arm severed, who was dressed in full uniform with the coveted Legion of Honor medal pinned to his lapel. "Where did you lose your arm?" Napoleon asked.

"At Austerlitz, Sire," came back the soldier's brisk reply.

"And for that you received the Legion of Honor?" asked Napoleon.

"Yes, Sire. It is but a small token to pay for the decoration," he said.

"You must be the kind of man who regrets he did not lose both arms for his country," Napoleon responded.

"What then would have been my reward?" asked the one-armed man.

"Then" Napoleon said, "I would have awarded you a double Legion of Honor."

In reply to that, the proud old fighter drew his sword and immediately cut off his other arm!

This story was told for years until one day a man asked, "How did he do it?"

Okay, what more can be said other than that you should never believe everything you hear. Check it out! Is it real or is it fiction? Test it against truth! A person with a sense of humor doesn't have to make jokes out of life, just recognize the ones that are!

Moreover, when God gives any man wealth and possessions, and enables him to enjoy them, to accept his lot and be happy in his work—this is a gift of God (Ecclesiastes 5:19).

150. COOKIE

Harry "Cookie" Lavagetto, a former major league baseball player and manager died on Friday, August 10, 1990. He was seventy-seven years old. *So what?* you may be thinking, *Why should I be interested in an old ball player?* Read some of his story:

Cookie managed the Washington Senators from 1957 to 1960 and became the first manager of the Minnesota Twins. Still no big deal. As a baseball player, he was a lifetime .269 hitter, which is no big deal either. There are lots of .200 hitters.

But Cookie's great moment in the sun came in 1947 as a member of the Brooklyn Dodgers. In the fourth game of the World Series, New York Yankees pitcher, Floyd Bevens, was throwing a no-hitter. It's down to the ninth inning and two Dodgers had managed to get on base . . . still a no-hitter. With two outs in the ninth, Lavagetto had a double that bounced of the right field wall (which also happened to be his very last hit in the majors), to drive in two runs and led the Dodgers to a three to two win!

Yes, that's exciting, but we're still not to the rest of the story. Years later, he was asked if he was thinking about breaking up that no-hitter when he hit the ball. Lavagetto replied: "I wasn't thinking 'no-hitter,' I was thinking double!"

Are you thinking the glass is half empty or the glass is half full? Are you thinking I can't do this or I can do this? Are you catching on?

If you say it can't be done, then it's likely you can't do it. If you think I can do it, then it's likely you can! Your success in life will depend on your attitude. Success comes in cans and failure comes in can nots!

A simple man believes anything, but a prudent man gives thought to his steps (Proverbs 14:15).

151. IT'S ALL IN HOW YOU SAY IT

A reporter had been assigned the task of writing up a life story about a local socialite because she had been very generous with her fortune. She was about to be honored for a huge gift that was being used to build a new hospital for the community. While doing some research into her background and her family tree, he came upon two relatives who had not been good citizens, to say the least.

He brought this to her attention and she replied, "Yes, I know about my great-grandfather as well as an uncle who was the black sheep of the family." She looked at the reporter and said, "If you must mention them, please write something that would be dignified and in good taste."

So the reporter wrote the following about her great-grandfather, who had been hanged for being a cattle rustler: "His demise came while participating in a public ceremony when the platform gave way under his feet."

He mentioned her black sheep uncle, who more recently had died in the electric chair for murder, with this sentence: "Uncle Harry graciously occupied the chair of applied electricity in one of America's great institutions. He died while in a harness."

I'm all for saying kind and gentle things about others. If the kind thing can't be said, say nothing! You see, our tongues are powerful weapons for good or destruction. The Bible is constantly warning about how destructive the human tongue can be and how difficult it is to tame the tongue. My word to you for today is this: think before you speak!

Out of the same mouth come praise and cursing.
My brothers, this should not be (James 3:10).

152. THE WEAK LINK

History is absolutely full of important life lessons if we are willing to learn from them. Not too many are willing for it's also said, "The only thing we learn from history is that we do not learn from history." Enough already. Come with me to ancient China for this history lesson.

Ancient China had been invaded many times by enemies intent on conquering or pillaging the nation. They had battled with any number of barbaric hordes such as Genghis Khan and others. They became tired, particularly with this problem from the North. Desiring security, one of their leaders decided that the best protection for their nation would be to erect what we today call the Great Wall of China. It was to be built so high no enemy could climb over it and built so thick that nothing could break it down. It was quite an engineering feat, and today it stretches for thousands of miles and is one of the world's most visited tourist attractions. They say it's one of the few things that can be seen from outer space. Quite an achievement.

After the wall was built they settled down to enjoy their security. However, during the first hundred years of the wall's existence, China was invaded three different times through the Great Wall! Not once did the barbaric hordes break it down or climb over it. Each time they had bribed a gatekeeper and then marched right through a gate!

All the protection in the world is worthless if the people in charge can be bought off or bribed. Lack of integrity in our leaders today is making our society unsafe for the next generation. What will you do about this lack? And always remember, the Chinese were so busy relying on their walls of stone that they had forgotten to teach integrity to the youth who grew up to guard the gates!

Train a child in the way he should go, and when he is old he will not turn from it (Proverbs 22:6).

153. KING TUT'S CURSE

King Tut is likely the world's best known teenager from the ancient world. Perhaps you've seen his amazing exhibit that has traveled the world.

It's been established that this legendary Egyptian pharaoh Tutankhamen died at age nineteen in 1324 BC. How he died has been a huge controversy since his tomb was discovered by Howard Carter in 1922. However a new study published in the *Journal of the American Medical Association* found that King Tut most likely died after a severe bout of malaria and complications from a fractured leg. This evidence was obtained through DNA testing done by Egyptian, German, and Italian researchers. This now also explains the mystery of why a hundred or so walking sticks were found in his tomb.[17]

The writer, James Patterson, has just released a book in which he goes into great detail about how King Tut had been murdered; this new finding contradicts the old theory about his murder.

This is an amazing story. DNA reaches all the way back to the thirteenth century before Christ and can determine the cause of death in a mummy. Have you ever thought about how it would be possible for God to know and remember everything about your life and my life when you and I must stand before His judgment seat and give an account of our lifestyle? In fact, the Bible says it has a record of everything we have done or said in life. If DNA can do what it does, surely God has a better record keeping system. Therefore, when you live your life, keep an eye on eternity and how you need to live your life so you don't need to fear the coming judgment!

And I saw the dead, great and small, standing before the throne, and books were opened. Another book was opened, which is the book of life. The dead were judged according to what they had done as recorded in the books (Revelation 20:12).

154. HUNGER STUNTS 200 MILLION KIDS

Nearly 200 million kids under the age of five who live in poor countries have stunted growth because of malnutrition, according to a report published by UNICEF. More than 90 percent of these kids live in Africa and Asia, and more than a third of all kids who die in that age group have a link with poor nutrition.

Progress is being made in Asia where rates of stunted growth dropped from 44 percent in 1990 to 30 percent today. The rate of stunted growth in Africa was about 38 percent in 1990 and is about 34 percent today. South Asia is the hotspot for this problem with Afghanistan, Nepal, India, Bangladesh, and Pakistan accounting for 83 million kids under the age of five.

So why should you as a teenager be concerned about little kids? Did you go to bed last night without your dinner? Did you go to school today just so you could get a free school lunch because there was nothing to eat at home? Have any of your teeth been falling out because of poor nutrition? If not, then be thankful for the country in which you live and the home in which you live that provides the very basics of life.

Again, why should teens be concerned about starving little kids? What's wrong with well-nourished teens helping out little kids who need a hearty lunch tomorrow? All of us can be of help in lots of ways—we could easily sacrifice and go without that extra McDonald's Big Mac. We can also give some of our abundance to our church or other reputable organizations who will feed and help these little guys. God tells us to help the poor. How about beginning today?

He who mocks the poor shows contempt for their Maker (Proverbs 17:5).

155. NATIONAL BIBLE BEE WINNER

Isaac Ward from Binghampton, New York, was the junior winner in the first National Bible Bee contest. Isaac, fourteen years old, won a $50,000 scholarship for taking first place in the eleven- to fourteen-year-old category in the 2009 contest held in Washington, D.C.

The National Bible Bee is for the purpose of motivating kids and youth from age seven to eighteen years of age to memorize the Bible. This contest began with more than 17,000 contestants who signed up to participate nationwide. There were 340 local Bible Bee contests before they narrowed the field down to the final 300 participants.

How did Isaac win? Isaac, who is a homeschooler, has memorized the following books of the Bible: James, Galatians, Ephesians, Philippians, Colossians, Philemon, and the Gospel of Mark. Awesome!

And what about you? How much of the Bible have you memorized? Bernie Elliot, National Bible Quiz coordinator, said, "The discipline and training make it easier once you do it for the Lord and in the power of the Spirit."

Why go to this effort? Sure, to win a $50,000 scholarship! Who wouldn't? But there are any number of other reasons why we should be memorizing the Word of God. One excellent reason was written by the psalmist who said, "I have hidden your word in my heart that I might not sin against you" (Psalm 119:11). That's a powerful and a fabulous reason! How about this? "They overcame him [the devil] by the blood of the Lamb and the word of their testimony" (Revelation 12:11). That's a secret to living a life of victory and freedom from sin. Bible memorization is an opportunity while you are young! The Word of God will guide you through the rest of your life.

For the word of God is living and active. Sharper than any double-edged sword, it penetrates even to dividing soul and spirit . . . it judges the thoughts and attitudes of the heart (Hebrews 4:12).

156. SLED DOGS TO THE RESCUE

How would you have liked to grow up in a part of the world that is so remote and rugged that you could not get out of town by cars, trucks, trains, boats, or airplanes? Not many places like this are left in the world. In 1925, though, this was the situation in Nome, Alaska. Transportation was a huge problem, but that's not all. During the winter of 1925 many kids and teens became deathly sick with diphtheria, a very rare disease today, but a real problem back then. The problem gets more difficult when this town discovered they had no medicine or vaccine for the treatment of diphtheria. Without help many of these kids and teens were doomed. Telegrams were sent out asking for immediate help.

How would vaccines get there? A plan was devised. The medicine would be sent by plane as far as Nenana, Alaska, but it was still more than seven hundred miles to Nome. The only possibility was by dogsled!

The medicine was carefully packed to protect it, and teams of dogs and their drivers, called mushers, took turns carrying the precious cargo. They battled snowstorms, high winds, and below zero temperatures. Then in the final few miles another snowstorm struck. The trail was lost in the snow, visibility was down to nothing, it looked like the plan might fail. But the lead dog Balto knew the way; he kept on leading the team until they arrived in Nome in time to save the sick kids!

A great story, but are you aware that not only sick kids in Nome needed to be saved? We have a whole world that needs to be saved! How about you? Do you need to be saved? How is a person saved? It's when we accept Jesus as our Savior that we are saved!

Christ Jesus came into the world to save sinners (1 Timothy 1:15).

157. ARE YOU SURE?

Do you know where you would spend eternity if you were to die in your sleep tonight? There are really only two possible places to spend it: in heaven with Jesus Christ and all the saints or in hell with the devil and all his demons. Talk about a choice, it's either black or white; there is no in between place you can spend eternity. This is to the point, only two choices. If you don't choose, you have made a choice. If you choose to go to heaven, there are specifics you need to know and act on.

First you must admit you are a sinner. The Bible says, "There is no one righteous, not even one . . . for all have sinned and fall short of the glory of God" (Romans 3:10, 23).

Second, you must ask God's forgiveness and repent of your sins. The Bible promises, "Everyone who calls on the name of the Lord will be saved" (Romans 10:13).

Third, believe in Jesus. This is simply putting your trust in Him as your one and only hope of salvation. The Bible again says, "For God so loved the world that he gave his one and only Son, that whoever believes in him shall not perish but have eternal life" (John 3:16).

Fourth, you will become a child of God by receiving Christ. We go to the Bible again for this promise, "To all who received him, to those who believed in his name, he gave the right to become children of God" (John 1:12).

And finally, confess that Jesus Christ is your Lord! The Bible tells us, "That if you confess with your mouth, 'Jesus is Lord,' and believe in your heart that God raised him from the dead, you will be saved" (Romans 10:9).

The choice is yours. You can make the right choice right now! I'm praying for you and this important life choice, and I welcome you to the family of God!

How shall we escape if we neglect such a great salvation? (Hebrews 2:3).

158. BUILDING A BUSINESS ON ICE WATER

In 1936 North America was experiencing some of the hottest temperatures ever recorded. Nobody ever said anything about global warming back then. The heat was just part of life's difficult circumstances. For example, some parts of South Dakota during July had temps as high as 120 degrees with no air conditioning, especially in cars! There was a couple, Dorothy and Ted Hustead, who were struggling to establish a drug store in Wall, South Dakota, right near the Badlands. Customers were few and far between.

Dorothy was attempting to take a nap on one of those hot July days, but it was no use. She felt the heat and was disturbed by the cars rumbling by on the highway in front of their small store. She knew the drivers and passengers were feeling the same kind of heat with no relief in sight. She had one of those bright ideas!

She told her husband, Ted, about her idea. They made up some signs for the highway promising free ice water. The customers came pouring in and soon wanted more than the free ice water. Ted hit the road and posted signs farther and farther from Wall, South Dakota. The business today is still growing. The little drugstore with the free ice water has not changed. In fact, today, if you go through Wall, you can still get free ice water! This little store has grown into a five hundred seat restaurant and all kinds of mall stores.

So what's the big deal? Today's world is full of people in a hurry to get a drink of cool water. Who is going to offer them a drink of the water of life? How about you and me who may have already drunk of this water that brings eternal life?

Whoever drinks of the water that I shall give him will never thirst. But the water that I shall give him will become in him a fountain of water springing up into everlasting life (John 4:13-15 NKJV).

159. DISTURBING TRENDS AGAINST WOMEN

A study by the Los Angeles based Parents Television Council shows that storylines on primetime television are graphically depicting violence against women as never before. The report, "Women in Peril," revealed that incidences of violence against women on ABC, CBS, FOX, and NBC shows rose 120 percent between 2004 and 2009. Overall, other violence on the same networks during the span increased only 2 percent!

This study reported that females were depicted as victims of violence 429 times in 2009 compared to 195 times five years earlier. The most frequent type of violence was being beaten, 29 percent; next was a credible threat of violence, 18 percent; shootings, 11 percent; rape, 8 percent; stabbings, 6 percent; and torture, 2 percent. During 19 percent of these depictions, the woman died.

CBS had the highest number of instances with 118, but NBC had the highest increase of violence during this period, 192 percent. This report also noted a 400 percent rise in violent portrayals against teenage girls.

"In depicting violence against women and teenage girls with increasing frequency on television, or as a trivial, even humorous matter, the networks may be contributing to an atmosphere in which young people view aggression and violence against women as normative, even acceptable," this study concluded.

This is a challenge facing the next generation. When you become the next television programming personnel, what will you do to change this trend? Our pattern is Jesus Christ, who when He walked this earth elevated women to the same level of men! We all become equal when we gather at the foot of the cross.

There is neither Jew nor Greek, slave nor free, male nor female, for you are all one in Christ Jesus (Galatians 3:28).

160. MOTHER HAS THE LAST WORD

This true story happened during the American Revolutionary War. An army officer was sent around the Virginia countryside to confiscate horses that were needed for military use in the war effort. He came to a fine old mansion on a plantation. He rang the bell and asked to speak to the mistress of the house.

"Madam," he said in his most polite manner to the dignified lady he met in the parlor, "I am claiming your horses for the use in the army on order from my commander."

"Sir," she replied, "You cannot have my horses. I need them for the spring plowing and planting. By the way, who is your commander?"

He replied, "General George Washington, commander of the American army."

She then said, "You just go back and tell General George Washington that his mother says he cannot have her horses!"

Leave it to a mother! I hope you have been privileged to have a mother who is forceful enough to tell you no now and then.

But even more important, have you learned how to say no to temptations, to friends who might lead you into trouble, to advertisements that seek to entice you to take up smoking or consuming alcoholic beverages or to premarital sex? All kinds of decisions in this world are best handled with a firm no. If Adam and Eve in the garden of Eden had learned how to say no, it might have saved this world a whole lot of trouble.

"Simply let your 'Yes' be 'Yes,' and your 'No,' 'No;' anything beyond this comes from the evil one" (Matthew 5:37).

161. HOW OFTEN DO YOU LAUGH?

Comedian Jerry Lewis calls humor a safety valve. "The peoples of the world who have the ability to laugh at themselves are those who survive," says Lewis.

The late Bob Hope said that laughter has constructive power. "A laugh," he said, "can transform almost unbearable tears into something bearable, even hopeful."

The late country humorist, Jerry Clower once said, "God doesn't want his children to walk around unhappy. He wants them to be happy. I am convinced that there is just one place where there is not any laughter and that is hell. And I've made arrangements to miss hell, so, ha, ha, ha, I ain't goin' to have to ever be nowhere some folks ain't laughin'."

A recent survey indicates that the average child laughs about 150 times a day, but adults laugh less than ten times a day. If you're a teen in the process of becoming an adult, please don't lose your ability to laugh!

I have a theory that people who can laugh together are people who will last together. Have you noticed? Dictators and political leaders cannot stand to be laughed at. I have this theory that if the German people had had a sense of humor, Hitler never would have come to power. If the first time they had seen the goose stepping and heil salutes and laughed, there would have been no Third Reich!

The Bible really has a lot to say about living with joy and happiness. Living with joy and laughter and good humor will make you a much better person! I'm for living with joy and laughter today, and the rest of your life and mine. Be happy!

A cheerful heart is good medicine, but a crushed spirit dries up the bones (Proverbs 17:22).

162. ARE WE INTENDED TO FLY?

Many years ago a most interesting conversation took place that is really quite memorable, and I shall tell you why later.

A church bishop of the United Brethren was visiting a friend who happened to be the president of a small college. In time, their conversation turned to the progress that was being made in the world, and they speculated about the next big invention or the next great advancement for society and science.

The bishop made the pronouncement that he believed that everything that was worth inventing had already been invented!

The college president disagreed and voiced his hope like this, "For one thing, I believe that some day men will be able to fly in the air!"

"Nonsense, complete nonsense," the bishop objected, "If God had intended man to fly in the air, He would have given us wings in the first place."

This conversation likely would have been easily forgotten in time nor ever reported except for one important fact: the bishop's name was Wright, and he had two sons named Orville and Wilbur! Of course, these two guys were the first men to fly. Their flight took place at Kitty Hawk, North Carolina, and now you know the rest of this interesting story.

This bishop was wrong; God did intend for all of us to fly!

I remind you of an ancient Chinese proverb, "Man who say it cannot be done should not interrupt man doing it!"

Now it's your turn. What do you think is still to be invented?

But those who hope in the Lord will renew their strength. They will soar on wings like eagles; they will run and not grow weary, they will walk and not be faint (Isaiah 40:31).

163. HOW DID ALEXANDER BECOME "THE GREAT"?

Alexander became "The Great" because his influence outlasted his battlefield victories. His troops adored him. One instance of his leadership stands out. They had been on a forced march without water in the hot desert sun for two days. He sent out his scouts to find water, and they returned at the end of the day with a little bit in the bottom of a helmet. No one had had water in days; they enviously looked at their leader as he took the helmet to drink, then he poured it out and said, "It's no good unless we can all drink!"

He was raised with a sense of duty. At age twenty Alexander inherited the throne of Macedonia from his father. He then set out with 35,000 troops to conquer the world. In the next eleven years he marched more than 11,000 miles, never lost a battle, and sent Greek culture through out the then known world.

But by 324 BC, Alexander's own power became too intoxicating. He withdrew from the life of a soldier and declared himself the son of the Greek god Zeus. He began drinking heavily because there were no more worlds to conquer.

He was in Babylon with his army in 323 BC, preparing for his next campaign, and got into a drinking contest at a celebration banquet. He is believed to have gulped down at least six quarts of wine. The next day he was sicker than a dog; he had caught a cold that turned into pneumonia. From his bed he continued to issue orders. Within ten days of Alexander's drinking fest, the world conqueror was dead.

He managed to conquer the world, but he could not conquer himself! Alexander had always believed he was also descended from Achilles. If that's true, then Alexander's "Achilles' heel" was his ego.

What good is it for a man to gain the whole world, yet forfeit his soul? Or what can a man give in exchange for his soul? (Mark 8:36-37).

164. A SPECIAL PRAYER FOR A SON

Please think about the following prayer that was written by a famous world leader. I think it bears repeating, and then I shall identify the writer:

World, take my son by the hand; he starts school today! It is all going to be strange and new for awhile, and I wish you would sort of treat him gently.

To live in this world will require faith and love and courage. So, world, I wish you would sort of take him by his young hand and teach him the things he will have to know.

He will have to learn, I know, that all men are not just, that all men are not true. Teach him that for every scoundrel there is a hero, that for every enemy there is a friend.

Teach him the wonder of books. Teach him that it is far more honorable to fail than to cheat.

The man who wrote those words was Abraham Lincoln. These are more than beautiful words strung together. They express a prayer, one that is still valid today. It's a prayer that I hope your fathers have been praying for you!

Along these same lines, John Wooden, probably the best and most successful college level basketball coach who ever coached, said, "It's what you learn after you know it all that counts."

Listen to advice and accept instruction, and in the end you will be wise
(Proverbs 19:20).

165. THE ULTIMATE SEDUCTION

Leo Tolstoy told this story about a Russian young man who became heir to his father's small farm. One morning as he stood near the home on his homestead, a stranger—a person of great authority—told him that he could have, for nothing,

117

all the land he could walk around in one day. The one condition to this deal was that at sundown, he had to have returned back to the starting point.

The young man was excited and eager to begin! The plan was to meet the next morning at sunup and begin his adventure. His first plan was to cover a tract of land 6 miles square; but when he'd walked the first 6 miles, he decided to make it 9 miles square. After the 9 miles, he decided 12 miles. Then he decided he would make it 15 miles square. This was a walk of 60 miles in one day, before sundown!

By noon he covered the first 30 miles. He didn't bother to stop for food or even water because he was so eager to complete his journey. He forced himself to walk as fast as he possibly could. Fatigue began to set in; his legs were burning. The sun was beginning to set, so he forced himself to hurry. The last mile was agony. A few hundred yards from the finish he started to feel faint but managed to force himself to stagger across the finish line where the stranger was standing to meet him. He made it, but fell at the government authority's feet—dead!

The stranger said, "I offered him all the land he could cover. Now you see what that is—6 feet long and 2 feet wide."

The person who thinks money and possessions are everything has never been sick or faced their death!

Then he said to them, "Watch out! Be on your guard against all kinds of greed; a man's life does not consist in the abundance of his possessions"
(Luke 12:15).

166. THINKING BACK

When Jeff had died and arrived at the Pearly Gates, he didn't have long to wait for his entrance interview. Quickly he found himself standing before a very impressive angelic being with a clipboard in his hand who started his entry data. The angel asked, "Jeff, it would be of help if you could share with me an experience of yours of a totally purely unselfish deed from your life on earth."

Jeff thought for a few moments and replied, "Oh, yes. One day I was driving along the street and came upon a little old lady who was being robbed and beaten by a huge motorcycle gang type of guy. I drove my car into and over his motorcycle. I jumped out of my car after distracting him. I grabbed the little old lady and shoved her behind me, and faced him as he came charging at me. Then I kicked him as hard as I could in the shins and shouted at the lady to run. Then I hauled off and gave the guy my best right hand shot to his jaw!"

Impressed, the angel said, "That's quite a story. Tell me, just when did this experience happen?"

Jeff looked at his watch and said, "Oh, about two or three minutes ago!"

Yeah, I know, it's just a story and not very theologically correct either. So let's take this story another step and consider what it might be that you would be willing to risk your life for. Would you be willing to risk your life for the safety of a family member or a friend? What about risking it as a patriot for your country? What about risking your life as a missionary in a dangerous part of the world to tell someone else about the sacrifice Jesus Christ made for all of us?

[Jesus said,] *"For whoever wants to save his life will lose it, but whoever loses his life for me will find it"* (Matthew 16:25).

167. WHAT DO YOU THINK HEAVEN IS LIKE?

What do you think heaven is like or will be like? Perhaps this is a subject you haven't thought about much lately. Here's an old poem that reads like this:

The angels from their thrones on high
Look down on us with wondering eye,
That where we are but passing guests
We build such strong and solid nests,
And where we hope to dwell forever
We scarcely send up any building materials.
—*Author unknown*

So what is heaven like? Someone has written it like this, "You land at the airport, and God is waiting to greet you." If you are a traveling person, you are also familiar with the sinking feeling that comes when you try to show people videos of the places you've been. You ask, "Who would like to see my travel videos?" And there is usually silence. All travelers have experienced that problem with family and friends.

But with heaven, it will be completely different. God, who stands to meet and greet you, will also say, "I would love to see your videos!"

Okay, so what is your picture of heaven like? Do you see lots of angels and golden streets and mansions and light? Or what else do you see?

More importantly, it's not what you think heaven may be like. The bigger question is how do you make sure you will go to heaven when you die? There is only one way you can get to heaven. In the Bible, Thomas asked this same question: "Lord, we don't know where you are going, so how can we know the way?" (John 14:5).

Here's the specific answer: Jesus answered, "I am the way and the truth and the life. No one comes to the Father except through me!" (John 14:6). It's that simple, but you must know it's the only way to heaven, so you can someday really know what heaven is like!

Trust in God; trust also in me. In my Father's house are many rooms; if it were not so I would have told you. I am going there to prepare a place for you
(John 14:1-2).

168. SNAKE BITTEN

Jason was an active, outdoorsy, thirteen-year-old who lived with his family in the Deep South on the edge of a wooded, swampy area. They were the last farm place on their road before you would have plunged off into the wilderness. Jason, in his growing up days, had developed an avid interest in snakes of all kinds, poisonous and non-poisonous. He studied everything he could find concerning them. One of his favorite things to do was to go hunting for snakes. He carried an old sock or small flour sack in which he could carry home another snake or two or three.

On this particular day, even though he was careful, he missed seeing the coiled water moccasin. But he felt the hard hit on the back of his upper calf! Almost instantly the searing pain began running up his leg. He knew immediately what had happened. He walked a few short steps to get away from the snake and dropped to the ground. The effects of the adult snake's venom were already starting to work! No one knew where he was. How could he get help?

He cried out for help with heard no answers. Then he prayed, desperately. Almost immediately a man appeared, a very ordinary looking man, who picked him up and carried him all the way to his farm home. Mom and Dad immediately called 9-1-1, put him in their pickup, and rushed to the local hospital emergency room. With an injection of snake anti-venom, Jason survived. The doctor said without the help of the anonymous stranger, Jason would have died! Who was this stranger? They knew everybody in their area, but not this man. No one knew, but they concluded it was a guardian angel who showed up to help. Angels can appear when you need them most!

"For he will command his angels concerning you to guard you in all your ways; they will lift you up in their hands (Psalm 91:11-12).

169. MOTHERS STILL KNOW BEST

A recent survey was taken of several hundred mothers. The question asked was this one: "As a mother, do you have golden rules to live by?" Out of the hundreds of answers, they were boiled down to these simple commonsense rules. If they worked for mothers, they may just work for you:

1. If you open it, close it.
2. If you turn it on, turn it off.
3. If you unlock it, lock it back up.
4. If you break it, admit it.
5. If you can't fix it, call in someone who can.
6. If you borrow it, return it in good shape.
7. If you place value on it, take good care of it.
8. If you make a mess, clean it up, now.
9. If you move it, move it back.
10. If it belongs to someone else and you want to use, get permission.
11. If you don't know how to operate it, leave it alone.
12. If it's none of your business, don't ask questions.
13. If it ain't broken, don't fix it.
14. If it will brighten someone's day, say it.
15. If it will tarnish someone's reputation, keep it to yourself.

Well, there you have them, fifteen commonsense rules for living from mothers. Really, it's about all you'll need to get along in this life with others. In fact, they are so good, use them yourself and pass them along to others. Tell them they are compliments of Mom!

Therefore encourage one another and build each other up, just as in fact you are doing (1 Thessalonians 5:11).

170. WOMEN IN UNIFORM

Catherine G. Lutes of Tallmadge, Ohio, writes about her experience:

During our basic training to become Army nurses, we were required to spend one week out in the field, roughing it. It just so happened that during our week it rained the entire week, every day and night! In spite of the rain, training kept right on going. In the morning we got up in our swampy, damp tents, took a cold-water beauty bath from our helmets, strapped on our pistol belts and ponchos, grabbed our field backpacks, and trudged through the mud to set up field hospitals. Obviously, our personal appearances frequently left a whole lot to be desired.

The final blow to our feminine pride happened while we were standing in line in the mess tent, in the mud and rain. A really young Army private came by with his digital camera and asked if he could take our pictures. We said, "No way!"

He asked again, but this time explained, "This picture will prove to my girl back home that she has no reason at all to be jealous of you women."

First off, I think it's time we share a positive word of appreciation to all the young women and men who are serving in the armed forces of our countries around the world. They do it at great sacrifice so that we can remain free and enjoy our lifestyles.

Then, what is real beauty? Is it on the outside or on the inside? In today's world, a great premium is placed on outward personal appearances and the clothes we wear. But from the Bible's perspective, real beauty is on the inside. What have you been working on? Your inner person or only the outer person? I remind you, God looks on the heart while others look on the outside.

> *As for those who seemed to be important—whatever they were makes no difference to me; God does not judge by external appearance* (Galatians 2:6).

171. A ROAST CAMEL RECIPE

In my observations, teenage guys never think about such things, but teenage girls may have given lots of thought and planning to this special occasion—the wedding dinner. Brides usually are pretty fussy about every detail of a possible wedding, including the menu. How about this for your consideration?

One of the most complicated single dishes ever prepared by chefs is roast-stuffed camel. About now, I'm losing some of you, but let's go on. This large, tasty delicacy is often served at large Bedouin marriage feasts.

The recipe reads, "To prepare this delicacy, first take 100 gutted Mediterranean trout and stuff them with 200 hard-boiled eggs; then stuff the trout into 50 cooked chickens; the chickens are then placed into a body cavity of a sheep, and the sheep into the carcass of a camel. Then roast over a charcoal fire until done. This meal will serve at least 300 hungry guests!"

I kid you not, this recipe is taken from *The Book of Strange Facts and Useless Information*. There you have it, young ladies; this recipe will cause a real sensation with your guests at your upcoming wedding dinner.

On a more serious note, the possibility of a marriage and building a family is the most important decision you will make in your life—next to that of your relationship to Jesus Christ. Give your decision lots of prayer and choose wisely.

I remind you that psychiatrists tell us that girls tend to marry men who are like their fathers, so now we know why it is that mothers cry at weddings.

Tell those who have been invited that I have prepared my dinner: My oxen and fattened cattle have been butchered, and everything is ready. Come to the wedding banquet (Matthew 22:4).

172. EVOLUTION

Evolution versus creation versus intelligent choice is a hot subject in teaching circles. There's an interesting history surrounding this debate.

When Charles Darwin's *Origin of the Species* was published in 1859, most Christians didn't know how to react. His supposed research offered a shocking scenario that seemed to contradict the biblical version of God's creation. Many church people feared this new scientific theory might have a profoundly negative impact on the church and world in general. They were right. Today it's still an issue, especially in schools and universities.

Here's a four line poem entitled "Roots" by Ruth Tucker that you might enjoy:

Great Granddad was a jellyfish; his folks were just pure slime.
And Gramps, he was a lizard who was on the upward climb.
My daddy was a monkey, and mom a chimpanzee.
And here I am, a human, with a Ph.D!

Here's a question for your consideration: If in fact we descended from monkeys, why is it that monkeys are still here?

Darwin's theory of evolution suggests that the baboon came first and then came mankind. In today's world, politics and politicians are proving that it can go either way.

God has the last word on this subject, "So God created man in his own image, in the image of god he created him; male and female he created them" (Genesis 1:27).

And that settles it for me! How about you?

Then God said, "Let us make man in our image, in our likeness, and let them rule over the fish of the sea and the birds of the air, over the livestock, over all the earth, and over all the creatures that move along the ground"
(Genesis 1:26).

173. THE TEN CANNOTS

Perhaps all of us have some acquaintance with the Bible's Ten Commandments. Some of us would rather not be bothered by these rules for life, but they still apply whether you like it or not. But I digress. Instead of reading for you the Ten Commandments, I suggest you read these Ten Cannots:

1. You cannot bring about prosperity by discouraging thrift.
2. You cannot help the "small" people by tearing down the "big" people.
3. You cannot strengthen the weak by weakening the strong.
4. You cannot help the poor by destroying the rich.
5. You cannot keep out of financial trouble by spending more than your income.
6. You cannot further brotherhood or sisterhood by inciting race hatred.
7. You cannot establish financial security on borrowed money.
8. You cannot build character by taking away initiative and independence.
9. You cannot help people by doing for them what they could do for themselves.
10. You cannot have a meaningful life without God!

Do you know any politicians who need a copy? I must say this is pretty good stuff to live by. The writer, Oliver Wendell Holmes said, "The greatest thing in this world is not so much where we are, but in what direction we are moving."

Do not let this Book of the Law depart from your mouth; meditate on it day and night, so that you may be careful to do everything written in it. Then you will be prosperous and successful (Joshua 1:8).

174. WORLD'S FASTEST FAILURE OF A DRIVING TEST

One of the major rites of growing up is getting a driver's license. A test to prove your ability as a driver is given, so you have to earn the right to drive. The legal age to be able to drive varies from country to country; but universally, it's a special rite of passage. But not all driving tests turn out the way they should. Consider these . . .

Until recently the world record for the fastest failure was held by Helen Ireland of Auburn, California. She failed her driving test in the first second! How? By cleverly mistaking the accelerator for the brake pedal! She stomped it to the floor and shot straight ahead—through the wall of the local driving test center.

This record seemed an unbeatable one until an English auto mechanic from Lanarkshire named Thomas failed the test before the driver's license examiner had even stepped into the car. He arrived at the test center and Thomas tooted the horn to summon the examiner, who promptly strode out to the vehicle and announced, "It is illegal to toot your horn while your car is stationary!" He wrote out a ticket for disturbing the peace, told Thomas he had failed the test, and strode back into the driving test center again!

Genius of this kind cannot be taught, it must be a natural gift! It's true that we are all human and subject to messing up, but this too can be overdone. How can such goof-ups be avoided? It's quite simple. It's called careful preparation and study. It's called paying the price first, then the rewards come later. All right, how much have you been studying lately?

Listen, my sons, to a father's instruction; pay attention and gain understanding (Proverbs 4:1).

175. IS TV WATCHING HAZARDOUS TO YOUR HEALTH?

If Dr. William Dietz has his way, another well-loved product found in homes all over the world would carry the following warning label: television may be hazardous to your physical and mental heath.

Dr. Dietz, who is the chairman of the Academy of Pediatrics' subcommittee on children's and teen's television, says that TV is hazardous because too many parents have no control over its use and have no idea what kind of messages are being televised.

Surveys have shown that the average child and young teen watches three to five hours on average per day. This amounts to approximately 15,000 hours spent in front of a TV by the time he or she reaches the age of eighteen. Compare this to only 11,000 hours that will be spent in the average classroom!

According to his research, the boob tube instructs kids to be aggressive toward others because each child will have witnessed at least 18,000 televised murders while growing up. It also teaches that drugs, booze, and cigarettes are ways to deal with the problems of life. TV also teaches that sex, while it is always exciting, enticing, and mysterious, is wonderful because there is no personal responsibility to it.

As a result, this academy and Dr. Dietz recommend severe limitations on TV viewing or no TV watching at all! He recommends no more couch potato kind of lifestyle, and wants us to become physically active, fill our mind with positive kinds of input, and discipline ourselves to read good books. I agree with his recommendations, and I would challenge you to take it one step further: have a regular time of Bible reading every day.

The god of this age has blinded the minds of unbelievers, so that they cannot see the light of the gospel of the glory of Christ, who is the image of God (2 Corinthians 4:4).

176. WHICH IS WORSE?

We are going to read one of those serious daughter-to-mother talks, the kind that really gets down to where we live. The daughter is quite thoughtful and asks her mother, "Mom, which is worse—to tell a lie or steal something?"

The mother replied, "Well, both are sinful activities. They are both bad and I'm not sure which one is the worse." The daughter is quiet and the mom is thoughtful.

"Mom," the daughter replies, "I've been thinking about this a lot and I think it's worse to lie than to steal."

Then the mother asks, "Okay, please explain."

"Well, you see, Mom, it's like this," replies the daughter, "if you steal something, you can take it back, unless you have eaten it; and in that case you can pay it back. Or if you used it and ruined it, you can always buy another one and give it back. But when you tell a lie, it is forever!"

She's a smart, thoughtful daughter and I believe I agree with her thinking. A lie can easily destroy reputations, ruin relationships, and destroy trust.

I'm delighted to tell you that both lying and stealing can be forgiven, and that eternal forgiveness is found by repentance and accepting the forgiveness that is only found in our relationships with Jesus Christ.

Other people can usually determine our character by observing what we stand for, what we fall for, and what we will lie for. As you me, I am for living without lying or stealing. How about you?

You shall not steal. You shall not give false testimony against your neighbor
(Exodus 20:15-16).

177. THE WRONG PLACE AT THE WRONG TIME

Have you ever been at the wrong place at the exact wrong time? Usually we realize this after it's too late. Let's consider the wrong place for the following people who were at the wrong place at the wrong time.

Patricia Spahic was sitting in the third row during a production of the stage play, *Hamlet*, and was deeply cut in the head. How? When swinging his dagger, the actor who was playing the role of Hamlet allowed it to slip out of his hand, and the knife sailed into the audience and stabbed Patricia. She survived after a trip to emergency room.

Or consider Joan Raeburn who was traveling in her car on a rural road near the border of Ohio and Indiana when she was the victim of a hit-and-run pilot! She was minding her own business when the pilot grazed the roof of her car with his single-engine plane and flew off into the night! After a trip into the ditch, she too survived.

Or how about the lady who was shot and killed while sleeping in her apartment in Austin, Texas. The man downstairs was cleaning his pistol, didn't realize it was loaded, and accidentally fired the pistol up through the ceiling.

All three of these three young women had no idea of what event was just ahead of them. How can you be prepared for the accidents of life? There's not much you can do other than to make sure your life insurance is current. And how about doing a checkup about your eternal life assurance plan?

James Stewart wrote, "Let us live as people who are prepared to die, and die as people who are prepared to live!"

Just as man is destined to die once, and after that to face judgment, so Christ was sacrificed once to take away the sins of many people; and he will appear a second time, not to bear sin, but to bring salvation to those who are waiting for him (Hebrews 9:27-28).

178. ETERNAL VIGILANCE

Dean Niferatos was riding the number 22 CTA bus in Chicago, his normal mode of transportation on his way home from the university. He tells the following story:

The bus was full of people on their way home from work, and many of them were dozing off. The bus riders included working mothers, college students, teen high school students, some restless street punks, and a few affluent shoppers.

At the bus stop at Clark and Webster, two men and a woman climbed on the bus and paid their fares. The bus driver, a crusty, seasoned veteran driver, immediately bellowed out, "Everybody watch your valuables! Three pickpockets are now on board!"

The reactions were immediate: women clutched their purses, teens grabbed their shoulder bags, men transferred wallets from back pockets to front pockets, and all eyes were staring at this infamous trio of petty thieves. The trio looked insulted and harassed and didn't even slow down as they promptly exited through the back exit doors on this bus.

How about that for being politically incorrect? The Bible gives us many clear warnings that we are to be eternally vigilant always because evil is less likely to overtake us when we are on the lookout! The devil has been described as a roaring lion on the prowl seeking whom he may devour. The answer is always for us to be on the watch.

Teens can become wise by watching what happens to them when they haven't been watching and on guard so it doesn't happen again. Live with constant vigilance.

"Why are you sleeping?" he [Jesus] *asked them. "Get up and pray so that you will not fall into temptation"* (Luke 22:46).

179. WHAT IS MORE VALUABLE?

A monk who was traveling by foot in the mountains found a precious stone in a clear stream. The next day he met another traveler who was hungry, so the monk opened his knapsack to share his food.

The hungry traveler saw the precious stone in the monk's bag, asked to see it, admired it, and boldly asked the monk to give it to him. To his astonishment, the monk handed it over without hesitation.

The traveler left happy and rejoicing in his good fortune. He knew the jewel was worth enough to provide him with financial security for the rest of his life. But he couldn't stop thinking about the monk. A few days later, he returned to the path he had traveled before and searched for the monk.

When he found him, he gave the stone back to the monk and said, "I have been thinking. I know how valuable this stone is and that you also knew it to be very valuable. But I give it back to you in the hope that you will give me something more precious than this jewel. If you can, let me have whatever it is that enabled you to freely give me this stone."

What is more valuable than an uncut precious stone and financial security? The attitude of unselfish giving . . . the inner something that allows someone to give without asking for anything in return. What makes a person a giver? There's a simple and short answer—the change of heart that comes through an encounter with the God who gave the most precious gift he could give to us— his Son. If we accept this gift, we will see that it can change any hard heart into a caring one.

For God so loved the world that he gave his one and only Son, that whoever believes in him shall not perish but have eternal life (John 3:16)

180. DON'T QUIT

What's your first thought when things go wrong? Do you want to quit? Do you want to give up? Do you want to blame others? Or do you make a quality decision? The following has been a bit of encouragement to lots of people, so I want to share it with you if you happen to think about quitting.

When things go wrong as they sometimes will,
When the road you're trudging seems all uphill,

When the funds are low and the debts are high,
And you want to smile but you have to sigh.
When care is pressing you down a bit, rest if you must, but don't quit!
Success is failure turned inside out,
The silver tint of the clouds of doubt.
And you never can tell how close you are; it may be near when it seems far.
So stick to the fight when you're hardest hit,
It's when things go wrong that you mustn't quit!
(Author unknown)

Samuel Johnson wrote, "Consider the postage stamp; its usefulness consists in the ability to stick to one thing until it gets there."

Love does not delight in evil but rejoices with the truth. It always protects, always trusts, always hopes, always perseveres (1 Corinthians 13:6-7).

181. THE BEAUTY OF A MOTHER

T his little story happened on a gorgeous fall day. A street named Lovers Lane Boulevard happened to be lined with maple trees that were in the height of fall colors. It was one of those seasons too beautiful for words.

A lady was walking with her elderly mother, and they were talking about the beauty of nature they were enjoying. The daughter commented, "Isn't it wonderful of God to take something just before it dies and is gone and make it so beautiful?" as she looks at the falling leaves of gold, yellow, and red.

Her elderly mother replied, "Wouldn't that be nice if He also did that with people?"

The younger lady turned to look at the stooped, aged, white-haired, gentle faced mother beside her. She smiled and answered so softly that her mother struggled to hear her soft words, "Sometimes He surely does."

Have you taken the time to appreciate your mother, whether she's young or old? Think of all that your mother does for you to make life wonderful. You know, I finally found the right Mother's Day card that expresses my feeling for my mother in real terms. It said, "Now that we have a mature relationship, there's something I'd like to tell you. You're still the first person I think of when I fall down and go boom!"

I say, it's time to make every day a special Mother's Day. Let's all give Mom a word of thanks every day. And you might be surprised at what happens.

A wise son brings joy to his father, but a foolish man despises his mother (Proverbs 15:20).

182. IS PERFECTION ATTAINABLE?

Are you one of those people who could be described at a perfectionist? Such people expect or strive toward perfection. Are you concerned about perfection? This is a tough goal for human beings, but let consider the following.

If things were right only 99.9 percent of the time, there would be:

- One hour of unsafe drinking water every month if you live in a major city of the world.
- Two unsafe crash landings every day at Chicago's O'Hara Airport.
- Sixteen thousand pieces of lost mail, worldwide, every hour.
- Twenty thousand incorrect drug prescriptions dispensed every week.
- Five hundred incorrect medical surgeries every day.
- Five hundred newborn babies would be dropped on their head at birth every day.
- Thirty-two thousand heartbeats per person would be missed per year.
- The number of checks that would be deducted from the wrong account every hour would be 122,000.

Now the scenarios listed above would happen if these things were right only 99.9 percent of the time. I'm very thankful that as many things in this world work as well as they do.

Only one person I know is 100 percent right, 100 percent of the time. He's divine and He's God! His name is Jesus Christ, the Son of the Living God! And what's so fabulous is that all of us can have a relationship with perfection. We need to strive for perfection in this life because we are to follow His pattern for living; it should be our goal. It can be done! The biblical word for perfection is best translated as being mature. You're a teen, but you too can attain maturity, which in God's sight is moving toward perfection according to His definition.

Before Me no god was formed, nor will there be one after me. I, even I, am the Lord, and apart from me there is no savior (Isaiah 43:10-11).

183. THE TOUGHEST TWO YEARS OF EXISTENCE

This is a word of warning! Are you aware that according to psychologists and psychiatrists who study such things, the two most difficult years in life and growing up are the thirteenth and fourteenth years of your life! Why? Maybe you have passed these two years and may or may not agree with their findings. You may be caught in them or you are ready to enter them. Why are they considered to be so tough?

Let's break their findings down so that we can deal with this. First, it's a time of life that is marked by rapid physical and emotional changes. It's called adolescence and it's very much a part of growing up. Everything is changing, mentally as well as physically. Second, feelings of self-doubt and inferiority reach an all-time high during these years. This too is understandable and not the end of the world. Third—this may be one of the most difficult to deal with—because an adolescent's worth as a human being hangs too much on the fickle influence of a peer group. Relatively minor evidence of being rejected for any reason, or no reason at all, becomes significant to those who may already see themselves as failures. An example of this would be not being invited to an important event and how devastating that would be.

So what can be done? You need a support system, particularly your family, believe it or not. Don't abandon your future resources to that fickle peer pressure. Share an encouraging word with your fellow teens.

And most importantly, remember that Jesus Christ was thirteen and fourteen in His earthly life; therefore, you have the best friend you can have. He understands and loves you in spite of what is happening. His love is unconditional. With His help, you can do it!

Remember your Creator in the days of your youth, before the days of trouble come (Ecclesiastes 12:1).

184. HONKING HORNS

The following could have easily happened in the town where you live. It seems this teen driver, a girl, was stopped at a light; when the light changed to green, her car sputtered and stopped. She tried and tried to get it started again. She was embarrassed. But to make matters worse, the gentleman, using the term very loosely, immediately behind her insisted in expressing his impatience with her by loudly and repeatedly blowing his horn.

Finally, this brave girl, who was by now completely worn out with his thoughtlessness and her car refusing to start, stepped out of her car and walked back to the honker's car. He rolled his window down.

With hands on her hips and a bit of fire in her eyes, she said, "I am having a bit of a problem in getting my car started. If you would be so kind as to see if you can get it started, I will be most happy to sit in your car and honk your horn for you!"

Don't you just love it? A whole lot of people in your school, in your town, in your church, do a whole lot more honking than helping! Have you noticed there are always more talkers than workers? More critics than builders? More gripers than encouragers?

Any one who drives a car very much will have someone honk at them at one time or another. (Did you know that a split second is the time between the traffic light turning green and the car behind you honking?) And anyone who tries to accomplish something of value for others in this world will usually find a loud horn. By the way, will you be a starter or a honker?

We also rejoice in our sufferings, because we know that suffering produces perseverance; perseverance, character; and character, hope (Romans 5:3-4).

185. HOW TO LIVE LONGER

How often do you think about living healthy? Probably not too often because you are young and life is filled with other urgent things. However, now is the time to begin lifelong habits that will guarantee a long and happy life. Here are ten things you can do beginning today.

1. *Exercise.* Just thirty minutes a day for three times a week can cut your risk of developing heart disease, cancer, stroke, or diabetes—the four leading causes of death.

2. *Eat fruits and veggies.* Ugh, you may be thinking. But these are packed with the nutrients that keep your body and brain functioning properly with antioxidants.

3. *Get your chocolate fix.* Cocoa contains antioxidant flavonoids that decrease buildup in blood vessels and lowers blood pressures. Not too much, though.

4. *Adopt a pet.* Why? Interacting with a pet lowers your blood pressure and stress hormone levels, says Dr. Johnson of The Center for Human-Animal Interaction.

5. *Get enough sleep.* The National Sleep Foundation says that sleep deprivation has lasting bad effects on your health. Good sleep helps you test better.

6. *Brush and floss daily.* There is a connection between gum disease and potentially life-threatening problems such as cardiovascular or bacterial pneumonia.

7. *Drink green tea.* Want a real wonder drink? Try green tea! It has a powerful antioxidant known as polyphenol EGCG. Live long like the Japanese.

8. *Make lifelong friends.* Having close friends now and when you get older helps you live longer and happier.

9. *Wear your seat belt.* A study of car occupants between ages thirteen to thirty-four who were killed in car accidents were not wearing seat belts. Buckle up!

10. *Cultivate a positive life attitude.* An optimistic outlook on life decreases your risk of early death by up to 50 percent compared to pessimistic people.

Better a meal of vegetables where there is love (Proverbs 15:12).

186. WHY ARE SPIDERS IMPORTANT?

Do you remember the nursery rhyme about little Miss Muffet who sat on a tuffet eating her curds and whey? But as soon as a spider came along little Miss Muffet ran away. Have you run away from a spider lately? Sure, why not? Spiders are creepy with all those legs. But spiders can also bite. Not all spiders bite, but the ones that do can pack a wallop.

All right, why are spiders important to us? Because they build their webs in order to trap their food. And their favorite food is other insects. They keep our world from being totally overrun by insects.

Their webs are made of the silk they produce in their bodies. The next time you see a spider at work building a web, take some time to look at the detail and the beauty, especially when the sun shines through one.

Scientists tell us that spider silk, according to its weight and size, is proportionately five times stronger than steel! A spider and what it can do is another example of God's creation at work. One more thing: most spiders have eight eyes but can't see very well so they rely on other senses like taste and touch. Amazing!

If a little spider can do all of this, what can you accomplish? You may seem small and insignificant, but with God's help all things become possible! In the Bible, David was a teen who killed the giant Goliath and freed his nation from the bondage of the Philistines. Just think, a teen with a slingshot and God! Awesome! What will you and God accomplish?

Everything is possible for him who believes (Mark 9:23).

187. WHAT ABOUT YOU AND VIDEO GAMES?

Video games are everywhere and seem to be played by just about everybody, even some of your grandparents. So how many of you have played a video game today? A study by the Kaiser Family Foundation has, not surprisingly, found the following information:

Of people ages eight to eighteen, 71 percent have played "Guitar Hero/Rock Band." Sixty-five percent have played "Super Mario." Sixty-four percent of you have played "Wii Play/Wii Sports." Fifty-six percent have played "Grand Theft Auto," and 45 percent have played "Madden NFL."

But that's not all you are spending your time on. According to the Pew Internet Life Project, 75 percent of teens are spending lots of time on social network sites.

Now that doesn't take into account the time spent on TV watching or cell phone usage. Wow! So the question that comes to mind is, how much family time do you have? How much thinking, meditating, praying, or reading God's

Word do you do? It's easy to get trapped into day's hi-tech world so that we forget some of the really important values of life.

Studies have also shown that a typical teen now spends between five and six hours per day playing video games, watching TV, and texting. Perhaps it's time to think about resetting priorities. Yes, I also know that all your friends are doing the same so it's tough to change. How about setting aside an hour or two that is yours without the interruption of the hi-tech world? Just your private time, quiet time, or time to spend one-on-one with other important people in your life. And time with your God!

God will bring into judgment both the righteous and the wicked, for there will be a time for every activity (Ecclesiastes 3:17).

188. PREVENTING TEEN TOBACCO USAGE

Do you know what I'm talking about when I refer to bidis, kreteks, or dip? Odds are that teens know but adults don't. Each of these is a form of tobacco and pose a serious risk to teens.

Cigarette smoking among teens has decreased over the past ten years; however, not all tobacco products are following this trend. A national survey found that eight percent of high school seniors reported using smokeless tobacco in the past thirty days.

Parents in particular should be concerned about kids who are experimenting with other forms of tobacco including snuff, chewing or dip tobacco, cigars, bidis (bee-dees: flavored, leaf-wrapped cigarettes from India) and kreteks (kree-tex: clove flavored tobacco cigarettes). Surveys show that many teens experiment with several of these according to *Medicine* magazine.

It's not enough to talk about the dangers of cigarette smoking, it's also necessary to know of and to understand that other forms of tobacco can be just addictive and no easier to quit than cigarettes. These other forms also contain nicotine and have serious health effects such as cancer and cardiovascular disease.

Is this of interest to you? It should be. The statistical information in this devotional was provided by Phillip Morris, the largest tobacco manufacturer in the world. Talk about hypocritical. They manufacture and provide tobacco products and at the same time talk about prevention. This is another of those life choices you must make for yourself. Just say no. You'll be glad you did!

Do you not know that your body is a temple of the Holy Spirit, who is in you, whom you have received from God? You are not your own; you were bought with a price. Therefore honor God with your body
(1 Corinthians 6:19-20).

189. WAS GANDHI A FAILURE?

What is stopping you from getting involved in your church, your school, or your community? Too many of us have the mistaken idea that to be involved we have to be one of those special people—you know, a larger-than-life figure.

Yet even some historic larger-than-life figures often started in very modest, simple, and little ways. Some have more failures than successes. The grandson of Mahatma Gandhi tells the story of how his grandfather's family mortgaged everything they had to send Gandhi to law school. He graduated and passed the bar to practice law in India but was so shy that when he stood up in court, all he could do was stammer. In fact, he lost every one of his cases. He was considered a total failure.

His family then sent him off to South Africa, where he found his voice by challenging the racial segregation he observed and the rest is history. When thinking of Gandhi, consider him not as the master strategist of social change but as someone who first was tongue-tied, shy, and intimidated.[18]

When you look at his life from our perspective, given what he became in this world, how he ended up, who knows what might be possible in your life and for all the rest of us? It's not so much where you start, it's where you end!

Success is nothing more than failure turned inside out. Mark was a young man who followed Jesus Christ but experienced failure. He was mentored by a more mature Christian and later became one of the writer's of the gospel accounts of the life of Jesus Christ. Failure? He failed, but was not a failure. He became a success! Don't give up. Life success is getting up one more time than you might have fallen down.

Choose my instruction instead of silver, knowledge rather than choice gold,
for wisdom is more precious than rubies, and nothing you desire can compare
with her (Proverbs 8:10-11).

190. THE NEXT BIG IDEA

Are you aware that an inspiration can strike anywhere or at any age! Igor Sikorsky was born in Russia in 1889. In 1919, six years after designing and flying the world's first multi-engine airplane in his native Russia, Sikorsky immigrated to the United States.

After becoming a US citizen, he turned his attention and efforts to building the helicopter. He designed and flew the first usable helicopter that proved to be the world standard for all the others that followed.

So when did his big idea happen? He designed and built his first experimental helicopter and powered it by rubber bands at age twelve!

Got time for another big idea? How about assembly line manufacturing? Henry Ford adapted the meat packing industry's concept. Ford perfected this model for mass production in order to produce a motor car for the great multitudes. By 1914 his company had a 48 percent share of the automobile market. His big idea happened when he went shopping at the meat market for his mother while still a teenager! And the rest is history.

When will your big idea happen? When did it become clear in the mind of the boy Jesus as to His life's work? How about when he was twelve years of age and spent three days with the religious thinkers of his day in the temple at Jerusalem? The Bible says He listened and asked questions, and they were astonished at His understanding. What was his big idea? He told his parents, "I must be about my Father's business."

What is your big idea?

Praise be to the Lord, the God of Israel, because he has come and has redeemed his people (Luke 1:68).

191. WHAT'S IN A PRANK?

P ranksters have a long history beginning in the 1400s with Thomas Betson, the prankster/monk. His is the first documented practical joke when he hid a beetle inside a hollowed out apple and fooled his fellow monks into believing the mysteriously rocking apple was possessed!

In 1835 "The Great Moon" hoax was the first media trick. The *New York Sun* printed an article claiming astronomers have discovered life on the moon. More bogus articles appeared over the next few weeks until the country was caught up in moon fever.

In 1938 Orson Welles' radio broadcast of *War of the Worlds* convinced millions that our earth was under attack by aliens. People fled their homes, prayed in churches, and eventually came to curse Orson Welles' prank.

On April 1, 1957, a BBC telecast showed the "Swiss Spaghetti Harvest" with farmers pulling strands of spaghetti from trees. The network was deluged with callers asking where to buy the spaghetti tree! *(See devotion #314 for more details on this one.)*

In 1962 the broadcasting technician for Sweden's only television station made an appearance on the newscast to announce, "Thanks to a new technology, viewers can convert their existing black and white TVs into color. All they have to do is pull a nylon stocking over their TV screens." Thousands tried it!

Is it better to be the prankster or the prankee? Just don't leave home without your sense of humor! Even the Bible tells us that when we laugh, it's good medicine for the soul.

A cheerful look brings joy to the heart (Proverbs 15:30).

192. HONEST ABE

Perhaps you have heard the story of the time Abraham Lincoln bought something at the country store and the clerk gave him two cents—imagine only two cents—too much change. Young Abe didn't realize the mistake until he had walked two and a half miles home. When he arrived home and put his change on the dresser, he noticed the extra two cents. Now here's where the story gets to us. Abe didn't keep the extra money. He didn't pretend the mistake didn't really happen. He didn't ignore it and think it was too bad for the clerk. He didn't think, *Nobody will notice only two cents short.*

No, he put the two cents back into his pocket and walked the two and a half miles to the store to return the money. Then he walked back home again—five extra miles for only two measly cents! But he returned home with a crystal-clear conscience.

In today's world, two cents doesn't amount to much. But let's say the counter guy at McDonald's gives you two dollars or even twenty dollars too much in change. When you discover the mistake, what will you do? Will you go out of your way to return the extra or simply pocket it? Will you think, *It's their mistake, too bad.* Would you walk an extra five miles to return two bucks?

Do people trust you? Do you trust yourself? Temptations to steal or break trust are presented to us almost every day. Has somebody lied to you or stolen from you? Will you trust that person again? Never give anybody a reason to never trust you. Begin now and make it a lifetime habit. Be honest in all things. Be squeaky clean!

Direct my footsteps according to your word; let no sin rule over me
(Psalm 119:133).

193. THINK ABOUT IT

In 1923 an important meeting was held at the Edgewater Hotel in Chicago with nine of the world's most successful financiers. They were the president of the largest steel company, the president of the largest utility company, the president of the largest gas company, the greatest wheat speculator, the president of the New York Stock Exchange, a member of the President's cabinet, the greatest investor on Wall Street, and the president of the International Bank of Settlements.

These people had all found the secret of making money. However, let twenty-five years pass and let's see where these men went or became:

Charles Schwab, president of the largest steel company died bankrupt and had to live on borrowed money the last five years of his life. Samuel Insull, president of the largest utility company died a fugitive from justice in a foreign country. Howard Hopson, gas company mogul, went insane. Arthur Cutten, the wheat speculator, died abroad without a penny to his name. Richard Whitney, of the New York Stock Exchange, spent time in Sing Sing Penitentiary. Albert Fall, of the President's cabinet, was pardoned from prison to die at home. Jesse Livermore, of Wall Street investments, committed suicide. And Leon Fraser of the International Bank hung himself.

All of these men had learned well the art of making money, but not one of them had learned how to live! Lots of lessons can be learned from people and history. Most importantly, before you allow anyone to influence you with his or her value system, find out if that person actually lives by the same system! Paul the apostle told the young man Timothy, "Follow me as I follow Jesus Christ."

Don't let anyone look down on you because you are young, but set an example
for the believers in speech, in life, in love, in faith and in purity
(1 Timothy 4:12).

194. LITTLE THINGS ARE IMPORTANT

We are all faced with little choices every day. Some of these choices are obvious and may even be life-changing decisions. And then other choices seem so small we hardly even notice them. But little choices when made correctly can make a huge difference!

- For example, do you laugh at the kid who drops his or her books in the hallway, or do you stop and help him or her pick them up?
- Do you cheat on your tests, or do you discipline yourself enough to get the knowledge and talent to ace the next one?
- Do you help someone in need, or do you ignore that person's need? Do you take time to listen and encourage the person by offering real help?
- Do you always take the easy way out, or do you apply yourself enough to do the hard things that really count?

Okay, right or wrong, such seemingly little choices we make today have a way of compounding themselves into life habits. For example, if you jog for thirty minutes every day, after two or three days you will not notice much change. But if you do this for three or four months, you will notice a big difference in your body.

Knowing the right thing to do and doing it are two different things. The simple, kind, right things to do can be easy; but it's also not easy to do the right things too. It's as easy to fall into a bad habit of not doing the right things as it is to do the right things. It may not be easy, but know and do until it becomes your life habit!

Therefore, as we have opportunity, let us do good to all people, especially to those who belong to the family of believers (Galatians 6:10).

195. HOW TO BE NUMBER ONE

You know you have really made it in the world when an Adidas sneaker has been named after you. However, you need to know this is not named after a professional athlete. He's twenty-seven-year-old Chinese-born pianist Lang Lang (pronounced Long, Long). The argument can be made that he is the most successful classical pianist of our generation with more than a million CDs and DVDs sold as well as hundreds of sold-out concerts all over the world.

Superstardom in classical music didn't come easily. He left his home at age nine, in rural China in the town of Shenyang, to have access to the best teachers. He went with his father to a Beijing slum where they lived without heat. Nights were especially miserable. His father forced him to practice for most of his waking hours in an obsessive attempt to make Lang number one; he admits he feels he lost part of his childhood while honing his craft.

Lang has come a long way since those many years of privation and endless practice. Today his passion is to show young people the fun he finds in classical music. Adidas Originals designed a gold and black piano themed sneaker, with Lang Lang's name written in Chinese and a silhouette of the piano star in action. He says, "When you think of classical music's image, it's very serious and elite. I'm trying to interest young people in classical music, so it was really a good fit."

He's easy to spot with his spiked hair and tone-on-tone sleek suits. He's also proven that classical music doesn't have to be stuffy. But more importantly, he's proven that the journey to becoming number one begins with a single step![19]

So together, let's take that first step!

How long will you lie there? When will you get up from your sleep?
(Proverbs 6:9).

196. DO IT NOW!

How do you, as a teenager, make the secret of getting things done a part of your life and a lifetime habit? The answer is quite simple, by repetition. Perhaps you've heard this quote from philosopher and psychologist, William James, "Sow an action and you reap a habit; sow a habit and you reap a character; sow a character and you reap a destiny."

He was saying that you are and will become what your habits make you. But what is so exciting is that you can choose your habits. You can develop any habit you desire, especially when you use this special, secret self-starter!

So what is this self-starter that forces you to use this secret? It's simple but profound; the secret of getting things done is this self-motivator: do it now! This can be your secret for the rest of your life. Do it now! But first a word of warning. Never say to yourself "do it now" unless you follow this with a positive action. Whenever action is desirable to be taken and this phrase flashes through your mind, you must immediately take the action.

Make it a practice to quickly respond even in little things! This will help you develop the habit of an action that becomes so strong so that in times of emergency or when opportunities present themselves, you will act! [20]

When you should be reading your Bible, do it now! When it's time to pray for someone who is hurting, do it now! When it's time to get out of bed and go to church and you'd rather sleep in, motivate yourself by saying, Do it now, and follow with the actions!

For it is time to seek the Lord, until He comes
and showers righteousness on you (Hosea 10:12).

197. DO YOU WEAR A MASK?

Somewhere, in the course of your life journey, has someone taught you how to wear a mask? Maybe friends? Maybe school? Maybe society? Maybe your parents? Someone, somewhere taught most of us how to wear masks!

What does or did your mask look like? There can be several kinds of masks—the "everything-is-okay" mask; the "I-have-it-all-together" mask; the "I-can-do-it-all-by-myself" mask; the "don't-bother-me-now" mask; the "don't-ask" mask; or even the ultimate mask, "I-don't-need-God-in-my-life-now" mask.

What is your personal mask? I remind you, when you wear a mask, it means you have something to hide. So what are you attempting to hide behind your mask? Are you lonely, angry, disappointed, neglected, rejected, depressed, upset, guilty, fearful, or running from God? What is behind your mask? But even more importantly, is there help for the problem behind your mask?

Let's explore this a bit more and take it to the level where you can find help. Yes, you can be helped. It begins with being able to live with redemption, forgiveness, and love in a broken world. This is found in a person: His name is Jesus! He came to live among us as a relational, approachable, non-rejection God. You are not alone, you do not have to continue in your cover-up. Jesus came to set all captives free. Wouldn't you like to be free? You can live in freedom from this moment. Now, doesn't that sound wonderful? You can live as an authentic person; you can live in freedom; you can live a transparent life! All of this is made possible because of Jesus Christ and His sacrifice for you. Simply, invite Him to set you free. Yes, you can do it right now!

Therefore confess your sins to each other and pray for each other so that you may be healed. The prayer of a righteous person is powerful and effective (James 5:16).

198. WHO AM I?

I am your constant companion. I am your greatest helper or heaviest burden. I will push you onward or drag you down to failure. I am completely at your command. Half the things you do you might just as well turn over to me, and I will be able to do them quickly and correctly.

I am easily managed. You must merely be firm with me. Show me exactly how you want something done, and after a few lessons I will do it automatically. I am the servant of all great individuals, and alas, of all failures as well. Those who are great, I have made great. Those who are failures, I have made failures.

I am not a machine, though I work with all the precision of a machine plus the intelligence of a human. You may run me for a profit or run me for ruin; it makes no difference to me! Take me, train me, be firm with me, and I will place the world at your feet. Be easy with me and I will destroy you!

WHO AM I? I am habit![21]

He who heeds discipline shows the way to life (Proverbs 10:17).

199. DOGS IN THE COURTROOM?

The young woman in Seattle was having second thoughts about her testimony in a 2008 trial of the man accused of abducting and raping her. "That's when we brought Ellie on board," said King county senior prosecuting attorney Ellen O'Neill Stephens. Ellie isn't a counselor or a psychiatrist. She's an eight-year-old Labrador retriever! The King's county prosecutor's office uses Ellie to help calm victims and witnesses of violent crimes.

"When things got tough, the victim was able to focus on Ellie and describe the attack," Stephens said. "She told me that just holding the leash made her feel more in control." The attacker was found guilty, and Ellie accompanied the young woman to the sentencing.

This idea of using dogs to ease the tension of being in a courtroom is gaining popularity in the United States. Courthousedogs.com began in Seattle when Stephens took her son's service dog, Jeeter, to work and discovered that the dog had a calming effect on young witnesses. The practice is spreading to courts in Texas, California, Florida, Missouri, and Michigan.

These courtroom dogs go through at least two years of training, including learning basic commands as a puppy and then going to a special training center for six months to learn more advanced commands such as picking up dropped items, opening doors, or coping with crowds.[22]

If dogs can be trained to be helpful, you and I can also be trained as volunteers to help others. By the way, have you ever given thanks to God for His wonderful creatures?

At his gate was laid a beggar named Lazarus, covered with sores . . . even the dogs came and licked his sores (Luke 16:20-21).

200. THE TOP TEN STUPIDEST STATEMENTS

The following is a list of stupid statements made by so-called experts!

1. "There is no reason for any individual to have a computer in their home," said Kenneth Olsen, president and founder of Digital Equipment Corporation, in 1977.
2. "Airplanes are interesting toys but of no military value," said Marshal Ferdinand Foch, French Military Strategist and WWI Commander, in 1911.
3. "Man will never reach the moon regardless of all future scientific advances," said Dr. Lee De Forest, inventor and father of radio, in 1967.
4. "Television won't be able to hold on to any market it captures after the first six months," said Darryl F. Zanuck, head of Twentieth Century-Fox, in 1946.
5. "We don't like their sound. Groups of guitars are on their way out," said Decca Records, rejecting the Beatles in 1962.
6. "For the majority of people, the use of tobacco has a beneficial effect," said Dr. Ian G. MacDonald, Los Angeles surgeon, quoted in *Newsweek*, on November 18, 1969.
7. "This telephone has too many shortcomings to be seriously considered as a means of communication," said a Western Union internal memo in 1876.
8. "The earth is the center of the universe," said Ptolemy, the great Egyptian astronomer in the second century.
9. "Nothing of importance happened today," wrote King George III of England on July 4, 1776.
10. "Everything that can be invented has been invented," smugly spoken by Charles H. Duell, the U.S. Commissioner of Patents in 1899.

Who can speak and have it happen if the Lord has not decreed it?
(Lamentations 3:37).

201. YOU SAID WHAT?

This is not going to be a lecture on the evils of a foul mouth. Instead, this is a challenge to you. I dare you, just for fun, can you go for one day without swearing or cussing, or any talk to do with sex, violence, greed, or cutting another person to pieces? I dare you! Why not challenge your best friend to do this with you for just one day?

And I also will tell you, you might not make it through the first day without being successful. Now, this is an experiment, and there's no right or wrong on this test. Should you not be able to do this, you're quite normal. But it also may show you how much of what you say is geared to these things that may not produce any happiness in your life.

So, you may not pass the first day. My challenge to you is go for round number two. Give it a second try and my money will be that you will do much better! You might make it a whole day without such comments. If you're not able to complete a full day, go back for another try.

You might be successful on the third or fourth or twentieth attempt! When you are successful, observe how much happier your day has been. I believe your spirits will be higher and brighter.

My purpose in this simple exercise is to get you to see and experience the power of your words. What you will discover is that you will think more about the words you say. This is not perfect, but it's a great habit to live by. So my friend, you may also discover that when you speak peaceful words you will live a more peaceful life!

Take note of this: Everyone should be quick to listen, slow to speak and slow to become angry (James 1:19).

202. JIM RYUN, WORLD RECORD HOLDER

Today it really seems preposterous to think that athletics didn't look very promising for Jim Ryun early on in his life. In junior high he was cut from the basketball and track and field teams at school. But get this, he was even cut from the baseball team at his church! One of the reasons was that at age five, he had a bout with measles that left him with only half of his hearing.

Jim recalls, "I remember praying one night: 'God, if you have a plan for my life, please show it to me, because I could use it right now!'"

Jim Ryun could be exhibit A to show that God answers prayer! Just two

143

years later, in 1964, the Wichita, Kansas, native became the world's first high school athlete to break four minutes in the mile! He set an American record and went on to compete in three Olympics.

"It really did change everything," Ryun says when he reflects on the first time he ran a mile under four minutes. In 1966, as a college sophomore, he set his first world record at 3 minutes, 51.3 seconds and was named Sportsman of the Year by *Sports Illustrated*. He held the record for nearly eight years and set world records in five other events. In 1980 he was inducted into the U.S. Track and Field Hall of Fame.

In May of 1972, Ryun and his wife, Anne, became Christians through the witness of some friends. His newfound faith in Christ provided a fulfillment that his swift feet could not. He says, "I wanted the peace that only comes through Jesus Christ."

Not bad for a partially deaf kid who struggled as a teen to find his niche in sports and life. "Even failure God uses in your life," he said.

> *Forgetting what is behind and straining toward what is ahead, I press on toward the goal to win the prize for which God has called me heavenward*
> (Philippians 3:13-14).

203. FACEBOOK CAN GET YOU FIRED

Are you job hunting or do you already have a job? Here's a word of warning. What you put on social network sites such as Facebook may keep you from getting a job or can get you fired. Employees like to think that what they do on their own time is their personal business, but that is not always the case.

According to a 2009 survey by the American Management Association and the ePolicy Institute, 27 percent of companies now have policies about what employees can post on their personal blogs.

Nancy Flynn, executive director of the institute, says, "You have to think about whether this will come back to haunt you." This thought never crossed the mind of Nate Fulmer, a warehouse manager for a chemical supplier. Fulmer and his wife made fun of a local church sermon in a podcast they posted online in 2005. Fulmer says it received a great deal of attention. His boss listened to it, thought it was offensive, and fired him. "I was blindsided," he says.

According to Flynn's survey, more than 2 percent of companies have dismissed employees over the content of personal social networking pages. So her advice to you is to check company policy before posting anything that is potentially offensive, even if it has nothing to do with work![23]

The Bible tells us that the tongue is something hard to tame; it should also specifically include a blog on a computer is also hard to tame. As a part of healthy living we are always to speak well and write well of others.

An anxious heart weighs a man down, but a kind word cheers him up
(Proverbs 12:25).

204. IF ALL ELSE FAILS

An angry seventeen-year-old threw his wrench across the garage and rolled out from underneath his '87 Honda Civic. He had given up. He had been working for hours on his car to change the brake pads. Compounding the problem, he wasn't exactly a great mechanic. Mad and exasperated, he stomped into the house and announced to his dad that his car had serious problems, had been built wrong, and he couldn't fix it!

Then he shouted, "In fact, I don't know if anyone can fix it!"

Calmly, his dad called a mechanic friend on his cell and asked for help. Then they went to the library and found the manual and made copies of the pages on how to change the brake pads. They went to the dealership, talked with the service manager, and discovered they needed a specially made tiny tool that was necessary to complete this job. Back home at the car, it only took them about thirty minutes to complete the job. And he was one happy camper with grease on his hands.

What's the big difference? First he went to his father. Second, he discovered the right instructions. And third, he purchased the right tool for this particular job.

How about that? It's a pretty good formula the next time you are frustrated with a life situation when you have tried but failed because you had been sure you knew how to it.

So the next decision you are facing, use this formula: go to your heavenly Father, study your instruction manual—the Bible—and use the proper tools provided by the Holy Spirit. In changing brake pads or life, follow the instructions.

Pay attention and listen to the sayings of the wise (Proverbs 22:17).

205. CAN YOU OUTRUN A BEAR?

It's an old story with lots of variations, but here goes this version. Two teenagers were out hiking on top of the Grand Mesa Mountain in Western Colorado when they happened upon a mama bear with a set of twin cubs. The hikers were not aware of their presence, so they hiked and talked but without being aware that they walked between the cubs and their mama.

Mama Bear reared to her full height, roared in protection of her little ones, and dropped to her four feet and began a charge. There is no fury like a mama bear protecting her cubs! The situation was serious. The teens turned and began running. One of the boys stopped, pulled his heavy hiking boots off, and jammed on his running shoes!

His friend yelled at him, "Come on, man! We've got to get out of here! Why are you changing your shoes? We can't outrun this bear anyway!"

Jumping back to his feet and lunging into a full run, the first guy yelled, "I don't have to outrun the bear, I only have to run faster than you!"

Talk about a great friend! Well, let's look at friendship for a bit. What's the ultimate test of friendship? Jesus has given us the answer. Jesus tells us in the Bible that this ultimate test of friendship is when a friend will be willing to give up his or her life for a friend. Wow. He did and he showed us the way. He went to the cross and died for all of us calling us His friends!

So, what about you? Are you a fair-weather friend, one who is only a friend until the going gets tough, until there is risk involved? What kind of a friend are you?

My command is this: Love each other as I have loved you. Greater love has no one than this, that he lay down his life for his friends (John 15:12-13).

206. MULTIPLE CHOICES

How do you plan to get the money you will need in your life? Some of you will need more than others. Some of you will have more than you need. Still others will never have enough!

So where will you get the money you need in life? Hopefully, by now you have discovered that money doesn't grow on trees, right? Your parents have already been telling you that a money tree isn't growing in the backyard. You are left with only four methods: you can earn it, inherit it, marry it, or steal it. But stealing is illegal and could land you in the clink, and marrying it is highly unlikely. Inheriting it can take forever, so I'd say about 99.9 percent of you will have to earn your money.

How will you earn it? This is not so easy to answer. Okay then, when will you earn it? You will perhaps spend about forty hours a week for fifty-two weeks a year between the ages of twenty-two to sixty-five, so we're talking about 86,000 hours of your life. Awesome!

Take it from me: 86,000 hours is a long time to be miserable. Most of us don't like to do things we hate for even one hour. This choice is one of the biggest you will make. What will you do for a living that will not make your life miserable?

So you want a job that will make you rich—maybe not happy but rich. But how much is enough? Is 1 million or 10 million or 100 million enough? If you are fourteen, sixteen, or nineteen, everybody has the same basic needs: health and happiness. You need to know, though, money can't buy either one of these. My suggestion to you is to do what you love and the money will follow. Do what the Lord would have you do and health, happiness, joy, love, and a good life will follow!

> *I am the Lord your God, who teaches you what is best for you, who directs you in the way you should go* (Isaiah 48:17).

207. THINK YOU'RE READY TO GO ALL THE WAY?

Do you really think you're ready to go all the way? Are you sure? Think about the possibility of sexually transmitted infections, unplanned pregnancy, emotional doubts, and more! All good reasons to wait. But before you go too far, let's take a look at the following list or make up your own:

You're Not Ready To Have Sex If . . .
- You think sex equals love.
- You feel pressured.
- You're afraid to say no and mean it.
- It's easier to give in.
- You think everyone else is doing it. (They are not!)
- Your gut feelings and instincts tell you not to.
- You don't really know all the facts about a pregnancy.
- You think a woman can't get pregnant the first time. (She can, really!)
- It goes against your moral or religious beliefs.
- You will live to regret it the next morning.
- You feel embarrassed or ashamed.
- You can't support a child or yourself.
- Your idea of commitment is a three-day DVD rental.
- You believe sex before marriage is wrong.
- You don't want to get HIV, the virus that causes AIDS.
- You might contract a sexually transmitted infection, also called STDs.
- You think it will make your partner love you.
- You hope it will change your life for the better.[24]

You are not ready to have sex if any of the above fit your situation! Really, it's okay to wait until marriage.

> *The acts of the flesh are obvious: sexual immorality, impurity and debauchery* (Galatians 5:19).

208. GEESE CAN BE SMARTER THAN HUMANS

Have you ever watched a flock of geese heading to a warmer climate for the winter? Have you noticed they fly in a V formation? Scientists have learned interesting facts about the way they fly.

By flying in this V formation, the whole flock can fly 71 percent farther than if each bird flew alone. Why? When a goose flaps its wings, it creates an updraft for the goose that follows. As the lead goose gets tired it will rotate to the back of the V and allow another goose to take the lead position.

The geese in back honk to encourage those in the front. Whenever a goose falls out of formation, it immediately feels the resistance of trying to fly alone and quickly gets back into formation.

Should a goose get sick or wounded and fall out of the formation, two other geese will follow it down to help and protect it. They will stay with the wounded goose until it is better or dies, and they will then join up with a new formation or create one of their own to catch up with the group.

Smart birds, these geese. Where did they get such wisdom? Remember who was their Creator? The lessons are wisdom to live by. By sharing together we can all fly farther. By honking encouragement, we all experience a better lifestyle. By staying in formation, we become a team that gets the job done. By taking care of their hurting and wounded, they build a loyalty that lasts a lifetime. They teach the lesson on synergy, which we all need to learn.

Who is wise and understanding among you? Let him show it by his good life, by deeds done in humility that comes from wisdom (James 3:12).

209. HERO WORSHIP AND FALLEN SUPERSTARS

Who is your hero? Who do you worship? Who do you want to pattern your life after? The rise and fall of superstars seems to go on forever. Not long ago, a hubbub surrounded the lifestyle of the world's best golfer and his infidelities. However, if you listen to the news or check out the tabloids or YouTube, you will discover an almost daily regimen of more stars who have fallen. If it's not athletes, it's politicians, educators, leaders, movie stars, and even preachers!

Maybe it's only an American trait, but somehow I believe it's worldwide that we seem intent on believing that our superstars live in a pristine universe where they will be sheltered from the temptations of the seven deadly sins. We want to believe they are a bit better than we who are so common.

"Alas, for every movie star who enthralls us, for every athlete whose last-second heroics brings glory to a team or town, there are distressing few whose personal lives can bear the light of public scrutiny and remain untarnished. The same might be said of all too many of our politicians from both national parties," wrote Lou Jacquet, editor of *The Catholic Exponent.*

What is it about celebrity status that seems to render such people incapable of making or acting with clear judgment and moral clarity? There is a powerful lesson out of this whole sorry mess for any of us who would be a person of faith. We need to look beyond celebrities for someone we would like to pattern our life after. We need someone who is really and truly worthy of following! For this someone, I nominate Jesus Christ, the King of all Kings, the Lord of all Lords! The one perfect, sinless One who never failed anyone.

The Word became flesh and made his dwelling among us. We have seen his glory, the glory of the One and Only, who came from the Father, full of grace and truth (John 1:14).

210. WOULD YOU LIKE TO LIVE TO BE 100?

Joe Rollino, a 104-year-old strongman, has died; he was run over by a minivan. Rollino once lifted 3,200 pounds at Coney Island and was still bending quarters with his bare fingers at age 104! In his heyday, Rollino hobnobbed with the likes of the famed magician Harry Houdini and performed feats of strength on his shows. So what was his secret? According to his family he was a lifelong vegetarian, didn't drink, didn't smoke, and exercised every day.

In 1990 there were some 37,000 Americans who lived to be 100 plus! Projections are that by 2040, more than half a million will be 100 or more. So what are their secrets that could become your keys to living that long? I know, you are too young to think about such things as old age, but why not? Here's another fascinating fact. Of the people who reach 100, fully 90 percent of them were still physically and mentally healthy, and about half of them still live on their own or with their families. How about that?

Their secrets are quite simple. First, don't outlive your savings. So plan well in the area of finances. Second, change your lifestyle to avoid sickness and mental decline. Only 30 percent of longevity is because of genes. The rest is up to you. Eat right, don't smoke, don't drink, and eat your veggies and fresh fruit. Stay socially engaged. Third, learn how to deal with worry, anxiety, depression, and stress. Control what you can and let the rest roll off your back. Go to church regularly, pray, worship, be positive, and live for the Lord. You can be the next generation of centenarians!

Honor your father and mother that it may go well with you and that you may enjoy long life on the earth (Ephesians 6:2).

211. HUMOR IN A JOB PERFORMANCE

One of the things you will face in your future, if you have a job, is that dreaded annual job performance evaluation. Yes, you likely will be evaluated on an annual basis—we're talking about the real world here. The following quotes were taken from actual job performance evaluations of real employees. Enjoy!

- "Since my last report, this employee has reached rock bottom and has started to dig deeper."
- "His men would follow him anywhere, even to the ends of the world, but only out of morbid curiosity."
- "I would not allow this employee to breed. This associate is really not so much of a has-been, but more of a definitely won't be."
- "Works well when under constant supervision and cornered like a rat in a big trap."
- "When she opens her mouth, it seems that this is only to change whichever foot was previously in there."
- "He would be out of his depth in a parking lot puddle. He sets low personal standards and then consistently fails to achieve them."
- "This young lady has delusions of adequacy. She is depriving a village somewhere of an idiot."
- "This employee should go far; the sooner he starts, the better."

Well, it just doesn't get much better than this. Welcome to the job performance evaluation. It might be easy to get a job but tougher to keep it!

Lazy hands make a man poor, but diligent hands bring wealth
(Proverbs 9:4).

212. CAREFUL EVALUATIONS

Many years ago, an executive of the Standard Oil Company made a very wrong decision that cost the company more than $2 million. John D. Rockefeller was the president. On the day the news leaked, most of the executives of the company were finding various ingenious ways of avoiding the wrath of Mr. Rockefeller, lest his wrath descend on their heads.

Edward T. Bedford, a partner in the company, was the exception. He was scheduled to see Rockefeller and kept the appointment, even though he was prepared to hear a long tirade against the man who made the error in judgment. When he entered the office, the powerful head of the gigantic Standard Oil empire was bent over his desk, busily writing with a pencil on a pad of paper. Bedford stood silently, not wishing to interrupt. After a few moments, Rockefeller looked up.

"Oh, it's you, Bedford," he said calmly. "I suppose you've heard about our loss?"

Bedford replied that he had.

"I've been thinking it over," Rockefeller said, "and before I ask the man in to discuss the matter, I've been making some notes."

Bedford old the story this way, "Across the top of the page was written, 'Points in favor.' There was a long list of the man's virtues, including a brief description of how he had helped the company make the right decision on three separate occasions that had earned many times the cost of this recent error."

This is a great lesson. Before you rip into somebody, list their good points first.

Stop judging by mere appearances, but instead judge correctly
(John 7:24).

213. I BELIEVE IN YOU

Danny wanted to earn a varsity letter and have a letterman's jacket more than anything else in this world. Unfortunately, Danny was small for his age and not very athletic. He had had asthma as a youngster but had managed to build back his endurance by running. So he decided to go out for the track team as a distance runner. He ran all summer to get his time down in the mile to make the team.

His mother constantly encouraged him. She told him if he wanted it badly enough, he should go for it. She continually told him, "I believe in you!"

As a tenth grader he barely qualified for the team, but he didn't get to compete enough to earn his letter. That summer his mother contracted leukemia and Danny ran harder than ever, hoping to earn his letter so he could present it to his mother. Each day he'd tell her what his times were and she'd say, "You're getting better; you can do it. I believe in you!"

The next year Danny made the team and was on his way toward earning his letter when his mother died. A month later, when the varsity letters were being awarded, Danny's coach gave him an envelope with his mother's handwriting on it. Inside was a note that read, "I knew you could do it. I'm so proud of you."

The coach said, "Your mom bought this for you last year and asked me to hold it for you." Then he handed Danny a letterman's jacket. Inside was a message that had been embroidered, "I believe in you!"

Who do you know that needs your good words of encouragement?

Do not withhold good from those who deserve it,
when it is in your power to act (Proverbs 3:27).

214. LOSING YOUR MONEY OR YOUR PATIENCE

There's an old story the Hassidic Jews tell of a man who once made a bet of five hundred dollars with a friend that he could get a certain Rabbi, who was famous for his patience, to blow his stack. So the man went loudly banging on the rabbi's door at midnight and to further irritate him, he asked a stupid question: "Why do the Babylonians have round heads?"

To this rude, inconvenient, and vulgar shout, the rabbi smiled and quietly answered, "Because they have inexperienced midwives."

Frustrated, the man left. He returned later at an even more inconsiderate time, banged on the door, and bellowed, "I want to know why rabbis have weak eyes." This time, he thought the rabbi would lose it.

But no. The undisturbed rabbi quietly answered, "Because they live in the desert and the wind drives sand into their eyes."

He had tried again and failed. The man left. But he was ready to try once more, but now afraid he was losing his money, he decided to directly insult the patient rabbi: "May there never be another man in the world like you!" he screamed.

"Why?" patiently answered the rabbi.

"Because I just lost five hundred dollars on you!" he shouted back.

"Oh," replied the rabbi, "it is not entirely lost, because it will teach you not to be so impatient. Besides, it is better for you to lose five hundred dollars than it is for me to lose my patience!"

How quickly or easily do you lose your patience or become angry? Think about it.

A man's wisdom gives him patience; it is to his glory to overlook an offense
(Proverbs 19:11).

215. WHY WAIT UNTIL MARRIAGE?

Jaime Rau is a professional photographer and founder of Purely Committed, International, which was established in 2001. This is an organization encouraging peers to save sex for marriage. She writes the following:

Watching my single mother rushing into relationships blindly, giving away her body and losing pieces of her heart, I was always pretty sure I wanted to wait until marriage to have sex. But after hearing a camp counselor share how wonderful it was to give herself as a wedding gift to her husband, I was positive I wanted my wedding night to be as amazing as hers!

As I got older, my reasons for commitment became ever deeper. I started to realize the physical, emotional, and relational risks involved in sex outside of marriage. I witnessed the self-esteem of my girlfriends and mom plummet as guys slept with them.

I love knowing that someday when I get married, I will be able to have a level of intimacy with my husband that I have never had with anyone else. This intimacy will bond us together for life.

If you have already shared your gift and had your heart broken, you can still reap the benefits of recommitting to purity. Wrap your gift back up with a tag that says, "Reserved for Someone Special" and vow to save it for your wedding night!

I couldn't have said it better. Thank you, Jaime! Abstinence means refraining from all sexual activity, including oral sex. Purity means saving yourself mentally, emotionally, and physically until marriage and after marriage remaining faithful to your spouse.

Who can say, "I have kept my heart pure; I am clean and without sin?"
(Proverbs 20:9).

216. DATING DOS AND DON'TS FOR GIRLS

It's okay for guys to read this chapter. Are you aware that according to studies, one in six women has been a victim of rape and that among female rape victims, 54 percent are under the age of eighteen? Here are some important tips on how to protect yourself.

DO keep a cell phone and contact information with you at all times. DO keep an emergency stash of money for a taxi with you in case your date goes sour. DO make sure someone knows where you are at all times. DO learn some self-defense moves.

DON'T go out with a guy if you don't know him very well. DO get to know him in a group setting first. DON'T go on a blind date alone. Insist on double dating with a couple you know. DON'T go to quiet or secluded spots with your date. DO insist going somewhere public if he really wants to get to know you. DON'T leave your drink unattended at a party or eat anything questionable. Drugs can be slipped into your food or drink. DON'T go to a guy's place alone with him.

DO develop high standards and set boundaries of personal space. DO let your date know where your boundaries are. DON'T allow your date to violate any portion of your boundaries; if he does, tell him to stop. If he doesn't stop, leave immediately!

DON'T try to explain things, just leave and call your parents or a friend to pick you up. DO trust your instincts. If you sense something isn't right, get out of the situation.

Even a child is known by his actions, by whether his conduct is pure and right (Proverbs 20:11)

217. THE COLD WITHIN

The following poem has a very interesting message for our day. It's from an unknown source, which is too bad. But it's about what happens when people prejudge each other. Hopefully, this makes all of us think.

The Cold Within
Six humans trapped by happenstance, in bleak and bitter cold,
Each one possessed a stick of wood, or so the story's told.

Their dying fire in need of logs, the first man held his back,
For of the faces 'round the fire, he noticed one was black.

The next man looking 'cross the way saw one not of his church,
And couldn't bring himself to give the fire his stick of birch.

The third one sat in tattered clothes; he gave his coat a hitch,
Why should his log be put to use to warm the idle rich?

The rich man just sat back and thought of the wealth he had in store,
And how to keep what he had earned from the lazy, shiftless poor.

The black man's face bespoke revenge as the fire passed from sight,
For all he saw in his stick of wood was a chance to spite the white.

The last man of this forlorn group did naught except for gain,
Giving only to those who gave was how he played the game.

Their logs held tight in death's still hand was proof of human sin,
They didn't die from the cold without, they died from the cold within!

But I'm happy to tell you, this world is still full of people who are really warm on the inside and who value the diversity in the world and in the church. Now think about this question for the rest of today: Are you warm within? And without?

A man of many companions may come to ruin, but there is a friend who sticks closer than a brother (Proverbs 18:24).

218. PLAYING SOCCER AT THE HIGHEST LEVEL

He grew up playing soccer in the streets of Gioia del Colle, Italy, but he had one dream—to play soccer at the highest world level. Today he is doing exactly that.

"I really didn't dream of being anything else," says Nicola Legrottaglie, a defender and considered one of the world's best players. "I started playing in my hometown, a small town in Apulia, in southern Italy. Kids thought about football because there were no other areas to dream about making it big. There were never other dreams." For Legrottaglie, soccer—or football, as it's known by most of the world— is the world's number one sporting event.

He says, "For me, it's another way of proclaiming Jesus' name. Everything I do, everything anyone does, who is a Christian, must be done to proclaim the name of Jesus, to give Him glory. Not for personal boasting, but for Him!"

Legrottaglie's passion for the sport and for God was evident by age thirteen when he made a promise to God. He says, "I did make a promise to God, that if He gave me the opportunity to become a footballer, I would become a missionary for Him. So today I find myself keeping that promise that I made to God to become a missionary in the world where He sends me!"[25]

And pray for us, too, that God may open a door for our message, so that we may proclaim the mystery of Christ (Colossians 4:3).

219. SOME MYTHS ABOUT STEM CELL RESEARCH

Medical technology is advancing at an incredible pace, but along with this advance are some difficult bioethics dilemmas. The use of human embryos for this research and cloning represents a critical crossroads in the life of our culture and society. What will we do? How are we to come to the right moral decisions? Let's explore some of the misunderstandings and myths about his subject.

Myth 1: Stem cells can only come from embryos. The fact is that stem cells can be taken from umbilical cords, the placenta, amniotic fluid, and adult tissues and organs such as bone marrow, fat from liposuction, regions of the nose, and even from cadavers up to twenty hours after death.

Myth 2: Christians are against stem cell research. There are four categories of stem cells: embryonic stem cells, embryonic germ cells, umbilical cord stem cells, and adult stem cells. Given that germ cells can come from miscarriages that involve no deliberate interruption of pregnancy, Christians in general oppose the use of only one of these four categories, embryonic stem cells. In other words, most Christians approve of three of the four possible types of stem cell research.

Myth 3: Embryonic stem cell research is against the law. In reality, there is no law or regulation against destroying human embryos for research purposes. Anyone using private funds is free to pursue it.

The above facts are provided by the Family Research Council, founded in 1983 and dedicated to articulating and advancing a family centered philosophy of public life.

So God created man in his own image, in the image of God he created him; male and female he created them (Genesis 1:27).

220. THE CAMEL TAKES REVENGE

The camel is a very unusual animal. It has some very bad habits—it bites, it kicks, it spits, it stinks, and it takes revenge! The camel has a deep seated DNA of revenge. The camel always wants to "pay back" anybody who injures or hurts it.

Camel drivers and anyone who care for these animals as they travel through the desert know well about this nasty habit. Plus camels have long memories! To deal with this problem, camel jockeys and herders have come up with an interesting way of keeping themselves from being hurt as the camel takes revenge.

When a driver has in some way made his camel angry, he immediately runs out of sight of the camel. He then chooses a place of hiding near the road or trail on which the camel will soon pass. Just before the beast comes by, the camel jockey throws down some of his clothes and arranges them in a heap that looks like a sleeping man.

So along comes the camel, who sees and smells this heap of empty clothes. and the camel thinks it is the person who hurt him. He pounces on the pile, shakes every piece of clothing, stomps all over the clothes, and even bites each one.

Finally, when the camel has done a thorough job and tires of the revenge, the camel walks away. Then the jockey comes out of hiding, mounts the now placated beast, and merrily rides away!

Even a camel is smart enough to teach us a lesson. At least the camel gets over it and gets on with life. But the best way I know of dealing with the desire to take revenge on people who hurt us is to forgive and get on with life. Oh, yes, the best way to learn to forgive is by practicing forgiveness!

For if you forgive men when they sin against you, your heavenly Father will also forgive you. But if you do not forgive their sins, your Father will not forgive your sins (Matthew 6:14-15).

221. CHARACTER OR SELF-ESTEEM?

Which is most important, character or self-esteem? Which comes first, self-esteem or character? Which are you more concerned about?

As societies, when we lost track of character and focused on making sure everybody has a good self-esteem, the experts made a huge mistake! Character is a foundational issue, a bread and butter concept, a meat and potatoes thing to live by and build your life on. However, contrast that to this thing called self-esteem, and you have a cotton candy kind of concept.

Myriads of dissertations have demonstrated the supposed correlation between low self-esteem and virtually every problem that can be faced in life. Some of this research is really trivial—slow learners, unwanted kids, abused kids, and even obese teens have low self-esteem.

It's assumed that if you have low self-esteem, you will be a low achiever; if you have high-self esteem, you accomplish more in life. But in fact, there is nothing about causality. It's the opposite of popular opinion. People who have skills, education, and life accomplishments have good self-esteem. Self-esteem is really the result, not the cause of good work and a solid character.

If your work is meaningless, your education is without focus, and your relationships are broken and messed up, all the self-validations will only go so far! Build your character, build your skills, build your relationship with the God of creation, and you will also discover you have a balanced and self-fulfilling life experience, as well as a good self-esteem.

I say to every one of you: Do not think more highly of yourself than you ought, but rather think of yourself with sober judgment, in accordance with the measure of faith God has given you (Romans 12:3).

222. HINTS FOR CAMPERS

Are you one of those people who love the outdoors, hiking, fishing, hunting, and camping? You know, getting back to nature. The following are some hints for all of you outdoorsy types:

- Get even with a bear who raided your food bag by kicking his favorite stump apart and eating all those juicy ants.
- A hot rock placed in your sleeping bag will keep your feet warm. A hot enchilada works almost as well, but the cheese sticks between your toes.
- When camping, always wear a long-sleeved shirt because it gives you something to wipe your nose on. And remember, a two-man or two-woman pup tent does not include two men or two women or even a pup.
- A potato baked in the coals for an hour makes an excellent veggie, but a potato baked in the coals for three hours makes an excellent hockey puck.
- Take this simple test to see if you qualify for solo camping. Shine a flashlight into one ear. If the beam shines out the other ear, do not go into the woods alone.
- In emergency situations such as getting lost, you can survive in the wilderness by shooting small game with a slingshot made from the elastic waistband of underwear.
- The next time you go camping, remember to always take a well-developed sense of humor along with your tent, sleeping bag, and lots of grub! A camper without a sense of humor is like a car without a bumper.
- And most of all, when in the outdoors, always remember to give thanks and praise to the Creator who made this wonderful, exciting, beautiful, and bountiful world!

And God blessed the seventh day and made it holy, because on it he rested from all the work of creating that he had done (Genesis 2:2).

223. GOOD THINKING

W hat goes through your mind as you are watching Olympic athletes compete on TV? I'm thinking especially about the swimming events. Do you catch the incredible focus these athletes exhibit? They are in fabulous physical condition, but in each event hundredths or even thousandths of a second separate the winners from the losers. So what is the element besides strength and athletic ability that separates the winners from the losers?

Flip Darr, collegiate swimming coach who played a vital part in eight different Olympic winners, sheds some light on this topic. "I felt in my coaching career that if I would work on the swimmers' heads, their bodies would come along." He paused and goes on, "A lot of coaches work on their bodies and then at the last moment try to do their heads. The thing is, if they are working with their heads all the time, and working with their head over the body, mind over matter, they will have more confidence when they walk up to the starting block."

This is a fabulous illustration of the value of good thinking. Athletic ability is important for a swimmer, but preparation for the biggest race of your life is as much mental as it is physical, if not more. Bill MacCartney, former head football coach at the University of Colorado said, "Mental is to physical what four is to one."

This is a powerful concept in making the case for good thinking—in the swimming pool or at school or at home. The specific thoughts you think that increase your effectiveness might not be the same as what are required for an Olympic medal, but the overall commitment to good thinking is identical.

Whatever is true, whatever is noble, whatever is right, whatever is pure, whatever is lovely, whatever is admirable—if anything is excellent or praiseworthy—think about such things (Philippians 4:8).

224. THINKING OUTSIDE THE KNOT

An ancient Greek history and mythology, Gordius, who was King of Phrygia and Mida's father, had declared that whoever could untie the Gordian knot was destined to become ruler of all Asia. Many, maybe even hundreds, had attempted to solve the puzzle and untie this Gordian knot, but no one had been successful.

When Alexander the Great came to Phrygia, he was challenged with the impossible knot, so he too attempted to solve the puzzle and untie the knot. Like many before him, he was unsuccessful. Eventually he became impatient and frustrated. In his impatience, he drew his sword and smashed it down on the knot and cleanly cut it in half.

Even though he had not untied the knot in the way that Gordius had expected, it had to be said that he solved the puzzle. He had done what had been asked of him—solve the puzzle and undo the knot. Alexander was then awarded the prize, and he became the ruler of all of Asia. He conquered the then known world by the age of twenty-five.

In today's world, you and I have been challenged many times to "think outside of the box." It means bring some new and creative thinking to solve many of life's problems. Think the unthinkable. Think outside of the conventional wisdom. Be unique. Become a problem solver! Follow the example of Jesus, who did the impossible more than once in His earthly ministry. One major breakthrough of His life was to introduce this world to a kind, loving, caring, wonderful heavenly Father!

No one has seen the Father except the One who is from God; only He has seen the Father (John 6:46).

225. SAY THE JUST RIGHT WORDS

Mary Ann Bird wrote the following story in her book, *The Whisper Test*:

I grew up knowing I was different and I hated it. I was born with a cleft palate, and when I started school, my classmates made it clear to me how I looked to others: a little girl with a misshapen lip, crooked nose, lop-sided teeth, and garbled speech.

When schoolmates asked, "What happened to your lip?" I'd tell them I'd fallen and cut it on a piece of glass. Somehow it seemed more acceptable to have suffered an accident than to have been born different. I was convinced that no one outside my family could love me. There was, however, a teacher in the second grade whom we all adored, Mrs. Leonard, by name. She was short, round, happy . . . a sparkling lady.

Annually we had a hearing test. Mrs. Leonard gave the test to everyone in the class and finally it was my turn. I knew from past years that as we stood against the door and covered one ear, the teacher sitting at her desk would whisper something and we would have to repeat back things like: "The sky is blue" or "Do you have new shoes?" I waited there for those words God must have put into her mouth, those seven words that changed my life forever. Mrs. Leonard said, in her whisper, "I wish you were my little girl!"

The Bible speaks about how important the right word spoken at the right time are like gold or silver. Words are powerful and words have meaning and words can change a life for somebody else. So, just for today, how about speaking an encouraging word into the life of somebody who needs your good words!

Reckless words pierce like a sword, but the tongue of the wise brings healing
(Proverbs 12:18).

226. THE FROG WHO COULD

There once was a convention of frogs that had a cross-country running meet. The goal was to reach the top of this mountain. A huge crowd had gathered to watch this race and cheer on the competition.

The race began, but no one in the crowd believed any of the frogs would manage to climb this mountain. Shouts were coming from the crowd, "This run is too tough for little frogs!" Or "this is an impossible climb." And "It can't be done!" No encouragement came from the crowd, only negative comments.

Then the frogs began collapsing and dropping out from exhaustion, except for the few with a steady run. Some broke through the "wall" and caught a fresh burst of energy. But the crowd was still yelling, "This is impossible! No one will make it to the finish line!"

More frogs became exhausted and gave up. But one tiny frog continued to climb higher and higher; this one did not give up!

The persistent frog crossed the finish line, the only one to finish the race. He put out the effort and never gave up. He was the winner.

All the other frogs wanted to know the secret of how this frog had managed to finish the race and become the winner. Another frog asked this little frog how he had managed to find the strength to succeed and reach the goal. It turned out, the winning frog was deaf! He could not hear the shouts of discouragement. His so-called handicap turned out to be the advantage! Success is nothing more than a failure turned inside out.

The Lord is my strength and my defense; he has become my salvation. He is my God, and I will praise him (Exodus 15:2).

227. DO NOT TALK TO MY PARROT!

A lady named Rachael had a faulty dishwasher that quit working, so she called a repairman. Since she had to go to work the next day, she gave specific instructions to the repairman: "I'll leave the house key under the front mat. Fix the dishwasher, leave the bill on the counter, and I'll mail you a check."

But that wasn't all the instructions. In capital letters, she continued, "OH, BY THE WAY, DON'T WORRY ABOUT MY PIT BULL DOG, SPIKE. He won't bother you. But whatever you do, DO NOT—UNDER ANY CIR-CUMSTANCES—TALK TO MY PARROT! I repeat, DO NOT TALK TO MY PARROT!"

When the repairman arrived at Rachael's home the following day, he discovered the biggest, meanest looking pit bull he had ever seen. But, exactly as she said, the dog just lay there on the carpet watching the repairman do the repairs. No bother, no problem.

The parrot, however, drove him nuts the whole time with his incessant yelling, name calling, and screeching. Finally, the repairman couldn't contain himself any longer and yelled, "Shut up, you stupid, ugly bird!"

To which the parrot replied, "Go get him, Spike!"

Oh, well. So much for not following specific orders. It's like not reading the instructions before you attempt to assemble your next gadget. Instructions exist for a purpose. What about an instruction book on how to have a fulfilling lifestyle? The instruction manual for living is called the Bible, God's Word. You should not only read it, but also follow the specifics given! Your life is too important for a do-it-yourself-project.

I seek you with all my heart; do not let me stray from your commands
(Psalm 119:10).

228. THE REAL PRESIDENTIAL VETO

The former first lady of the United States, Laura Bush, recalls one overnight visit with her husband, George W. Bush, in the home of his parents, the former President and Mrs. Barbara Bush.

"George woke up at about 6:00 a.m., as was his usual practice, and went downstairs to get a cup of coffee," Mrs. Bush explains.

"Then he sat down on the living room sofa with his parents and put his feet up on the coffee table," says Laura.

All of a sudden, Barbara Bush yelled, "Put your feet down!"

George's dad then replied, "For goodness sake, Barbara, he's the President of the United States."

And Barbara said, "I don't care. I don't want his feet on my coffee table!"

The President promptly did as he was told as Mrs. Barbara Bush observed, "Even Presidents have to listen to their mamas!"[26]

I think all of us can probably relate. Would you like to live a long and exciting life? The Bible tells us that one key to living a long time is to obey your mother and father, so that your days may be long on this earth. This is such an important life key that the Bible explains it's a command with a special promise. This promise apparently has no time limits; therefore, whether we are young or old—just ordinary or a world leader—the Bible, God the Creator, and a former Presidential First Lady all give the same important advice: listen and obey your mama!

Honor your father and your mother, as the Lord your God has commanded you, so that you may live long and that it may go well with you in the land the Lord your God has given you (Deuteronomy 5:16).

229. SOLVING THE PAPER PROBLEM

A family moved into a new town, and one of their first things to do was to order a daily paper to be delivered to their home. The next day they began receiving the paper but became annoyed when they had to search for the newspaper every day. When the paper boy would toss it toward the house, it would land in the yard, the bushes, the driveway, under the porch, or even on the porch roof!

162

The man of the house called the number to the paper boy's home and spoke with him. But he did not complain about the way in which it was delivered, he thanked the thirteen-year-old for delivering his paper on a daily basis. He stayed on the phone and had conversation. In this phone call he learned that the young man loved basketball. That was all this perceptive man needed to know. That same day, he went to the local hardware store and bought a basketball hoop and fastened it to a post on the front porch.

The next morning, as the family was having breakfast, they heard a "ker-plunk" and a thud as the newspaper landed exactly right on the porch next to the front door. Oh yes, they never had to search for a wayward paper again!

Pretty clever! Talk about solving a problem without having it escalate into a full-blown conflict. Are you faced with a problem, maybe not a big issue, but one of those things that just annoys you, drives you nuts, and never seems to be resolved? Here's the solution. Understand the motivations of those with whom you might be in conflict. There's always an answer, but armed with this simple idea, together we might have solved the problem. I'm for innovation and good problem solving!

The fear of the Lord is the beginning of wisdom; all who follow his precepts have good understanding (Psalm 111:10).

230. SOME SHORT SHOTS OF WISDOM

Don't let your worries get the best of you.

- Remember, Moses started out in life as a basket case.
- A wise teenager will never play leapfrog with a unicorn.
- God will put us through many different kinds of life tests, but they are always open book tests.
- In life go as far as you can see and when you get there, you will be able to see a whole lot further.
- An optimist is a person who takes the cold water thrown on his good ideas, heats it with enthusiasm, and uses the steam to push on ahead.
- The future belongs to those who are willing to make painful short-term sacrifices for the possibility of long-term gains.
- Confidence comes from doing a little thing well because you know that you can do bigger things well too.
- Some people have all the confidence of a kamikaze pilot who is about to take off on his tenth mission.

- In this life the bad news is that time flies. The very good news is that you are the pilot.
- Never consider yourself a slow learner. Perhaps it may be that teaching just may come hard to most of your teachers.
- Christianity is the I crossed out. Just think of that every time you take a look at a cross.

Great are the works of the Lord; they are pondered by all who delight in them (Psalm 111:2).

231. TEACHING A BLIND PERSON TO TRUST

It's a fascinating process to witness. She is about eighteen or nineteen years old. She stands at a street corner waiting for the light to change so she could cross the street. But she's afraid, she seems disoriented, she hears the cars and obviously she is afraid. Then it dawns on the observer—she is blind and can't see the red light making it safe to cross.

He watches her Seeing Eye dog pull at the harness to encourage her to follow its leading. Finally she walks with the dog across the street because there is a man beside her talking to her, encouraging her to trust her Seeing Eye dog.

If you were to follow them, you would see the same picture all over town. The blind girl, the Seeing Eye dog, and the sighted man will be walking through parking lots, down sidewalks, crossing streets, going into a mall, across train tracks, and even going into restaurants.

Finally it dawns on the observer again. Working with the dog is a new experience for the blind girl. The dog knows what to do. The sighted man is along to encourage the woman to trust in her guide, a dog who becomes the eyes for the blind girl. It's the girl who needs to know how to trust. She is learning how to place her trust in an animal with a greater perspective.

We are like that! Faith is not a blind leap but a trust that is built up over time in the trustworthiness of someone else. The Bible doesn't command faith, it tells us to "taste and see that the Lord is good" (Psalm 34:8). David was not taking a blind leap of faith when he faced the giant Goliath because he knew what God would do from his past and previous experiences. The Bible says to trust and then to obey.

All those gathered here will know that it is not by sword or spear that the Lord saves; for the battle is the Lord's (1 Samuel 17:47).

232. BAD THREADS

A shoe manufacturing company in Thailand discovered their productivity in their factory had dropped. Perhaps a better way to say it was that their output had fallen off the cliff. And there was another problem; their customers were complaining about the quality of their shoes—they were coming apart.

So the company called in a consultant to figure what was going wrong. The first step this consultant took was the last thing that most management people think to do. He went out on the factory floor and began talking with the assembly line workers. He asked them what they thought had gone wrong with their production.

They told the consultant exactly what had gone wrong. They told him that putting shoes together takes a lot of thread. The sewing machine operators said that recently the new thread they were using kept breaking. They were spending too much of their production time rethreading their machines and therefore production was shut down.

The consultant checked out the thread problem. He learned that one of their purchasing agents had found a cheaper price on thread. The company was able to save pennies per each bobbin of thread, which added up to a substantial savings. The only problem was that productivity dropped in half and their customers refused to buy their shoes!

In making shoes and in making your life, it's important to pay attention to the small threads in your life that hold it together. Build with quality materials that will not break under the stress of real life. The quality materials to build your life on are found in God's Word, in His church, with His people! Build well for the long journey.

Consequently, you are no longer foreigners and aliens, but . . . built on the foundation of the apostles and prophets, with Christ Jesus himself as the chief cornerstone (Ephesians 2:19-20).

233. SOMETHING MUST BE WRONG

This story is about a seventy-three-year-old farmer who lived in Iowa near the town of Bettendorf. He was single and lived alone but still worked his very large farm. In an accident, on a Sunday afternoon, his tractor tipped over and pinned him beneath it for four days and four nights. Nobody had seen the accident. He went four days without food or water, lying in pain. A concerned friend went to check on him and rescued him. He was taken to the local hospital for treatment. He lived, he survived, but he lost his leg below the knee.

Several newspapers picked up the story expressing amazement that a seventy-three-year-old farmer could survive such an ordeal. Even more unique is the reason why his friends went looking for him. One neighbor said it best, "He never missed Wednesday night prayer meeting at church. Last night he missed so we knew something was wrong." Simply missing one church service saved his life.

Not missing a single church service just might be the thing that will save your life too! Why bother with church? It's quite simple but also compelling. People need people. Teens need teens. God's people need God's people in order to know God in a better relationship. God's life in Christ is a corporate kind of an affair. All God's promises were made to God's people in the plural. Just show me the story of a Bible Christian who was isolated and alone. The Bible doesn't teach about becoming isolated, it teaches about all of us about becoming together in a group, a special body called the church. By the way, have you missed church lately?

> *And let us consider how we may spur one another on toward love and good deeds. Let use not give up meeting together, as some are in the habit of doing, but let us encourage one another—and all the more as you see the Day approaching* (Hebrews 10:24-25).

234. AN OFFER FROM ELVIS

This is an interesting and little known page of American history. Not everybody liked former President Richard Nixon, but the King did. I'm not talking the king of some foreign country, I'm talking about the King, Elvis Presley. Elvis thought J. Edgar Hoover was the greatest living American, and Richard Nixon wasn't far behind.

On December 21, 1970, Elvis dropped by the White House unannounced, requesting an audience with the President. To make sure Nixon knew who he was, he brought along a letter to introduce himself. It seemed Elvis was interested in becoming a federal agent to help fight the drug problem—the country's, not his.

In his letter he wrote that "the drug culture, the hippie elements, the SDS, and Black Panthers" did not consider him as part of the establishment; therefore, he would be able to easily infiltrate their ranks to act as an undercover agent. To help Nixon realize what he was talking about, Elvis wrote that he had done an "in-depth study of drug abuse" as well as "Communist brainwashing techniques." Nixon agreed to see Elvis, who was stoned on painkillers during the meeting. Needless to say, his request to become a federal agent was denied.[27]

What a fascinating scene of history of two people who are now dead and gone. Is there a lesson here for us today? Yes, too often Christians are mistaken in believing that their sin experiences in their past or even present makes them a better Christian, when in reality it is their current relationship to God, without sin, that makes us all better Christians!

No one who is born of God will continue to sin, because God's seed remains
in him; he cannot go on sinning, because he has been born of God
(1 John 3:9).

235. IT'S NOT ALL BAD

This world is not falling apart just because the media is filled with stories of riots, crime, corruption, aggression, drug usage, and how bad this generation of today's teens are compared to the last generation. I'll have you know this kind of reporting has always made news and probably always will.

This world, however, is held together by something more positive, more constructive, but less spectacular than sensational news. It is the everyday lives of the greater mass of people who never make the news but who are helping make the world a better place for everyone!

Every day millions of teens all over this world get up and go to school and study hard to prepare themselves for a better life. It makes no difference where this takes place, just know it takes place. Many teachers teach with love and the efficiency of a dedicated person.

Every day millions of teens resist temptations to lie, cheat, or steal for personal gain. These are the ones for whom honesty is a way of life. These have made the decision to live with respect, moral values, and decency.

Every day millions of teens purposely go out of their way to be helpful to others. Good deeds are a natural response to others in need.

Every day millions of teens have chosen to live a life that is pleasing to others but most importantly a life that brings honor, praise, and glory to the God whom they have chosen to serve. You are not alone. Live it right!

And whatever you do, whether in word or deed, do it all in the name of the
Lord Jesus, giving thanks to God the Father through him (Colossians 3:17).

236. BUILDING WITH INTEGRITY

Maybe you are too young to begin thinking about retirement, but how about a retirement story? A carpenter has worked his lifetime and now it's time to retire. He goes to the contractor/builder who employed him for thirty years and tells his employer he plans to retire—to live in leisure, spend more time with his wife and family, and watch the grandkids grow up. He would miss the regular paycheck, but it's time to retire.

The builder was saddened to hear this announcement and let such a good worker go. But he asked him to please build just one more house as a personal favor. The carpenter agreed, but in time it was easy to see his heart was not in his work. He resorted to shoddy workmanship, he cut corners, and used inferior materials—an unfortunate way to end a dedicated career.

When the house was completed, his employer came to inspect the house. As they were ready to enter the house, the builder handed the keys to the carpenter and said, "This is your house! This is my retirement gift to you."

The carpenter was shocked! What a shame. Now he will live out the rest of his life in a second-rate built home. If he had only known he was building his own house, he would have done it differently.

So, my young friend, that's how it is. We build our lives a day at a time. Hopefully, we are using the best habits, the best thoughts, the best actions and the best materials. It may be a shock to you, but the life you build is the life you will have to live in the rest of your days. Build wisely! Life is a do-it-yourself-project.

> *Therefore everyone who hears these words of mine and puts them into practice is like a wise man who built his house on the rock* (Matthew 7:24).

237. THE WORLD'S GREATEST RÉSUMÉS

Hello! My name is Jesus, the Christ. Many call me "Lord." I am presenting my résumé because I am seeking the top management position in your heart and life. Please consider the following accomplishments as listed in my résumé:

Qualifications: I founded the earth and established the heavens (Proverbs 3:19). I formed mankind from the dust of the ground (Genesis 2:7). I breathed into humanity the breath of life (Genesis 2:7). I redeemed all of mankind (Galatians 3:13).

Occupational Background: I've had only one employer (Luke 2:49). I have never been tardy, absent, disobedient, slothful, or disrespectful; and my employer has nothing but rave reviews (Matthew 3:15-17).

Skills and Work Experience: These include empowering the poor to be poor no more, healing the brokenhearted, setting captives free, healing the sick, restoring sight to the blind, and setting free those who are bruised (Luke 4:18). I am a Wonderful Counselor (Isaiah 9:6). I have the authority, ability, and power to cleanse you of your sins (I John 1:7-9).

Educational Background: I encompass the entire breadth and length of knowledge, wisdom, and understanding (Proverbs 2:6). My words are so powerful they are described as being a lamp (Psalm 119:105). I can tell you the secrets of your mind (Psalm 44:21). All treasures of wisdom and knowledge are in Me (Colossians 2:3).

In Summation: Now that you've read my résumé, I'm confident that I'm the only candidate uniquely qualified to fill this vital position in your life. I will properly direct your pathways (Proverbs 3:5-6), and lead you into everlasting life (John 6:47). When can I begin? Time is of the essence! I'm waiting for your answer.

Through him all things were made; without him nothing was made that has been made. In him was life and that life was the light of men (John 1:3-4).

238. THE ULTIMATE RECALL NOTICE

Cars can be recalled! Why not a recall notice from your Maker?

Recall Notice: The Maker of all human beings is recalling all units manufactured, regardless of make, year, or model due to a serious defect in the primary and central component of the heart. This is due to a malfunction in the original prototype units code named Adam and Eve, resulting in the reproduction of the same defect in all subsequent units. This defect has been technically termed "Subsequential Internal Non-morality," or more commonly known as SIN as it is primarily expressed.

Please check to see if you have one or more of the following symptoms:

• Loss of direction in life.
• Bad vocal emissions.
• Amnesia of original origin.
• Lack of peace and joy.
• Selfish or violent behavior.
• Depression or confusion in the mental or nerve components.
• Fearfulness.
• Rebellion against the Manufacturer.

The Manufacturer is neither liable nor at fault for this defect but is providing factory-authorized repair and service free of charge to correct this SIN defect.

The Repair Technician, Jesus Christ, has most generously offered to bear the entire burden of the staggering cost of these repairs. No additional fees or hidden charges are applicable.

The number to call for repairs in all areas is: P-R-A-Y-E-R. Once connected, please upload your burden of SIN through the REPENTANCE procedure. Next, download ATONEMENT from the Repair Technician, Jesus, into your personal heart, mind, and soul components. No matter how large or small the SIN defect is, Jesus will replace it with love, joy, peace, patience, kindness, goodness, faithfulness, gentleness, and self-control.

For God so loved the world that he gave his one and only Son, that whoever believe in him shall not perish but have eternal life (John 3:16).

239. A CARROT, AN EGG, AND A CUP OF COFFEE

Olga, eighteen years old, complained to her mother about how things were so hard for her. She whined and complained about school, her part-time job, her teachers, her boss, her lack of money, and all the problems of her life.

This was taking place in the kitchen, and as Olga talked her mother filled three pots with water and placed them on burners. Soon the pots came to a boil. In the first one she put carrots, in the second she put eggs, and in the last she put ground coffee. She let them boil and didn't say a word as Olga continued to complain.

About twenty minutes later she turned off the burners, fished out the carrots, took out the eggs, and poured a cup of coffee. Turning to Olga she asked, "What do you see?"

Olga replied, "Carrots, eggs, and coffee."

Then her mother asked her to feel the carrots, then break and peel the hardboiled eggs, and take a taste of coffee. "Okay, Mother, what now?"

Her mother explained that each of these three had all faced the same problem: hot boiling water. "But notice," she went on, "each had a different reaction. The carrots went in strong, hard, and unbending. The egg had been frail in the outer shell but the insides had become hard. The coffee grinds were different; after they had been in the water, they changed the water into something else." She paused, "Olga, which one of these are you?"

Okay, the next time you find yourself in boiling water, how will you respond? Are you the carrot that becomes soft or the egg that becomes hard or the coffee that changes your surroundings? Life can be tough, but with God's help you can change your world.

It is God who arms me with strength, and makes my way perfect
(2 Samuel 22:31).

240. SCARS TO LAST A LIFETIME

The following happened a few years ago on a hot summer day in south Florida. A thirteen-year-old boy home from the last day of school decided to go for a swim. He ran through the house, shedding clothes and shoes, put on his swimming trunks, and shot out the back door. He was soon swimming in the cool, refreshing water. As he swam away from shore, an alligator was swimming toward shore.

His dad, working in the yard, saw the two getting closer and closer. He ran to the water, shouting to his son as loud as he could to warn him. He heard the warning and made a quick turn back to shore. Too late! Just as he reached the dock, his dad reached for him and the gator got him. The dad grabbed his son just as the gator bit down on his legs, and an incredible tug-of-war took place. The gator was stronger than the dad, but the dad was more passionate! A neighbor heard the screams, raced to his house, got a gun and returned to shoot the reptile.

Remarkably, after weeks in the hospital, the teen survived! His legs were scarred by the vicious attack. Stitches were everywhere, and skin grafts and rehab had to take place. And his arms were also scarred with deep scratches where his dad's fingernails had dug into his flesh in the effort to hang on to the son he loved.

A newspaper reporter interviewed the boy after the trauma and asked if he could see the scars. The teen lifted his pants legs and then with obvious pride said, "But look at my arms. I have these because my dad wouldn't let go!"

We might have scars from a painful past, but there also might be some wounds because God our loving heavenly Father has not let go because He loves you!

For God did not send his Son into the world to condemn the world, but to save the world though him (John 3:17).

241. FIRST PRIME THE PUMP

The following note was found in a baking powder can that was wired to the handle of an old-fashioned pump that offered the only hope of drinking water on a very long and seldom used trail across the Amargosa Desert:

This pump is all right as of June 1932. I put a new sucker-washer in this pump, and it ought to last five years or more. But the washer dries out and the pump has got to be primed. Under the white rock just below, I buried a bottle of water and sealed the spout with a cork. There is just enough water to prime the pump. If you drink any of the water, there will not be enough to prime the pump. Pour one-fourth of the water in the pump and let it soak into the leather sucker-washer for about three minutes. Then pour the rest of the water from the bottle into the pump and pump like crazy! You will get plenty of cool, clear, clean water.

The well has never run dry. When you get all the water you want or need, please fill the bottle and put it back as you found it for the next person. Remember, don't drink the water first; prime the pump and you'll get all you can drink. Trust me!

Okay, trust me! Ever heard of this thing called delayed gratification? It's about paying the price first, then enjoying the reward later. You see, in life, the only place where success comes before work is in the dictionary. And the elevator to success is out of order; you must climb to success one step at a time. This might be a tough life lesson, but it's the only way. Think about Jesus Christ and His life. He spent thirty years of His life in preparation for only three years of ministry! Moses spent forty years in the palace of Pharaoh, then forty years in the desert for forty years of leadership/ministry.

A man's wisdom gives him patience (Proverbs 19:11).

242. BUMPER STICKER WISDOM

I don't know about you and where you live, but where I live, you can see all kinds of bumper stickers on cars that proclaim all kinds of things. Try these on for size:

- Into every life some rain must fall, usually when your car windows happened to be left down.
- It is cynicism and fear that freeze life; it is faith that thaws it out, releases it, and sets it free.
- Love is like a roller coaster . . . When it's good, you don't want to get off; when it isn't, you can't wait to throw up.
- Just remember, you have to break a few eggs to make a really big mess on your neighbor's car.
- Faith is to believe what we do not see, and the reward of this faith is to see what we believe.
- If you believe the doctors, nothing is wholesome. If you believe theologians, nothing is innocent. If you believe the military, nothing is safe.
- There are two positive ways to assure failure in any conflict. Always underrate your competition and always overrate yourself.
- You have not really lived today until or unless you have done something for someone else who cannot possibly pay you back.
- We cannot do everything that needs to be done at once, but we can do something at once.

- God grant me the serenity to accept the people I cannot change, the courage to change the one I can, and the wisdom to know that I'm the one I can change!

Blessed is the man who finds wisdom, the man who gains understanding, for she is more profitable than silver and yields better returns than gold (Proverbs 3:13).

243. THE 500 MILE WALK

Fifteen-year-old Mike Durbin isn't a man of steel, he doesn't leap over tall buildings in a single bound, nor can he stop a speeding bullet. However, Mike is a modern-day superhero. Why? He recently decided to step out of his comfort zone and walk 500 miles to find out what it means to be a "youth in ministry, reaching people for Christ." How did it happen?

This high school junior from Whitehouse, Texas, attended a special missions dinner where Chet Caudill spoke on the subject of real sacrifice. He challenged the students to make an extraordinary effort to raise money for missions so as to gain some understanding of true sacrifice in the process.

Mike was inspired to pray and asked God to give him an extraordinary something to do. The next morning he told his father, Big Mike, that God had given him a concept to walk 500 miles from Whitehouse, Texas, to Springfield, Missouri, in order to help his youth group raise $10,000 for missions. The walk took place June 1 through July 1.

He was joined by his nineteen-year-old uncle, Marcus Durbin. Big Mike and eight-year-old brother, Dalton, helped with the daily itinerary and logistics. Along the way, because of his blog and walk, he had opportunities to speak to churches, camps, youth groups, and several media outlets, all who gave him an opportunity to share his faith and raise money at the same time for this project.

Oh, yes, one more thing you must know: Mike is a survivor of childhood leukemia. He says, "My theme is 'I will walk. I will pray; I will fast; I will give; I will mow lawns; I will bake cookies. I will be passionate and get out there and do it!'"[28]

The path of the righteous is like the first gleam of dawn, shining ever brighter till the full light of day (Proverbs 5:18).

244. FROZEN THINKING

Nick was twenty-one years old, big, strong, and a very reliable employee. He got along well with everyone on the job. He had worked in the railroad yards for his company for the past three years. He had one major problem—his attitude was chronically negative, and he was known as the most pessimistic man on the job.

One summer day, on a Friday, his crew was sent home an hour early so they could celebrate the birthday of their foreman. All the workers left except Nick, who had somehow accidentally locked himself in a refrigerated boxcar that was empty. When he realized he was locked inside, he panicked. He beat on the doors until his arms and hands were bloody; he yelled until he was so hoarse he couldn't yell.

Aware of the danger, he knew the temperature in the unit was as low as five or ten degrees Fahrenheit. He feared the worst; he knew he would freeze to death! He found a scrap of cardboard and scribbled a note to his parents, "Getting so cold. Body numb. If I don't get out soon, these will be my last words."

They were. He was found in a fetal position, frozen! The autopsy revealed Nick's body temperature had lowered enough for him to die. But the refrigeration unit was not even on! The time he froze to death the temperature in the boxcar never dropped below sixty-one degrees Fahrenheit, which is only slightly less than normal room temperature. He had expected to die because he believed he would freeze to death.

Life is a self-fulfilling prophecy. Too many people today are like Nick—fearing the worst. Do you expect failure or do you expect success? Do you believe for the good things in life?

If a man digs a pit, he will fall into it; if a man rolls a stone, it will roll back on him (Proverbs 26:27).

245. SONGS FOR BIBLE CHARACTERS

If you were a songwriter, what kind of a song would you write in honor of some of the people found in the Bible? Well, you don't have to because songs and song titles have already been written that go well with the following characters. Enjoy!

Here's how this goes: if you were to write a song in honor of Noah, it would be: "Raindrops Keep Falling On My Head." Do you get the concept? And yes, these are real songs that have already been written.

- How about a song for Adam and Eve? I would nominate, "Stranger in Paradise."
- Try this one on for Lazarus: "The Second Time Around."
- Let's move on to Esther: "I Feel Pretty."
- Next is for Moses: "The Happy Wanderer."
- Now for Jezebel: "The Lady Is a Tramp."
- Samson: "Hair."
- Salome: "I Could Have Danced All Night."
- Daniel: "The Lion Sleeps Tonight."
- Joshua: "Good Vibrations."
- Peter: "I'm Sorry."
- Esau: "Born to be Wild."

If you're not getting the connections, perhaps you could ask your parents or a friend who is biblical literate. Or maybe, this is the time to get serious about your Bible study. How about some more?

- Jeremiah: "Take This Job and Shove It."
- Shadrach, Meshach, and Abednego: "Great Balls of Fire."
- The three wise men: "When You Wish Upon a Star."
- Jonah: "Got a Whale of a Tale."
- Elijah: "Up, Up, and Away."
- Methuselah: "Stayin' Alive."
- Nebuchadnezzar: "Crazy."
- And in conclusion, Jesus Christ, the Son of God: "What A Friend We Have in Jesus" and one more, "He's All I Need"!

They had harps given them by God and sang the song of Moses the servant of God and the song of the Lamb: Great and marvelous are your deeds
(Revelation 15:2-3).

246. HOW TO KNOW YOU BOUGHT A BAD COMPUTER

If you are a teen, likely you cannot remember life before computers, iPods, twitter, Facebook, or even cell phones. But at times, technology is not all it's cracked up to be. I'm getting off track, so let's get back to the top ten signs to know when you have purchased a bad computer:

TEN: The lower corner of your screen has these words that appear each time you boot up, "Etch-a-Sketch."

NINE: The celebrity spokesman who appears is that "Hey Vern" guy.

EIGHT: In order to start up your computer, you need some jumper cables and a friend's car.

SEVEN: It's "Pentium: Redefining Mathematics."

SIX: Your computer's quick reference manual is only 320 pages long.

FIVE: Whenever you boot it up, all the dogs in your neighbor start howling.

FOUR: The screen often displays the following message: "Ain't it about time to take a break?"

THREE: The manual contains only one sentence you understand: "Good luck!"

TWO: The only chip inside is a Dorito.

ONE: You have finally decided that your computer is an excellent addition to your fabulous paperweight collection.

Oh well, if you can't trust your computer, what can you trust in this world? Perhaps you have heard the saying, "The only sure things in this world are death and taxes." Let's say it like this: the only sure things in this world are death and eternity. Which brings up another question: Where will you spend eternity? In heaven or hell? Think about it, while you still have a choice and time to make it right!

It is better to go to a house of mourning than to go to a house of feasting, but death is the destiny of every man; the living should take this to heart
(Ecclesiastes 7:2).

247. WHAT HAPPENS WHEN A BABY COMES?

At the Roaring Mine Camp in northern California during the gold rush days of the late 1800s, the only woman in this particular camp, a woman of questionable reputation, had died. Then some of those rough, tough, gruff, miners—a rowdy bunch if there ever was one—discovered she had left behind a baby. They discovered the crying baby lying in a plain box.

They looked at that box and decided that this was no bed fit for the baby to be sleeping in. What did they do? They sent a man by mule to Sacramento, California, to get a rosewood cradle. When he returned, they put the baby in the cradle and said, "You know what? That baby doesn't look good in those ragged, dirty bedclothes. Get back on that mule and go back to Sacramento to get some proper blankets for the baby."

They moved the rosewood cradle with the baby in clean blankets into another bedroom and looked at the walls that didn't look too good either. They said, "Let's clean up these walls with new paint." And when they finished, they decided to fix the windows because of how cold it became at night. Next came curtains for the windows.

The baby needed some quiet time and a nap, so the rowdy, loud language stopped. On a nice day, they took the baby to the mine entrance. They noticed how bad it looked, so they cleaned the mess up and even planted some flowers so it would look nice for the baby. They walked the baby downtown and noticed the trash that was everywhere; so they cleaned it up for the baby to have a better environment.

Everything was changed by the presence of the baby. That baby who came to change everything was Jesus Christ at Christmas. Has this baby changed everything in your life?

And this is the testimony: God has given us eternal life, and this life is in his Son. He who has the Son has life; he who does not have the Son of God does not have life (1 John 5:11-12).

248. A SONG AND A SONGWRITER

One of the world's most popular songs is "Precious Lord," and it made Tom Dorsey one of the major composers in gospel music. The appeal of this song has crossed all kinds of borders and has been translated into thirty-two different languages. During the 1920s, Dorsey had achieved a measure of fame as a jazz musician, and it was during this time that he became intrigued with the idea of blending jazz and blues with church music.

In August 1932, Dorsey was scheduled for a gospel concert in a St. Louis church. Because his wife was pregnant, he worried about leaving her alone in Chicago but was assured she would be fine, so he kept this commitment. During the concert, a telegram came with four words, "Your wife just died." He quickly returned home to find that his wife had died in giving birth to a son, who also died the same night.

Dorsey said, "I buried Nettie and our son in the same casket. Then I fell apart. I felt God had done me an injustice." Then one day, in his anguish, as he sat down at his piano, he said, "My hands began to browse on the keys. Then something happened! I felt as though I could reach out and touch God. I found myself playing a melody I had never heard before, and the words came into my head. They seemed to fall in place: "Precious Lord, take my hand, lead me on, let me stand. I am tired, I am worn. Through the storm, through the night, lead me on, to the light. Take my hand, Precious Lord."

His pain was healed and he went to write more than four hundred more gospel songs. He said, "When we hurt the most, this is when God is closest and when we are most open to His restoring power!"

And the God of all grace, who called you to His eternal glory in Christ, after you have suffered a little while, will himself restore you and make you strong, firm and steadfast (1 Peter 5:10).

249. SAD CHILDREN AND A HAPPY, SMILING GOD

The late, great humorist and author, Erma Bombeck, told this story of what had happened to her while in church one Sunday morning.

I was intently watching a small child who was turning around and smiling at everyone. He wasn't gurgling, spitting, humming, kicking, or tearing up the hymnals or rummaging through his mother's handbag. He was just smiling!

Finally, his mother jerked him about and in a stage whisper that could be heard in a little theater off Broadway said, "Stop that grinning! You're in church!" With that she gave him a belt and as the tears rolled down his little cheeks, she added, "That's better," and returned to her praying.

We sing, "Make a Joyful Noise Unto the Lord" while our faces reflect the sadness of one who has just buried a rich aunt who left everything to her pregnant hamster.

Suddenly I was angry! It occurred to me the entire world is in tears, and if you're not, then you'd better get with it. I wanted to grab this child with the tear-stained face close to me and tell him about my God. The happy God! The smiling God! The God who had to have a sense of humor to have created the likes of us. One who understands little children who turn around and smile in church. I wanted to tell that little child that I too have taken a few lumps for daring to smile in an otherwise solemn religious setting.

What a fool, I thought, this woman sitting next to the only sign of hope, the only miracle left in our civilization. If that child couldn't smile in church, where was there left to go?[29]

Then Nehemiah said: "Go and enjoy choice food and sweet drinks, and send some to those who have nothing prepared. This day is sacred to our Lord. Do not grieve, for the joy of the Lord is your strength" (Nehemiah 8:10).

250. RESEARCH, SPIRITUALITY, AND WELL-BEING

A research report, "Spirituality and Well-being in Australia" strongly suggests that the drift towards a more secular mindset among Australians can be detrimental to the health. Dr. Peter Kaldor, the report's principal author, said the results suggest that in some vitally important areas, those with a more secular outlook have lower levels of well-being than those with a spiritual orientation.

"Those with a spiritual orientation tend to score higher on many of the well-being measures included in the study. They tend to have a greater sense of purpose in life, a greater openness to personal growth, and be more optimistic about life in general," he said.

This research is based on the "Well-being and Security Study" undertaken by researchers from Edith Cowan University and Deakin University. Dr. John Bellamy, a researcher for this study said, "For years, some have assumed that a more secular outlook on life would be positive for society. While no doubt a complex question, the opposite is true: religion and spirituality provide anchors for life.

"The lower levels of well-being among people with a secular mindset suggest that many Australians are not finding the well-being they aspire to. Why, then, with widespread affluence are Australians no happier than previously?" was a major conclusion of this study.

Dr. Bellamy said, "The results of the research suggest that with the decline of the significance of church life in Australia and the secularization of Christian festivals such as Christmas, we are losing something of the fabric of community well-being." Think about it. What can you do to change our world for the better?[30]

> *And let us consider how we may spur one another on toward love and good deeds. Let us not give up meeting together, as some are in the habit of doing, but let us encourage one another—and all the more as you see the Day approaching* (Hebrews 10:24-25).

251. I WAS CUT

American football has an annual Super Bowl game that is usually preceded by a gala Super Bowl breakfast attended by the football greats. At this particular event there is a speaker. This time it was Chris Carter, an All-American Ohio State graduate and All-Pro wide receiver for the Minnesota Vikings, now retired.

Read what Chris said:

Every stage of my life, I've always been the best football player. I've always been the best wherever I went, whether it was elementary school, junior high, high school, college, and even in the pros. But do you know what was the turning point in my life? It was when I was cut by the Philadelphia Eagles professional football team!

When he mentioned "cut," Chris Carter's voice cracked, and tears formed in his eyes. Suddenly this was more just a gala celebrity breakfast where people gathered to get autographs. This became a real event as people related to Chris at this point. He continued,

For the first time in my life, I looked around and realized there was a team that didn't want me, and I had to come face-to-face with an inventory of my life. I had to look around and ask the question, "What resources do I have to draw on?" In that moment, for the first time in my life I said, "God, I need help!"

There was nothing musical. No bright lights. But in a very calm and real way, God reached out to me in the weeks and months after I'd prayed that prayer, "God, I need help!" And God found me at my point of despair. He found me when I was at the end of my rope. He found me when I was spiritually bankrupt. He found me, and He restored my soul!"

He restores my soul. He guides me in paths of righteousness
for his name's sake (Psalm 23:3).

252. WHO IS REALLY RIDING IN THIS LIMO?

The story goes that the Pope was traveling to a much anticipated, important meeting with the Secretary General of the United Nations. As the pilot began his approach to the JFK airport in New York, he was redirected to land at the Newark, New Jersey, airport because of crosswinds. Now the Pope was behind schedule and a bit worried.

He was whisked away in a limo, but the driver was going too slow for the Pope, who asked him to speed up. The driver replied, "I'm terribly sorry, your Holiness, but I can't afford another speeding ticket because I'll lose my driver's license."

The Pope commanded, "Please stop the car, and I'll drive." So they quickly changed drivers, the limo driver in the back with the Pope driving!

Now driving much faster than the speed limit, weaving in and out of traffic, changing lanes, narrowly missing parked cars, the Pope attracted the attention of two police officers in a marked car with lights on and siren blaring.

The officer said, "I'm going to nail this guy!" as he got out of the squad with his citation book in hand.

After only a minute or two, the visibly shaken officer returned to the squad with his ticket book still closed and said to his partner, "This guy is big, I mean really big!"

"Who is it?" his partner asked. "The mayor of New York City, the governor of New York State, the President of the United States? Don't tell me we stopped the President?"

"No, he's bigger than all of them!" the first officer insisted.

"Who's bigger than the President of the United Stated?"

"Well, I'm not sure who he is, but the Pope is his chauffeur!"

Ascribe to the Lord, O mighty ones, ascribe to the Lord glory and strength.
Ascribe to the Lord the glory due his name; worship the Lord in his holiness
(Psalm 29:1-2).

253. FORGIVEN AND FORGOTTEN

There's a story written by the famous Arab writer, Tahan, who tells of two friends, Nahib and Mussa, who were traveling on a lonely, dark road in Persia. At some point, one of them lost his footing and fell into a whirling, foaming river. Without hesitation, the other leaped in and saved him from drowning. The friend who almost drowned in the rapids called his most skilled slaves and ordered them to carve these words on a nearby black stone: "Wanderer! In this place Nahib heroically saved the life of his friend, Mussa!"

After this had happened, these two friends continued on their journey. After many months went by, they came again to the very spot where the one had saved the other's life. They sat for a while and talked and then on some trifling matter they began to quarrel. Finally, in a fit of anger, the one who had almost drowned was struck in the face by his friend, Nahib.

The one who was struck stood up and used his stick to write these words on the white sand near the black boulder: "Wanderer! In this place Nahib, in a trivial argument, broke the heart of his friend, Mussa."

When one of Mussa's men inquired why he would record his friend's heroism in stone but his cruelty only in the sand, Mussa, the wounded friend, replied, "I shall cherish the memory of Nahib's brave assistance in my heart forever. But the grave injury he just gave me I hope will fade from my memory even before the words fade from the sand."

For if you forgive men when they sin against you, your heavenly Father will
also forgive you. But if you do not forgive men their sins, your Father will
not forgive your sins (Matthew 6:14-15).

254. A LAST WILL AND TESTAMENT

One morning in 1888, the Swedish inventor of dynamite, Alfred Nobel, awoke to read his own obituary. It was an error; it was Alfred's brother who had died and the paper reported the death of the wrong Nobel.

To Alfred, the shock was overwhelming because for the first time he saw himself as the world saw him. He had made a huge fortune from explosives and was called the Dynamite King, the merchant of death. He then resolved to change that to the true meaning of his life purpose. He set aside his fortune, which was to become the expression of his life, and created the most coveted Nobel Peace Prize, to be given annually to the persons who had done the most for world peace.

Contrast this to the story of Howard Hughes. At his death he was worth 2.5 billion dollars and was the richest man in America. His nearest relative, a distant cousin, was asked to claim his body and when he did, in astonishment he asked, "Is this Mr. Hughes?" Hughes had spent the last fifteen years of his life in seclusion as a hermit and a drug addict. His six-foot four-inch frame had shrunk to six foot one inch, and he weighed only ninety pounds.

Not a single acquaintance or relative mourned his death. The only honor he received was a moment of silence in his Las Vegas casinos. *TIME* magazine recounted the sad moment this way: "Howard Hughes' death was commemorated in Las Vegas by a minute of silence. Casinos fell silent. The blackjack games paused, the stickmen cradled the dice in the crook of their wooden wands. Then a pit boss looked at his watch, leaned forward and whispered, 'Okay, roll the dice. He's had his minute!'"

That's sad, but a reminder that we all will die someday, like we have lived!

The tender mercy of our God . . . will come to us from heaven . . . to shine on those living in darkness and in the shadow of death, to guide our feet into the path of peace (Luke 1:78-79).

255. WHAT GOES AROUND COMES AROUND

Have you ever had the privilege of inspecting an Australian boomerang? If so, you know it is made of hard wood, is about three feet long and curved almost into a right angle, and weighs about half a pound. It is thrown by holding it upright behind the head and then sending it forward with as much spin as possible.

It will travel about fifty yards upright before it flattens out. This is because one side is flat and the other side is curved, and the edges are sharp. It will begin to rise and can do three or four circles, going up to 150 feet and as far as 100 yards away. Then because it has a skew in it, this piece of wood does something that is strange. When you throw a piece of wood, it falls to the ground as far away as your strength can make it, but when an Australian throws a boomerang, it comes back.

Some things in life are like a boomerang. For example, the way you speak and act toward others will often be the way they will speak and act toward you. If you treat others with kindness and respect, you will find that kindness and respect will be shown to you by most of them. If you are not nice to others, then you will find that most of them will not have much to do with you.

The Bible is very explicit when using this principle in a life action. Jesus said, "Blessed are the merciful, for they will receive mercy" (Matthew 5:7). It's the boomerang effect in a positive way. Try it, you will find it works every time! Paul the apostle expressed it in a different way when he wrote, "A man reaps what he sows" (Galatians 6:7). It's the law of sowing and reaping! Remember, you will always reap more than you sow!

> *He who sows wickedness reaps trouble, and the rod of his fury will be destroyed. A generous man will himself be blessed, for he shares his food with the poor* (Proverbs 22:8-9).

256. THE POWER OF A SINGLE WORD

Can you quickly think of one word that will help you get what you want from other people? According to Dr. Robert Cialdini of Arizona State University, the answer is yes.

His theories are based on research of con artists and others who also contend that people will respond automatically and without thinking if they are given the proper trigger stimulus. And what might this stimulus be? What one word will help you to persuade people to give you what you want?

Check out the following example, cited as research by psychologist Ellen Langer:

When Dr. Langer asked people waiting in line to use an office copier, "May I use the copier because I am in a rush?" 94 percent of the people agreed.

However, when she merely asked, "May I use the copier?" only 60 percent agreed.

Then when she asked, "May I use the copier because I have to make copies?" 93 percent agreed and stepped aside to allow the action requested.

According to Dr. Langer: "The single word that triggered an automatic positive response was *because*."[31]

How interesting. How about giving this a try? The magic word when you ask for anything, according to this research, is because. Do you think it will work with your parents? How about using this word on your teachers? Or your friends? Because! How about using this word when you go in prayer to your loving heavenly Father? "Father, help me with this situation because of what Jesus Christ has done for me."

Pray also for me, that whenever I open my mouth, words may be given me so that I will fearlessly make known the mystery of the gospel
(Ephesians 6:19).

257. REAL BROTHERHOOD

Alfredo, a twelve-year-old Mexican boy had lost his family in a tragic fire. He was rescued, the only survivor, but it left his face horribly burned and disfigured in the fire.

Quite by chance, he came upon a home for boys, much like an orphanage, but it was run by a priest who created a real sense of family for the boys.

Alfredo watched the boys at play and wished he could be one of them, so he came to the priest and asked to become part of this home. The priest kindly explained that he could not settle the issue because the boys would make the decision. Alfredo waited nervously as the priest called a meeting and told them of Alfredo and his request.

The priest reminded them that if they accepted Alfredo, they would have to treat him as a brother, a member of their family. Then he brought in Alfredo; their faces registered shock, disbelief, and horror when they saw his face.

After what seemed an eternity to Alfredo, one of the boys stepped forward, went to Alfredo, shook his hand and said, "You are now my brother." And one by one all the others did the same.

This story made news on national TV. That evening a party was arranged to celebrate the additional new brother to the family. Alfredo's twisted face was washed, his hair was carefully combed, and his new clothes were spotless. But the most important thing about Alfredo was beautifully captured by the TV camera: on his horribly disfigured face, for the first time since the fire, there was an incredibly beautiful smile!

Are we willing to welcome new brothers and sisters into the family of God, even if they are different from us?

The Lord has anointed me to preach good news to the poor. He has sent me to bind up the brokenhearted, to proclaim freedom for the captives and release from darkness for the prisoners (Isaiah 61:1).

258. YOU ARE AN AWESOME MIRACLE OF CREATION

Dr. Deepak Chopra in his best-selling book, *Ageless Body, Timeless Mind*, describes the ongoing process taking in your body, right now: "Your body must live on the wings of change. At this moment you are exhaling atoms of hydrogen, oxygen, carbon, and nitrogen that just an instant before were locked up in solid matter; your stomach, liver, heart, lungs, and brain are vanishing into thin air, being replaced as quickly and endlessly as they are being broken down. The skin replaces itself once a month, the stomach lining every five days, the liver every six weeks, and the skeleton every three months. To the naked eye, these organs look the same from moment to moment, but they are always in flux. By the end of this year, 98 percent of the atoms in your body will have been exchanged for new ones!"

Awesome! Our bodies are living miracles, ongoing miracles. We are awesome miracles of God's creation. And maybe, the most astounding of all, each one of us is unique—one of a kind in this whole world of billions of people who were, who are, and who will be. We are unable to really comprehend our uniqueness.

You can begin to get your best possible look when you realize you are special in the creative plans of God! You are like this universe; your life is vast and always in motion. You are a necessary part of God's plan. You belong to the family of God. You belong in this wonderful, awesome family. God's plan for the fulfillment of His creation includes you—in fact, needs you! Do you appreciate the miracle of your mind? Do you appreciate the miracle of your spirit? Do you appreciate the miracle of your body? You are awesome and amazing!

For you created my inmost being; you knit me together in my mother's womb.
I praise You because I am fearfully and wonderfully made; your works are
wonderful (Psalm 139:14).

259. CONFESSION IS GOOD FOR THE SOUL

Father Murphy, a humble parish priest, was being honored at a special dinner celebration honoring the twenty-fifth anniversary of both his ordination and of being the parish priest. The scheduled main speaker was the leading local politician and also a lawyer, and a member of Father Murphy's congregation. It so happened that the speaker had been delayed because of a court case. Consequently, the master of ceremonies decided to open the program with a few words from Father Murphy himself. The emcee asked, "Tell us about your coming to this parish twenty-five years ago. What were your first impressions?"

Father Murphy stepped up to the microphone and said, "Because anything anyone ever told me in the confession box must remain secret, I can only hint gently at my first impression. Actually, when I first came here, my impression was that is was a terrible place. The very first man who entered my confessional recited just about every sin one could imagine short of murder. I was appalled. If that was only the first one, I thought, what were the rest going to be like? But as time went on, I discovered that I had come into a fine parish full of good and wonderful people."

At this point the politician arrived, was introduced by the emcee, apologized for being late and began his speech, "I'll never forget the day our beloved pastor arrived in our parish," he began. "In fact, I had the privilege of being the very first person to go to him in confession!"

Oh well, you can just be sure your sins will eventually find you out!

Live as free men, but do not use your freedom as a cover-up for evil;
live as servants of God (1 Peter 2:16).

260. WHO IS IN CONTROL?

The following story appeared in the *New York Times* on November 24, 1931:

The year was 1881. A man was to walk a wire strung across Niagara Falls, with another man on his shoulders! After weeks of preliminary practice, the moment for the event arrived.

The tight-rope-walker cautioned his young colleague: "We are about to risk our lives. I am to walk the wire. The whole responsibility is mine. You have nothing to do but match my movements. If I sway to the left, let yourself sway with me. If I sway to the right, do the same. Under no circumstances try to save yourself, for there must be only one will in this adventure. You must subordinate yours to ensure harmony. There is only one thing for you to do, sway with me."

As they drew near the opposite side, the unexpected happened. The long vibration of the wire broke in the center into two waves, and each of these broke again into two, and so on, in accordance with the law of vibration. And the shortened wavelike movements became so violent that the man could scarcely keep his feet where he placed them. It was a perilous moment, but the feat was accomplished and the spectacular escapade was a success!

After the event, the young man who had played the secondary role settled down, married, and became a church leader and a solid citizen. And he became quite fond of saying, "I learned more religion on that tight-wire that day than in all my life. I learned that the only safe and sane way to live is to sway with God!"

Lord my God, I take refuge in you; save and deliver me (Psalm 7:1).

261. THE POWER OF FRIENDSHIP

A university student spent a year living with a group of Navajo Indians on their reservation as part of his doctoral studies program. As he did his research, he lived with the members of a particular Navajo family, sleeping in their humble hut, eating their food, working with them, and living as any typical twenty-first century Navajo.

The grandmother of this family spoke no English, and this student knew no Navajo. Nevertheless, a close friendship developed between them. In the course of this year they spent a great deal of time together. Despite the language problems, they shared a common understanding of love and friendship. Over the months they managed to learn a few phrases from each other. And the year went by much too quickly.

Finally, the day arrived for the student to return to the university to write his doctoral thesis. In his honor and because of the wonderful time spent with him, the tribe held a special going away celebration.

The next day, as he packed his simple belongings into his pickup and prepared to get into his truck and leave, the grandmother came to give him a farewell hug and tell him a final goodbye. With tears in her eyes, she said, "I like me best when I am with you."

You are with the Lord when you are doing His will, following His example, living according to His teachings, devoting yourself to selfless ministry, and loving others as He loves you. This brings genuine joy into your life. And perhaps you can say to the Lord, "I love me best when I am with you!" And just maybe, someone will tell you: "I love me best when I am with you!"

You, my brothers, were called to be free. But do not use your freedom to indulge the sinful nature; rather, serve one another in love. The entire law is summed up in a single command: "Love your neighbor as yourself"
(Galatians 5:13-14).

262. WHICH IS BETTER, REVENGE OR FORGIVENESS?

When someone does you wrong, do you seek revenge or are you willing to forgive? Interesting question. Give it some thought, but while you do think about this. A team of researchers has reported that forgiveness can improve more than just your spiritual well-being. In fact, according to this research, forgiveness can reduce the risk of heart attacks, slow the spread of cancer, and prevent many diseases.

It's been a common knowledge that forgiveness is good for nations, communities, certain groups of people, and churches. Scientists have concluded it's also good for teens! New research, including Stanford University's "Forgiveness Project" wanted to find the scientific basis for such findings. Their studies demonstrated that forgiveness will lower high blood pressure, decrease depression, improve overall mental health, and make for better physical health. And the act of forgiveness improves cardiovascular health, lessens pain, and improves quality of life. Pretty impressive stuff!

But there's a problem. To forgive may not be easy, especially for victims of crime and abuse. Dr. Frederic Lusik, scientist and director of the Stanford "Forgiveness Project" said, "You can teach people how to develop the act of forgiveness as a skill."

The bottom line? The long-term effects of the act of forgiveness simply proves the Bible's claim that forgiveness is a good thing. Learning how to turn the other cheek is a powerful life benefit. None of us are too young or too old to learn how to forgive. So the concluding question is, what kind of a person do you want to become: bitter or better?

> *Then Peter came to Jesus and asked, "Lord, how many times shall I forgive my brother when he sins against me? Up to seven times?" Jesus answered, "I tell you not seven times, but seventy-seven times"* (Matthew 18:21).

263. WHAT REALLY IS DEATH?

Dr. Eric Fromm, a famous author/psychologist, when debating the argument of the day, "God is dead," argued we should be debating the question, "Is man dead?" He went on to explain, "Mankind has been transformed into a thing, a producer, a consumer, an idolater of other things"

We sit for hours in front of bad television without even knowing we are bored. We learn that millions of children around the world are literally starving to death without even relating this need to the teaching of the Bible about caring for the hungry. We have joined the rat race of material things that are measured in dollars and cents, all the time unaware of the anxiety we are enduring.

This represents death as far as Christians understand it to be. It is not true that physical death is the final enemy. The last enemy is hell—spiritual death, which can be conquered.

The *New York Times* writer, Russell Baker, wrote it like this: "It's all right to want it all. We have advertisements in which people who have it all torment people who don't have it all. They display their fantastic dental work, their stunning physiques, their incredible automobiles, beautiful mansions, tasty burgers and wine and pizza and beer, saying, 'It doesn't get any better than this.' Which is another way of saying, 'We've got it all.'"

Don't deceive yourself. If that's all there is to your fulfillment as child of

God, then it doesn't get any worse than this. If that's all it takes for you to say, "I've got it all," then what you really have is nothing!

> *What good will it be for a man if he gains the whole world, yet forfeits his soul? Or what can a man give in exchange for his soul?* (Matthew 16:26).

264. WHEN IS IT TIME TO LOVE SOMEBODY?

In the Broadway play *A Raisin in the Sun*, the father dies and is survived by his wife, a son, and a daughter. Each has a different idea on how to use the father's inheritance. The widow wants to buy a new home. The daughter sees it as her opportunity to go to medical school. The son wants it to go in business with a friend. He argues, "Don't you see, if I take this money I can do all these things for both of you."

So the son gets the money and gives it to his friend to go into business. But the friend takes the money and leaves town. Now the son has the difficult job of telling his mother and sister that all the money is lost. The mother is sympathetic and says, "Honey, I know you feel so bad."

But the sister asks, "How can you love him with what he has done? He doesn't deserve to be loved. He doesn't deserve any love."

To which the mother replies: "Honey, when do you think is the time to love somebody? Is it when they get a big promotion? Is it when they're successful? Is it when their investments pay off? Is that the time you love somebody? Honey, the time to love somebody is when that person is down and out. The time to love someone is when he or she has made a mistake in life and feel bad about it. The time to love somebody is when that individual has nobody to reach out to. The time to love somebody is when life has whipped and beaten that person. That's the time to love somebody!"

The ultimate expression of love is when we are willing to sacrifice our life so somebody else can live. That is the kind of love Jesus Christ modeled for you and me. Now, it's your turn to love somebody!

> *But I tell you, love your enemies and pray for those who persecute you*
> (Matthew 5:44).

265. TAKE CHARGE OF YOUR OWN LIFE

Have you ever read any of Aesop's Fables? If you haven't, make it a priority in your reading plan. These were written more than a couple of thousand years ago but have lots of life lessons for today. Let's read one of them, which goes like this:

An old man and his son were on their way to the marketplace leading a donkey when they overhear the conversation of two men who pass them, saying, "Look at that silly pair walking when they could be riding in comfort."

Taking this advice, the old man and his son climb up on the donkey's back and continue on their way to town. Soon they overhear another passerby who says, "Look at that lazy pair, breaking the back of that poor donkey, making him so tired no one will buy it. They should carry the donkey." Because of this, the old man and his son dismount and find a strong branch to which they tie the donkey's feet.

Then they sling the branch between them and carry the donkey, hung by his feet. When they cross a bridge, the angry donkey kicks until he breaks loose, then falls into the river and drowns.

What's the moral of this story? Aesop's fable reminds us that in every time and in every place of this world, people—especially teens—have had to learn to be themselves and take charge of their own lives!

And how about one more moral? You can't please everybody, and this is as true today as when this was written so long ago.

For me, to live is Christ and to die is gain. If I am to go on living in the body, this will mean fruitful labor for me (Philippians 1:21-22).

266. A SECOND LANGUAGE

Once upon a time, a mama mouse was leading her three baby mice across the street at a busy intersection. Before she stepped off the curb she looked both ways, saw no cars coming, and motioned for her three little ones to follow her across.

At about the same time, a cat stepped off the opposite curb. Closer and closer the cat crept until it was ready to pounce.

The mama mouse stopped and glared at the cat! The cat glared back. As they were eyeballing each other, the mama mouse let out a loud, terrific "WOOOF!"—a perfect imitation of a German shepherd. The frightened cat turned tail and ran!

Then the mama mouse turned to her little ones and said, "Didn't I tell you that a second language would come in handy someday?"

When it comes to the gospel truth about Jesus Christ, there are no second language possibilities. In the Gospels—Matthew, Mark, Luke, and John—Jesus talks about life and how to live it. However, you might like to put another twist to it. You cannot change His language of love and life into something else.

Jesus made it very plain when He said that He is the way, the truth, and the life! There is no other plan, no other Savior, no other way to heaven. It's your choice—either accept Him and His plan for life, making heaven your eternal home or reject Him and His message to spend an eternity in hell. His message is straightforward, simple enough for all of us to understand, and the choice to follow or reject is ours to make!

What if some did not have faith? Will their lack of faith nullify God's faith-fulness? Not at all. Let God be true and every man a liar (Romans 3:3).

267. WHAT DID I DO TO DESERVE THIS?

Have you ever wondered: "What did I do to deserve this?" Or how about this one: "Why did God do this to me?" Well join the club. But try this on for a bit of explanation.

A daughter is telling her mother how everything in her life is going bad. She's failing algebra, her boyfriend dumped her, and her best friend is moving away. While she is whining, her mother happens to be baking a cake and asks the daughter if she would like a snack. To which the daughter replies, "Absolutely, Mom, I love your cakes."

"Here, have some cooking oil," her mother offers.

"Yuck," says the daughter.

"Well, then, how about a couple of raw eggs?" Mom asked.

"Gross, Mom," the daughter answers.

"Would you like a cup full of flour, then? Or how about trying some baking soda?"

"Mom, those are all yucky!"

To which the mother replies, "Yes, I agree, all those things seem bad by themselves. But when you put them together in the right way and bake them, they make a delicious cake."

God works in the same way! Too many times we wonder why He would allow us to go through bad things and tough times. But God knows that when He puts these things all in His order, they always work out for good. Trust Him!

God is crazy about you. He sends you good things such as flowers in the springtime and a gorgeous sunrise every morning. Whenever you want to talk to Him, He listens. He can live anywhere and everywhere in this universe, but He chose to live in your heart and your life!

And we know that in all things God works for the good of those who love him, who have been called according to his purpose (Romans 8:28).

268. CAN WE SING?

In 1942 when Singapore fell to the Japanese invaders, more than four thousand civilians were captured and imprisoned in the Changi jail. Among these was Ethel Rogers Mulvaney, a young Canadian woman who was working for the Red Cross. This attack took place in the springtime, almost at Easter.

As their first Easter Sunday in this prison approached, Ethel asked the Japanese prison commandant if the prisoners might be able to sing in an Easter celebration in the courtyard on Easter Sunday morning. "Why?" he asked.

She replied, "Because Christ rose from the dead on Easter morning."

He barked his reply, "Request denied. Return to the compound." This little drama of the request and his refusal were repeated twelve different times. Then to their astonishment this order came, "Women prisoners may sing for five minutes in courtyard number one, in Changi jail, at dawn on Easter morning."

In the presence of the guards, they sang for five precious minutes, praising God for the resurrection of Jesus Christ, the only hope in a seemingly hopeless imprisonment. Then silently they marched back to the cells.

As they marched back, in the entryway, a guard stepped up to Ethel, reached under his brown uniform shirt, and gave her a tiny orchid. He placed it in her hand and spoke so softly that she had to bend over to hear, "Christ did rise!" Then with a smart military about-face he was gone down the passageway.

Ethel, her eyes brimming with tears, knew there was another believer and that she and the others were not forsaken—not even in Changi jail! Christ had not only risen, He had been remembered!

Why do you look for the living among the dead? He is not here; he has risen!
Remember how he told you while he was still with you . . . (Luke 24:5).

269. HOW TO RIDE A DEAD HORSE

What happens when logic is lost or when common sense is forgotten? Normal thinking says that when you discover you are riding a dead horse, the best strategy is to get off. However, we live in an interesting world where organizations such as schools, churches, companies, and most of all governments try other kinds of strategies such as the following:

The first strategy is to change riders. Buy a bigger or stronger whip. Or the best known fallback strategy: "This is the way we've always ridden our dead horse."

If none of these is working, we move on to the next ploy of arranging a visit to other sites to see how they ride their dead horses. Let's write a new manual for increasing the standards for riding dead horses. We can always appoint a group to revive the dead horse or create a training session to improve riding skills. We could compare the state of dead horses in today's environment or change the requirements so that the horse no longer meets the standard of being dead. If all else fails, we can hire an outside consultant to show how a dead horse can be ridden. We can always harness several dead horses together to increase our speed.

Eventually we come to the conclusion that increased funding will improve a dead horse's performance. Then we declare that no horse is too dead to beat. This is followed up by doing a study to see if outsourcing will reduce the costs of riding dead horses. And we can always buy a computer program that will enhance dead horse performance. This one works too, declaring a dead horse is less costly than a live one.

What is the moral of this nonsense? If you are riding a dead horse, get off!

> *You have circled this mountain long enough, now turn north.*
> *Give the people these orders* (Deuteronomy 2:3).

270. THE BUZZARD, THE BAT, AND THE BUMBLEBEE

How about some life lessons from the buzzard, the bat, and the bumblebee. The first lesson comes from . . .

The buzzard: If you put a turkey buzzard (like a hawk, slow and heavy in flight and eats dead animals) in a pen that is six feet by eight feet and open at the top, the bird, in spite of it's ability to fly, will be a prisoner. The reason is that a buzzard always begins a flight from the ground with a run of ten to twelve feet. Without space to run, it will not even attempt to fly but will remain a prisoner for life in this small jail with no top!

The bat: The ordinary bat that flies around at night and is so valuable because it eats hundreds of mosquitoes and other flying bugs is a remarkable and nimble flyer. However, it cannot take off from a level place. If you place a bat on the floor or flat ground, all it can do is shuffle about helplessly and maybe even painfully, until it reaches some elevation from which it can throw itself into the air. Then it takes off!

The bumblebee: If you can catch a bumblebee and drop it into an open drinking glass, it will stay there until it dies. Why? It never sees the means of escape at the open top but persists in trying to find some way out through the sides near the bottom. It will seek a way where there is no way until it destroys itself.

Consider the fact that too many of us are like the buzzard, the bat, or the bumblebee. We struggle with all our problems and frustrations, never realizing that all we have to do it look up to discover the way out. Trust in your Creator! Make that intentional decision every morning when you get up and talk to God.

Keep me safe, my God, for in you I take refuge (Psalm 16:1).

271. THE CHARGE OF THE LIGHT BRIGADE

Alfred Lord Tennyson wrote one of history's most famous poems, "The Charge of the Light Brigade." Do you remember it or have you studied it? It is based on the brave charge of a British cavalry unit during the Crimean War, and some of its most memorable lines run like this . . .

Half a league, half a league, half a league onward,
All in the valley of Death rode the six hundred.
Boldly they rode and well, into the jaws of Death,
Into the mouth of Hell rode the six hundred.
Theirs not to make reply, theirs not to reason why, theirs but to do and die,
Into the valley of Death rode the six hundred.
Cannon to right of them, cannon to left of them, cannon behind them
Volley'd and thunder'd; storm'd at with shot and shell,
    while horse and hero fell,
That they had fought so well, they that had fought so well
Came thro' the jaws of Death back from the mouth of Hell,
All that was left of them, left of six hundred.

What did you just read? I believe it's a picture of total obedience, reckless commitment, without hesitation, ignoring the odds, thundering toward the mouth of hell and death! Totally awesome, yet it's a beautiful picture of how to live and serve the Lord Jesus Christ! It's a challenge to all-out kind of living. We are in a life and death battle between evil and good, between God and the devil, between right and wrong. It's time we storm the very gates of hell! Today is no time for halfhearted living. Jesus died for us. Now it's time for us to rejoice, be joyful, and charge the gates of hell!

On this rock I will build my church and the gates of Hades will not overcome it. I will give you the keys of the kingdom of heaven; whatever you bind on earth will be bound in heaven, and whatever you loose on earth will be loosed in heaven (Matthew 16:18-19).

272. AN EIGHT-YEAR-OLD MAKES THE CASE FOR GOD

The following was written by an eight-year-old named Danny Dutton, who lives in Chula Vista, California. He wrote it for his third grade homework assignment to explain God. I really wonder if any of us could have done it better. Go for it, Danny!

One of God's main jobs is making people. He makes them to replace the ones that die, so there will be enough people to take care of things on earth. He doesn't make grownups, just babies. I think because they are smaller and easier to make. That way He doesn't have to take up His valuable time teaching them to talk and walk. He can just leave that to mothers and fathers.

God's second most important job is listening to prayers. An awful lot of this goes on, since some people, like preachers and things, pray at times beside bedtime. God doesn't have time to listen to the radio or TV because of this. Because He hears everything, there must be a terrible lot of noise in His ears, unless He has thought of a way to turn it off.

Atheists are people who don't believe in God. I don't think there are any in Chula Vista. At least there aren't any who come to our church.

Don't skip church to do something you think will be more fun like going to the beach. This is wrong. And besides the sun doesn't come out at the beach until noon.

If you don't believe in God, besides being an atheist, you will be very lonely, because your parents can't go everywhere with you, like to camp, but God can. I figure God put me here and He can take me back anytime He pleases, and that's why I believe in God.[32]

The name of the Lord is a strong tower; the righteous run to it and are safe
(Proverbs 18:10).

273. THAT'S GOD!

Have you ever wondered where God is or what God is doing? Perhaps you're just minding your own business, really doing nothing, when all of a sudden you feel like doing something nice for somebody else? That's God! He can speak to you through your mind and thoughts.

Have you ever been down in the dumps and needed somebody to talk to? Then you think of asking for help. That's God at work. He wants you to ask Him for help, to speak to Him as you would to a special friend.

Have you ever been thinking about somebody you haven't seen in a long time and the next thing you know, you see them or they text you? That's God at work wishing to remain anonymous.

Have you ever been given something wonderful, a surprise like money in the mail or a discount coupon at your special store for something you wanted but couldn't afford? That's God again! Why, because He knows your desires.

Have you ever been caught in a tough situation and had no clue how it would get better? But now you can look back at it with good memories? That's God! He's there in times of trouble too. He always has an answer and the way to make it better.

Have you wondered where and how He knows all? There's a special word that exactly describes God—it's called omnipresent. It means God is everywhere present at the same time. Now you know. If you already haven't, now is the time to invite Him and His Son, Jesus Christ, to come into your heart to be there 24/7!

Where can I go from your Spirit? Where can I flee from your presence? If I go up to the heavens, you are there; if I make my bed in the depths, you are there (Psalm 139:7-8).

274. WRONG ASSUMPTIONS

It happened again. Another forest fire was raging in the hills above Los Angeles, and a *Fox News* photographer had requested a private plane from his supervisor. It was granted and he called the local airport to charter a flight. He was told a twin engine plane would be waiting for him at the airport.

Sure enough, he arrived at the airfield and spotted a plane warming up outside of a hanger. He jumped in with his gadget bag, slammed the door, and shouted, "Let's go!"

The pilot taxied out, swung the plane into the wind, and took off. In the air, the photographer instructed the pilot, "Fly over the valley and make several low passes so I can take pictures of the fires on the hillsides."

"Why?" asked the pilot.

"Because I'm a photographer for *Fox Cable News Network*, and I need to get some closeup shots!"

The pilot was strangely quiet for a few seconds and finally stammered, "So, what you're telling me is that you're not my flight instructor?"

In this world, don't make any assumptions without all the straight facts.

Jesus said, "If you hold to my teaching, you are really my disciples. Then you will know the truth, and the truth will set you free (John 8:32).

275. A LETTER FROM GOD

Dear Friend,

As you got up this morning, I watched you and hoped you would talk to Me even if it were just a few words, asking My opinion or thanking Me for a good night of rest or something good that happened in your life yesterday. But I noticed you were too busy trying to find the right outfit to wear.

When you ran around the house getting ready, I knew there would be a few minutes for you to pause and say hello, but you were too busy. At one point you had to wait fifteen minutes for your ride, but no, you pulled out your cell and gossiped with your friend. I watched patiently all day but I guess you were too busy to say anything to Me.

You had a busy lunch . . . that's okay. But there still was more time left in the day, and I had hoped you would still talk to Me yet today. I noticed you were a bit embarrassed before your lunch. Maybe that's because you didn't even pause to bow your head and offer thanks for your meal.

At supper you ate your meal and again no thanks. But you had time for TV and more time to play games on your computer. I again waited patiently, but again you didn't talk to me. Bedtime came too quickly and you were too tired to spend a few moments before you dropped off to sleep. But I've got more patience than you will ever know.

I love you so much that I wait every day for a nod, a prayer, or even a thought from a thankful part of you. It's hard to have one-sided conversations. Well, it's almost time for another day, time to get up and again, today I'll wait and hope you might give Me a little time today. Have a nice day.

Your Friend,
God

In the morning, O Lord, you hear my voice; in the morning I lay my requests before you and wait in expectation (Psalm 5:3).

276. WHAT DO YOU BELIEVE?

I believe that a birth certificate shows that we were born. A death certificate shows that we died. Pictures show that we lived!

I believe that just because two people argue, it doesn't mean they don't love each other. And because they don't argue, it doesn't mean that they do!

I believe that no matter how good a friend is, they're going to hurt us every once in a while, and we must learn how to forgive them when they do.

I believe that true, real friendship continues to grow, even when there might be a separation and the same goes for true, lasting love!

197

I believe it is possible for us to do something in an instant, in a moment without thinking or counting the cost that could give us heartache for the rest of your life.

I believe that it's taking me a long time for me to become the person I want to be, the kind of a person that I should be, the kind of a person God wants me to be.

I believe that we should speak with kind words to the people whom we love and the people we are living with, because it may be the last time we see them.

I believe that we are responsible for what we do, no matter how we feel, and that we either control our attitudes or they will control us.

I believe that sometimes when I'm angry I have the right to be angry, but that doesn't give me the right to be cruel or mean or nasty or to hurt others.

I believe that God loves me no matter what happens in my life or what I do with my life, and I believe He will answer me when I ask Him for help.

Now it's your turn. What do you believe?

Whoever believes in me, as the Scripture has said, streams of living water will flow from within him (John 7:38).

277. WHAT ARE SIXTEEN GIRLS CAPABLE OF DOING?

On Saturday, May 15, 2010, sixteen-year-old Jessica Watson sailed into the harbor of Sydney, Australia, and docked her boat after her solo nonstop voyage around the world. She is now the youngest person in the world to complete this fantastic achievement. Three days later, she celebrated her seventeenth birthday. As she finished her journey, tears of joy and happiness flowed down her cheeks.

This was a 23,000-nautical-mile trip and took her 210 days. She began in Sydney and headed north across the equator. Then she dropped below South America and South Africa and sailed around the world. She did this in a thirty-four-foot sailing yacht named "Ella's Pink Lady" and was welcomed home in a special pink-carpet reception in the world famous Opera House.

As she reflected on her trip and what she had faced alone on the unforgiving ocean, Watson said, "Others don't realize what young people, what sixteen-year-olds and girls are capable of." Her yacht was overturned seven times by waves that reached as high as forty feet! Then with a confident smile she concluded, "It's amazing, when you take away those expectations, what you can do!" [33]

What an awesome feat against some very impossible obstacles. Never put yourself or other teens down because you or they or others don't have high expectations for you. You might surprise yourself what you could accomplish if you can overcome your expectations and set your goals higher!

Don't let anyone look down on you, because you are young, but set an example for the believers in speech, in life, in love, in faith and in purity (1 Timothy 4:12).

278. ARE YOU A FIRST TIME JOB HUNTER?

Are you a recent high school or college or trade school graduate and are job hunting? Here are some tips on job hunting to keep you from moving back home so you can live with and off your parents.

First, clean up your digital footprints. Have you "Googled" your name lately? This may be a whole lot more important than you think. J. T. O'Donnell, founder of Careerealism.com, a career development company, says, "Four out of five hiring managers say they search applicants' names online. Social networking sites like Facebook are most likely to pop up first. If the picture and stuff they see is unflattering, goodbye job."

Second, brand yourself. Social networking is not all bad because you can use sites like Twitter to show how serious you are about your chosen career field. Employers are looking for social media-savvy people. O'Donnell says, "In the workplace, social media will one day be as common as typing."

Third, never stop networking. Even in a lousy economy, keep at it. Be active in your field through volunteering, internships, and even pro-bono projects. The website, Monster.com shows that companies ranked word-of-mouth as the most effective recruiting method. So get out from behind your computer and take somebody in your chosen field out to share a cup of coffee. That's not a bad idea.

Fourth, never stop praying and asking for God's help. Believe it or not, God is interested in you and where you will be working. He needs you in the workplace too!

Whatever you do, work at it with all your heart, as working for the Lord, not for men, since you know that you will receive an inheritance from the Lord as a reward (Colossians 3:23-24).

279. A PRANK IS A MISCHIEVOUS TRICK

A prankster is a person who performs mischievous tricks on unsuspecting victims. The following are some memorable pranks:

• In 1996 Taco Bell announced it had bought the Liberty Bell and was renaming it the Taco Liberty Bell. Outraged citizens complained and overwhelmed the switchboard at the Independence National Historical Park in Philadelphia, where the bell is on display.

- In 1997 the chemical compound DHMO is colorless, odorless, and kills thousands of people every year through accidental inhalation, says a particular widely circulated email, calling for a ban. Furthermore, it's now "a major component of acid rain" and is "found in almost every stream, lake, and reservoir in America." One California town becomes so alarmed that residents debate banning foam cups, which are shown to contain DHMO. They nix the idea when they learn DHMO is actually water!

- In 2007 Google introduces "TISP" (Toilet Internet Service Provider), which supplies free broadband via the sewer system. A user flushes one end of a fiber optic cable down his toilet; an hour later, it's recovered and connected to the Internet by a team of "plumbing hardware dispatchers." Chat rooms were filled with interested parties asking, "Can this be true?"

Here's a question for you: Do you think God has a sense of humor or ever laughs? The Bible answers that for us in Psalm 2:4, "The one enthroned in heaven laughs." I don't know about you, but I'm glad I can serve a God who has a sense of humor. Living without a sense of humor is like driving a car without a bumper.

Our mouths were filled with laughter, our tongues with songs of joy. Then it was said among the nations, "The Lord has done great things for them"
(Psalm 126:2).

280. SOME INTERESTING FACTS ABOUT ISRAEL

If you are a Christian, Israel as a nation should be important to you! Why? It's the land of the Bible and the place of the birth and life of Jesus Christ. It's a fascinating place. Here are some things you may not know about Israel.

- Israel is only one sixth of 1 percent of the landmass of the Middle East.

  The Sea of Galilee, at 695 feet below sea level, is the lowest freshwater lake in the world, and the Dead Sea is the lowest surface point on earth at 1,373 feet below sea level. Israel is the only nation in the world that entered the twenty-first century with a net gain in the number of trees.

- The city of Jericho is the oldest continuously inhabited town in the world, and the Mount of Olives in Jerusalem is the oldest continually used cemetery in the world.

- Israel has the highest number of scientists, technicians, Ph.D's, engineers, and physicians per capita in the world.

- Israel has the highest ratio of university degrees per capita in the world and produces more scientific papers per capita than any other nation.

- Israel is the largest immigrant-absorbing nation per capita in the world.
- Israel is the only country in the Middle East where the Christian population has grown over the last fifty years and the only country in the Middle East where Christians, Muslims, and Jews are all free to vote.
- Israel's population is half the size of Metro New York City.
- Israel is the only country in the Middle East where women enjoy full political, religious, marriage, and occupational rights.[34]

Pray for the peace of Jerusalem: May those who love you be secure. May there be peace within your walls and security within your citadels
(Psalm 122:6-7).

281. MORE INTERESTING FACTS ABOUT ISRAEL

We hear so much today about the turmoil centered about Israel, but let's flip that coin and read some of the other side.

- Israel is the world's largest wholesale diamond center since 1970, and most of the cut and polished diamonds in the world come from Israel.
- The cell phone was developed in Israel along with voice mail technology. IBM chose an Israeli-designed computer chip as the brains for its first personal computers.
- The first antivirus software was developed in Israel; Windows NT and XP operating systems and the Pentium 4 and Centrino processors were designed and produced in Israel. Israel has the highest number of home computers per capita.
- Israel was the first Middle Eastern country to launch a satellite.
- Israel has more museums, orchestras, and publishes more books per capita than any other nation in the world.
- The most independent and free Arabic press in the Middle East is in Israel.
- Israel's dairy cows are the most productive cows in the world. They average 25,432 pounds of milk per cow per year compared to 18,747 pounds from American cows; 17,085 from Canadian cows; 13,778 from European Union cows; 10,207 from Australian cows, and 6,600 from Chinese cows.
- Israelis, per capita, are the world's biggest consumers of fruits and vegetables.

Would you agree with me? God is still blessing Israel in all kinds of ways so that they have become a world leader in many ways. Let's keep praying for the peace of Jerusalem![35]

Those who trust in the Lord are like Mount Zion, which cannot be shaken but endures forever (Psalm 125:1).

282. SOMETHING REALLY SPECIAL

If you had been alive when Jesus walked this earth and you had the opportunity to ask Him any question, what would you have asked? Maybe your question has already been asked. How about this one: "Teacher, which is the greatest commandment?" (Matthew 22:36). Is this question like the one you'd like to ask? Well, how did Jesus answer this very important question?

He told us about how God loves us and how we are to love as a response: "A new command I give you; Love one another. As I have loved you, so you must love one another" (John 13:34). So how do we really do this? Read the following essay about love.

- If I have mastered the language ever so perfectly and speak as a pundit, but have not the love that grows the heart, I have nothing.
- If I have decorations and diplomas and academic honors but have not the touch of understanding love, I am nothing.
- If I have great ideals and plans and wonderful visions but have not the love that sweats and bleeds and weeps and prays and pleads, I am nothing.
- If I can heal all kinds of sickness and disease but wound hearts and hurt feelings for want of a love that is kind, I am nothing.
- If I write books and publish learned articles but fail to transcribe the Word of the cross into the language of love, I am nothing!

(Author unknown)

I challenge you to love as God has loved us. Then we'll be something special in God's eyes, something like Jesus Christ!

A new command I give you: Love one another. As I have loved you, so you must love one another. By this all men will know that you are my disciples, if you love one another (John 13:34-35).

283. CAN HEAVEN WAIT?

The following is a timeless story about Satan, the master devil of deception:

Satan is seated on his throne, with all the minor devils surrounding him, waiting for instructions. Satan speaks, "Who will go and work to destroy the people on earth?"

One of the minor demons volunteers: "I will!" Satan asks, "And what will you tell them?" The minor demon replies, "I will tell them there is no God."

Satan is not pleased, "That's not good enough," he says. "People on earth know there is a God." Then a second devil volunteers, "I will work to destroy people on earth, and I'll tell them that they are too evil to come to God."

Again, Satan is not satisfied and replies, "That is not good enough either. They will be able to read in their Bibles that God invites sinners to come to Him."

Then a third devil speaks up, "I will tell the people that there is a God. I will tell them to listen to the gospel message as much as they want to. I will tell them it's all true. But I'll tell them also that there is plenty of time to make up their minds about accepting God's invitation to come to Him."

Satan is very pleased with this answer. Then he gives this order to all the minor and major demons and devils in hell: "Go out and tell the people on earth that heaven can wait. You don't need to make your decision today; tomorrow will do just fine!"

Is this your problem? You want God in your life, but you get distracted and put off the decision. Heaven can wait, but can you afford to wait?

For My Father's will is that everyone who looks to the Son and believes in Him shall have eternal life, and I will raise him up at the last day
(John 6:40).

284. TOO MUCH

Winnie the Pooh is a story in which Pooh, the friendly but sometimes not-so-bright bear, goes to see Rabbit, who lives in a hole in the ground.

Like a good host, Rabbit invites Pooh to have some honey from the honey jar. "Isn't it funny that bears like honey?" Rabbit says. Then Rabbit watches in dismay as Pooh proceeds to gulp down the entire jar and even licks the outside.

In his eat-and-run fashion, Pooh then says, "Goodbye" and starts up the hole to go on his way, but he gets stuck halfway out in the doorway.

Rabbit says, "What's the matter?"

Pooh replies, "The problem is, Rabbit, your door is too small."

Rabbit says: "The trouble is, Pooh, you've eaten too much!"

And that's the trouble with a whole lot of people, including a little man named Zaccheus, in the Bible, who became a rich little man—it's called greed! The story goes that Zaccheus has made a fortune out of using his position of power to exploit other people in order to line his own pockets. Then Jesus comes walking into his life and changed everything. Zaccheus turns his life completely around in the presence of Jesus. That's called repentance!

Zaccheus said to Jesus, "Look, Lord! Here and now I give half of my possessions to the poor, and if I have cheated anybody out of anything, I will pay back four times the amount" (Luke 19:8).

To which Jesus replied, "Today, salvation has come to this house" (Luke 19:19). To Pooh and all his greedy friends, this is the real answer to greed.

To those who sold doves he said, "Get these out of here! How dare you turn My Father's house into a market!" (John 2:16).

285. FINDING THE PERFECT JOB

My first job was working in an orange juice factory, but I got canned because I couldn't concentrate.

After that I tried to be a tailor, but I just wasn't suited for it, mainly because it was a so-so job.

Then I tried to be a chef because figured it would add a little spice to my life, but I just didn't have the thyme.

Next I tried working in a muffler factory in the automobile parts industry, but that was too exhausting.

I managed to get a good job working for a pool maintenance company, but the work was just too draining.

So then I got a job in a workout center, but they said I wasn't fit for the job.

After many years of trying to find steady work, I got a job as a historian until I realized there was no future in it.

My best job was being a musician, but eventually I found out I wasn't noteworthy.

I studied a long time and went to school for years in order to become a doctor, but I didn't have any patience.

I then attempted to be a deli worker, but any way I sliced it, I just couldn't cut the mustard.

My last job was working at Starbucks, but I had to quit because it was always the same old grind.

Where do you start deciding on what you will do for a job for the rest of your life? Now is your time to prepare, to plan, and to pray about your future because you will spend the rest of your life in it!

*So I saw that there is nothing better for a man than to enjoy his work, be-
cause that is his lot* (Ecclesiastes 3:22).

286. WHAT ARE YOU REALLY WORTH?

A well-known public speaker began a special school assembly program by
holding up a $20 bill. In the auditorium with about five hundred kids he
asked, "Who would like this $20 bill?" Hands went up everywhere.

Then he said, "I am going to give the $20 to one of you, but first let me do
this." He proceeded to crumple the $20 bill into a ball and asked, "Who still
wants it?" The same hands shot back up.

"Well," he replied, "What if I do this?" And he dropped it to the concrete
floor and started to grind it into the floor with his shoe. He picked it up, now
crumpled and dirty, "Now who still wants it?" Still the hands went into the air.

He reached back to the podium and produced a tiny pitcher filled with a
black substance. It looked like oil, and he poured it over the crumpled, dirty
bill. Then he asked, "Who still want this $20 bill?" The hands went back up!

He said, "Kids, we have all learned a valuable lesson. No matter what I did
to this money, you still wanted it because what I did to it did not decrease its
value. It was and is still worth $20! Many times in life we have been dropped,
crumpled, crushed, and dumped on. We may feel worthless and no good, but
no matter what has happened or will happen, you will never lose your value!
Dirty or clean, crumpled or creased, you are still priceless to those who love
you. The worth of our lives comes not in what we do or who we know but by
who we are. You are special. And most importantly, God loves you with an
everlasting, undying love!"

*For God did not send his Son into the world to condemn the world, but to
save the world through him* (John 3:17).

287. HOW FUNNY IS THIS?

It's funny how simple and easy it is for people to trash God and His Son Jesus
Christ and wonder why the world is getting worse and worse.

It's funny how we have removed the posting of the Ten Commandments
and removed prayer from our schools and wonder why bad things happen.

It's funny how we believe without questioning what the media tells us but
question everything about what the Bible says.

It's funny how everyone wants to go to heaven, provided they do not have
to believe, think, say, or do anything the Bible says.

It's funny how your friends will go with you to the movies, but when you ask them to go to church they always have an excuse.

It's funny how much easier it is for your pessimistic friends to drag you down to their level than it is for you, the optimist, to lift them up to your higher level.

It's funny how it is when you get up in the morning grumbling, whining, and complaining that the people you meet are also whining and complaining too.

It's funny how it works when we do nice things for other people that other people do nice things back to us.

It's funny how you can send a nasty joke through email and it spreads like wild-fire, but when you send messages about Jesus, people think twice about sending it along.

It's funny how when you become a Christian, everything in life takes on a new meaning and brings joy and happiness out of sadness and despair.

Grace and peace to you from God our Father and the Lord Jesus Christ, who gave Himself for our sins to rescue us from the present evil age
(Galatians 1:3).

288. I'M TIRED; MAYBE YOU ARE TOO

Many Americans have a problem whether they are young or old; it's a common complaint often heard: "I'm tired!" So let's take a good look at why we are so tired. I have heard people blaming this problem on the lack of sleep, not enough sunshine—and therefore not enough vitamin D—earwax buildup, poor blood, poor diet, too much homework, or anything else television ads tell me is my problem. But after some serious research, I have uncovered the real reason. I'm tired because I'm the only one doing anything and I'm over-worked.

Here's why. The population of the United States is about 350 million, but 214 million are currently retired. That leaves about 136 million to do the work.

There are 85 million in elementary schools, junior highs, senior highs, universities and colleges, which leaves 51 million to do the work.

Of this, there are 32 million employed by the Federal government, leaving 19 million to do the work. Those in the armed forces preoccupied with Afghanistan and Iraq total 2.8 million, leaving 16.2 million to do the work.

Then take 14.8 million people who work for state and city governments, and that leaves 1.4 million to do the work. At any time there are 188,000 people in hospitals, leaving 1,212,000 to do the work. But there are 1,211,998 people in prisons, and that leaves just two people do the work—you and me!

However, if you are reading these statistics while you are sitting down, that leaves only me. Nice, real nice! I need you to help me to work to make this world a better place.

Six days do your work, but on the seventh day do not work (Exodus 23:10).

289. HISPANIC HERITAGE MONTH

Did you know that a Hispanic Air Force Colonel and a Republican President combined forces to sign into law Hispanic Heritage Month in the United States? This is designated to take place each year from September 15th to October 15th.

In 1988 President Ronald Reagan signed Public Law 100-402 after Air Force Colonel Gil Coronado began working with the Congressional Hispanic Caucus to promote this nationwide celebration.

According to the official website for Hispanic Heritage Month, Hispanic influence in the Americas is extensive, from the founding of the State of Carolina in 1526 to founding the first free integrated public school in St. Augustine, Florida, in September of 1787.

There are many more accomplishments according to this website, and I list just a few of these:

• The first burglar alarm was invented and patented by Albert Silva in 1875.
• Cowboy gear—including the hats, boots, lassoes, chaps, spurs, and saddles—all were creations of Hispanic people, as were rodeos and cattle ranches.
• The $ symbol is taken from the Spanish Imperial Coat of Arms, and in 1775 the United States adopted the Spanish dollar as the basis of its monetary system.
• A donation of $12 million was made to the Revolutionary War effort by Hispanics when George Washington ran out of money.

Why the history lesson? To thank you if you are Hispanic; or if you have Hispanic friends, encourage you to tell them thanks for their help.

Be joyful always; pray continually; give thanks in all circumstances for this is God's will for you in Christ Jesus (1 Thessalonians 5:16-18).

290. DRUGS, NUMERICALLY SPEAKING

R esearch has indicated that illegal drug use among teenagers is declining—not by much, but it does show a decline. This is good! However, these same studies show the abuse of prescription drugs, especially pain killers, is increasing. This is bad! Too many teens make the wrong assumption that prescription drugs are safe, when in fact they are also highly addictive and can and do cause severe side effects and more.

The following are some statistics regarding teen drug and alcohol abuse:

- Underage drinking costs the United States more than $58 billion every year. This is just in one nation; think of what it must cost worldwide!
- Forty percent of those who started drinking at age thirteen or younger developed alcohol dependence later in life. Ten percent who began drinking at age seventeen developed dependence.
- Teens that drink are fifty times more likely to use cocaine or meth than teens who never consume alcohol.
- Alcohol kills seven times more teens than all other illicit drugs combined.
- More than sixty percent of teens said that drugs were sold, used, or kept at their school.
- Teens whose parents talk to them on a regular basis about the dangers of drug use are forty-two percent less likely to use drugs than those whose parents don't.
- Twenty percent of eighth graders report that they have tried marijuana.
- Sixty-three percent of teens who drink say they got it from their own or a friend's home.
- Those are some pretty scary statistics, although they probably don't surprise you. Take them for what they are, a word of warning to the wise. Learn to say no always. No is always better than addiction.[36]

> *Do you not know that your body is a temple of the Holy Spirit, who is in you, whom you have received from God? You are not your own; you were bought at a price. Therefore honor God with your body*
> (1 Corinthians 6:19-20).

291. THE WHALE SAID, "THANK YOU"

M aybe you read the story from the front page of the *San Francisco Chronicle* or watched it on television. This is the story of a female humpback whale. Somehow, she had become entangled in a spider web of crab traps, fishnets, and ropes. She had become so weighted down by these hundreds of pounds of debris that it had become a struggle for her to stay afloat, much less to swim free. The lines of rope had become wrapped around her body, her tail, her torso, and even a line across her mouth.

A commercial fisherman had spotted her just east of the Farallon Islands, a group of small islands on the ocean side of the Golden Gate Bridge. He immediately radioed for help from anybody or any group who was able to help with a rescue. Within a few short hours, a rescue team arrived and determined that she was so bad off that the only way to save her was to dive in the ocean with her and attempt to untangle her.

They worked for hours with cutters and curved knives, and eventually managed to cut her free. When she was free, the divers say she swam in what seemed to them to be circles of joy. She then swam back to each and every diver, one at a time, and nudged them and pushed them gently around. She was thanking them!

Some said it was the most incredibly beautiful experience of their lives. The guy who had cut the rope out of her mouth said her eyes were following him the whole time and that he will never be the same.

My hope is that you are so blessed with friends who will help you get untangled from the things that bind and trap you, and that you will also know the joy of giving and receiving thanks.

The Lord sets prisoners free, the Lord gives sight to the blind, the Lord lifts up those who are bowed down . . . the Lord watches over the alien and sustains the fatherless and the widow but He frustrates the ways of the wicked (Psalm 146:7-9).

292. THE PRISON PREACHER

More than four hundred years ago an uneducated and very poor common laborer believed God wanted him to become a preacher. No one considered him to be ministerial material. He lacked knowledge, he had no seminar training, and he had little charisma and no name recognition. Who would ever listen to him? What church would have him as their pastor? And how would this poor man ever support his large family because preachers were poorly paid in those days? As if these problems weren't enough, he chose the wrong church! In the 1600s England did not appreciate Baptists. In fact, the established state church officially forbade Baptists to preach because religious freedom had not been won by minority churches.

But such obstacles didn't stop John Bunyan! He would not be muzzled. He would not stop as crowds gathered outside his prison to listen to him preach. Finally, officials managed to isolate him totally from the people. Again he refused to quit. In his heart and mind, he had a passion to preach the gospel. How would he continue?

Bunyan had to preach, to express the message, so in desperation he began to write notes on bits and scraps of paper that were secretly passed through the bars to and from friends outside. He wrote about his personal struggle, and he wrote about a pilgrim named Christian. Soon the stories grew into a book. Who would read a religious allegory written by a Baptist in jail? Eventually, Bunyan borrowed money to pay for his book.

The rest is history! For more than three hundred years, *Pilgrim's Progress* has been the common person's commentary. No other book except the Bible has sold more copies. Have you read this book? If not, read it. You might be surprised!

Your word is a lamp to my feet and a light for my path (Psalm 119:105).

293. BE CAREFUL WHAT YOU WISH FOR

A woman and her teenage daughter had been out shopping, but when they returned home there were three quite old men with long white beards sitting in their front yard.

The mother said, "I don't think we know you. Are you hungry? How about some lunch?"

The men spoke up and asked, "Is the man of the house home?"

"No, but he'll be here after work."

"Then we cannot come in," one of them replied.

Later the man of the house came in the back door, and the mother and daughter told him about the three men out front.

He told the daughter, "Go and invite them in."

The daughter did as she was told.

"We do not go into a home together," said one.

"Why is that?" she asked.

One of the old men explained as he pointed to the others, "His name is Wealth, his name is Success, and my name is Love. Now you go inside and discuss with your mom and dad who you want to invite to come in."

The husband voted for Wealth, "Let him in to fill our house with wealth."

The mother said, "Why don't we invite in Success?"

But the daughter said, "Wouldn't it be better to fill our home with Love? Let's fill our house with love." The others agreed.

So the daughter went out and said, "Which one of you is Love? Please come in." Love got up and started walking into the house. And the other two also got up and followed him!

Surprised, the daughter asked, "I only invited Love, why are all of you coming?"

Wealth and Success answered, "If you had invited Wealth or Success, the other two of us would have stayed out, but since you invited Love, where he goes, we go because where there is Love there is also Wealth and Success!"

And now these three remain; faith, hope and love. But the greatest of these is love (1 Corinthians 13:13).

294. WHAT DO YOU KNOW ABOUT MICROBIA?

Have you ever had the opportunity to spend time with a microscope to visit the land of bacteria, fungi, viruses, and their myriad of relatives and friends? Let's just do that and consider some of the following fascinating facts.

- A teaspoon of dirt out of your backyard will contain more than one billion kinds of bacteria, which is about the same as a quart of dirty bathwater.
- A virus is nothing more nor less than a tiny bit of DNA or RNA wrapped up in a coat of protein.
- Antibiotics, the well-known drugs that are commonly used to kill bacteria, do not and will not have any affect on viruses at all.
- Many kinds of fungi are always living right with you. Bread mold, athlete's foot, yeast, and penicillin are all types of fungus.
- Scientists have revived bacteria that supposedly have been dormant for 250 million years! Now, how do they know this for sure?
- Free-floating viruses are said to be inert or inactive until they come into contact with a living cell. That's when they come back to life and can begin attacking your body.
- A giant type of an amoeba, called Chaos chaos, is so large you can see it with the naked eye and not even need a microscope.
- The Bible says that we humans have been wonderfully made. It sure seems that we are not the only creations that have been wonderfully, creatively made. So the question to ponder today is: Did God also create the wonderful world of microbes?

For you created my inmost being; you knit me together in my mother's womb. I praise you because I am fearfully and wonderfully made; your works are wonderful, I know that full well (Psalm 139:13-14).

295. HOW RICH ARE YOU?

Did you know that if your family owns even one TV set, you would be richer than a bit more than 99 percent of the population of Tanzania?

If you own a cell phone, you are richer than just under 70 percent of the people who live in Honduras.

If you have seen just a single movie in a theater in the last year, you are richer than at least half of the population of Turkey.

If you have access to at least one motor vehicle, even a motor scooter, for transportation, you are richer than most of the people of Madagascar.

If you live in the United States, you have about four times more room to breathe and stretch your legs, meaning that many less people live per given area of land than the people of Thailand have for their use.

If your family's monthly bills and other expenses average more than ten dollars a day, you live in an average sized apartment or house, and you eat three meals a day and have at least one car, cable connections, cell phones, and an Internet connection, you are among the richest 20 percent of all the people in the world!

Over half the population in countries such as Bangladesh, Cambodia, Ethiopia, Haiti, Niger, Pakistan, and Rwanda live on under two U.S. dollars a day.[37]

Is it time for all of us to express, "Thank You, God." Or is it time to look around, take a good look at the rest of the world, and find a better way to use what God has allowed us to have? We are told in the Bible to share with those caught in poverty!

He who is kind to the poor lends to the Lord, and He will reward him for what he has done (Proverbs 19:17).

296. DO YOU KNOW ABOUT BETHANY HAMILTON?

Bethany Hamilton was interviewed on ABC TV and was asked, "Do you think you'll ever surf again?"

The thirteen-year-old's response was an immediate, "Think? I know that I will surf again!"

Just days before this interview, the surfing prodigy lost her left arm in a shark attack. Early on Halloween morning in 2003, Bethany's father went to Wilcox Memorial Hospital for knee surgery. She went with her best friend, Alana, and Alana's father and brother. They paddled out about two hundred yards to their favorite surf spot, called the Tunnels and rested.

"I was lying sideways on my board," she recalls. "The shark came up and grabbed my left arm. It was pulling me back and forth. Then it let go and went under. I looked down at the water and it was really red from all the blood." And her left arm was gone!

Her friends got her to shore where she passed out. At the hospital, Bethany replaced her father on the operating table already prepped for surgery. She had lost more than 60 percent of her blood. She amazed the staff with her positive mindset and was released six days and several operations later. Back home she began relearning living skills.

Bethany told Chris Cuomo on ABC News, "If I don't get back on my board, I'll be in a bad mood forever."

She did and eight months later won the ESPY award for Best Comeback Athlete of the Year and the Teen Choice Award for special courage.

Bethany says, "I just know that God is using me in way bigger ways than I could have ever done."

I have learned the secret of being content in any and every situation
(Philippians 4:12).

297. WHAT IS SO SPECIAL ABOUT AN EAGLE?

Have you ever watched a bald eagle? Around the world there are many different kinds of eagles, but the bald eagle is the most spectacular. It's a huge and impressive bird with a wingspan of just a bit over thirteen feet. It can fly as high as 10,000 feet in the air and when it dives to catch a meal, it can reach speeds up to 100 miles per hour.

Adult bald eagles can weigh up to thirteen pounds. One distinctive feature of eagles is the way in which they can catch warm updrafts of rising air. They seem to glide without much effort; in fact, they use this system to fly long distances when they migrate from season to season. When they migrate, usually they follow rivers and lakes so they are not too far from fishing for their next meals.

Once in a while, an eagle will catch a fish that is too heavy to fly away with, so they have been known to hold that fish in their talons and swim to shore. These amazing birds will use their huge wings as paddles.

The bald eagle gets its name from its hood of white feathers. *Balde* is an old English word meaning "white." When baby eagles are hatched, they have mostly dark brown feathers, dark beaks, and dark eyes. As they grow, however, the feathers on their heads and tails turn white, and their beaks and eyes turn yellow.

The most amazing thing is that the Bible tells us we can be like eagles! When we trust in God, He gives us strength for each day—a renewed strength. This supernatural power allows us to soar above the temptations of life and to overcome its challenges. Remember the bald eagle when you face various struggles!

Those who hope in the Lord will renew their strength. They will soar on wings like eagles; they will run and not grow weary, they will walk and not be faint (Isaiah 40:31).

298. THE REAL MUTINY ON THE BOUNTY

The *Mutiny on the Bounty* is considered by many people to be a classic in literature. The mutineers from the ship Bounty, with a number of Tahitian women and some more men, decided to make their home on what they called the Rock of the West, better known as Pitcairn Island. They believed it would be the perfect place to hide because it was away from the main shipping lanes, and it had only one place to land a ship.

The Rock was an excellent place to hide from others who would hunt them down, but they could not hide from themselves! Eventually their evil ways overcame them. Several years of brawling, immorality, drunkenness, and murder took place until John Adams found he was the only man left on the island along with the women and children.

He really didn't know what to do, but knowing he had to do something, he dug into the old ship's chest and brought out the ship's old Bible. He began reading it and soon discovered his heart and life changed. Then every day he gathered the women and children together, read to them, and taught them the ways of Jesus.

Then one day, a ship finally landed and discovered that Pitcairn Island had become a community of Christians who were busy and productive, living joyful lives at peace with each other. If you've never read this book, today might be a good time to start. It's another story of how the grace and mercy of God can and will change people who will take the time to read and obey the Good Book. Have you read your Bible today?

Sanctify them by the truth; your word is truth (John 17:17).

299. THE WORLD'S MOST MIXED-UP THINKER

Dr. Norman Vincent Peale wrote, "Do you know who was the most mixed-up thinker who ever lived? It was the poor neurotic named Karl Marx." The following is what Peale had to say about Karl Marx.

Marx had been born into a very well-to-do family with everything a boy or young man could hope to have in life. He was sent to an exclusive school where he managed to flunk out. He was constantly fighting and quarreling with his schoolmates. He later said that he never had a real friend in school or growing up. His father got him a good job, but since he could not get along with the people he worked with, he was fired.

Finally, Marx managed to persuade a girl to marry him, but he couldn't get along with her. They had four children, but three of the four eventually committed suicide.

Karl Marx was a man who hated and resented the world, but mostly he hated all the people who had become successful in life. He did persuade a capitalist, Frederick Engles, to support him while he wrote a book that changed the world, *Das Kapital.* It was Marx who divided the world into two classes: capital and labor. He pitted these two classes against each other, and his writings became the foundation upon which communism was founded and his revolution began.

Contrast his writings and philosophy to another world leader who proclaimed freedom for all who had been held as captives, to set at liberty all who had been bound up! His name was Jesus and He still sets all captives free today!

For unto us a child is born, to us a son is given, and the government will be on his shoulders. And he will be called Wonderful Counselor, Mighty God, Everlasting Father, Prince of Peace. Of the increase of his government and peace there will be no end (Isaiah 9:6-7).

300. CHECK OUT THESE NUMBERS

If you happen to be an average teenager of about average height and average weight, here's what you and your body will be doing in the next twenty-four hours:

- Your heart will beat about 103,689 times.
- Your blood will travel through your body's veins, arteries, and vessels about 168,000,000 miles.
- You will normally take approximately 23,040 breaths, unless you are engaging in vigorous sporting events.
- You will inhale 438 cubic feet of air with all those breaths.
- You will eat 3.25 pounds of food, more or less, but some of you might be gluttons and change this statistic.
- You should drink about 2.9 pounds of liquids.

- You will lose 5.34 pounds of waste, which also depends on how much food you have taken, it could go higher and maybe lower for girls.
- You perspire about 1.43 pints; in the summer time, much more.
- You will give off 85.6 degrees or units of heat.
- You will toss and turn in your sleep between 25 to 30 times.
- You will likely speak about 60,000 words for females, about 48,000 for males.
- You will move 750 major muscles.
- Your hair will grow .01717 of an inch.
- You will have exercised 7,000,000 brain cells.

So we can conclude it pays to take good care of this fabulous machine called the body because there just aren't many if any used parts for sale.

My frame was not hidden from you when I was made in the secret place. When I was woven together in the depths of the earth, your eyes saw my un-formed body. All the days ordained for me were written in your book before one of them came to be (Psalm 139:15-16).

301. THE DART TEST

A young lady named Sally related the following experience she had in one of her classes in Bible college. Her teacher, Dr. Lavang was known for his object lessons.

On this particular day, Sally walked into class and just knew they were in for a fun day. On the wall was a big target and on a table were lots of darts. Dr. Lavang instructed the students to draw a picture of someone they disliked or who had made them mad, and they were to throw darts at them.

One of Sally's friends drew a picture of a girl who had stolen her boyfriend. Another drew a picture of her little brother. Sally drew a picture of a former friend who had betrayed her. Her picture was detailed, even down to dimples. She was quite pleased with the likeness.

Eagerly the class lined up and began throwing darts. Some threw darts with such force that their targets were ripping apart. What fun they all had!

Then when time was up, Dr. Lavang asked the students to return to their seats. Some class members were still quite angry but had enjoyed the fun.

Dr. Lavang began removing their pictures from the wall. He then slowly removed the target from the wall. Underneath the target was a picture of Jesus. A hush came over the room as each student viewed the mangled picture of Jesus; holes and jagged marks covered His face and His eyes were pierced.

Then Dr. Lavang spoke only these words, "Whatever you did for one of the least of these brothers of mine, you did for me!" No more words were necessary as the students sat with tear-filled eyed before slowly making their way out of the classroom.

I was hungry and you gave me something to eat, I was thirsty and you gave me something to drink, I was a stranger and you invited me in, I needed clothes and you clothed me, I was sick and you looked after me. I was in prison and you came to visit me (Matthew 25:36).

302. NO PEACE AND NO JOY

When he was a young theology student, John Wesley wanted to be a good Christian and help others too. Together with his brother Charles, he organized a little group of young men at Oxford University who soon became dubbed "The Holy Club." With lots of willpower, John Wesley attempted to impose on himself and his club members a stringent code of conduct. But he and they soon discovered no peace and little joy in their efforts.

Frustrated and seeking help, John and Charles traveled across England to visit with William Law, who told them their problem was that they were attempting to make Christianity something complicated and burdensome.

William Law told them, "Religion is the plainest and simplest thing in the world. It is just this: we love because He first loved us!"

Are you making something difficult, complicated, or joyless out of your practice of your religion? Really it's as easy as ABC to simplify and live in joy.

A: *Admit you are a sinner.* The Bible says, "There is no one righteous, no not one . . . for all have sinned and fall short of the glory of God" (Romans 3:9, 23) Here's where it all begins. Ask God's forgiveness and repent of your sins!

B: *Believe in Jesus.* "For God so loved the world that he gave his one and only Son, that whosoever believes in him shall not perish but have eternal life" (John 3:16). Become a child of God by receiving Christ Jesus into your life.

C: *Confess that Jesus is now your Lord.* "If you confess with your mouth, 'Jesus is Lord,' and believe in your heart that God raised him from the dead, you will be saved" (Romans 10:9).

In him was life and that life was the light of men. The light shines in the darkness, but the darkness has not understood it (John 1:4-5).

303. NUMERICALLY SPEAKING

From Mumbai to Madrid, where you are living will likely influence how much or how often you pray, according to a global survey done by *Reader's Digest*. There is a significant difference between the East and in the West.

At least 66 percent of people who live in Malaysia, the Philippines, and India say they pray every day. However, just the opposite is true in Europe. Of the people who responded in the Czech Republic, 65 percent never pray, followed by a large number of those in the Netherlands, France, Spain, and the United Kingdom who also never pray.

The trend is different across the Atlantic where 55 percent of Americans say they pray daily. So how often do you pray?

Of those who were surveyed, the following shows the percentage of people who pray daily in these countries:

Australia: 23 percent	Mexico: 31 percent
Brazil: 50 percent	Netherlands: 19 percent
Canada; 40 percent	Russia: 19 percent
China: 33 percent	Singapore: 24 percent
Germany: 28 percent	Turkey: 62 percent
Italy: 20 percent	United Kingdom: 25 percent
Malaysia: 76 percent	

I'm sorry if your country was not mentioned, the *Reader's Digest* only did this survey in nineteen countries. Even more important than how many people pray in your country, how often do you pray?

Nothing was said about who or what these people prayed to. How about you? Who do you direct your prayers to? How often do you pray? Perhaps you're like the man, Jonah, caught in the belly of the great fish who prayed in disaster, "From inside the fish Jonah prayed to the Lord" (Jonah 2:1). And when do you pray? Often or only when you are in trouble?

Therefore I tell you, whatever you ask for in prayer, believe that you have received it and it will be yours (Mark 11:24).

304. JASMINE

In 2003 police in Warwickshire, England, opened a garden shed to find a whimpering, cowering, female greyhound dog. She had been locked in, abandoned, abused, and now left to die.

With compassion, the police took the dog to the Nuneaton Warwickshire Wildlife Sanctuary run by Geoff Grewcock. This was known as a haven for animals of all kinds who had been abandoned, orphaned, injured, or in need. Geoff and his staff had two aims with this dog: to restore the greyhound to full health and to win her trust. It took several weeks, but both goals were achieved. They named her Jasmine and began looking for an adoptive home.

But Jasmine had other ideas. She started welcoming all animal arrivals at the sanctuary. No matter what kind of an animal appeared, she would look into the box or cage and when possible would deliver a welcoming lick. She would take puppies by the scruff of the neck and put them with her on the couch to cuddle with them. She is like this with all the animals; she takes all the stress out of them. She has done the same with fox and badger cubs. She also licks the rabbits and guinea pigs, and even lets the birds perch on the bridge of her nose. She has cared for 5 fox cubs, 4 badger cubs, 15 rabbits, 15 chicks, 8 guinea pigs, 1 roe deer fawn, 2 stray puppies, and 1 injured barn owl! Jasmine—the timid, abused, and deserted creature—has become the sanctuary's surrogate mother, a role for which she may have been born.

What a lesson for all of us! Can we put aside the pains of our past and care for the hurting and less fortunate among us?

I tell you the truth, whatever you did not do for one of the least of these, you did not do for me (Matthew 25:45).

305. A LESSON THAT SHOULD BE TAUGHT EVERYWHERE

On the first day of school in September 2005, Martha Cothren, a social studies teacher at Robinson High School in Little Rock, taught an unforgettable lesson.

On this first day of school, with permission of the superintendent, the principal, and the building supervisor, she had all the desks removed from her classroom.

When the first period kids entered, they discovered no desks. They asked, "Mrs. Cothren, where are our desks?"

She replied, "You can't have a desk until you tell me what you have done to earn the right to sit at a desk." During this day the answers were all over the board.

"Because of our good grades" some said. Or others tried, "Maybe it's because of good behavior."

And so they came and went. By early afternoon television crews had gathered in the classroom to report on this crazy teacher who had taken all the desks away.

During the final period of the day Martha Cothren said, "Throughout this day no one has been able to tell me just what he or she has done to earn the right to sit at the desks ordinarily found in this classroom. Now I am going to

219

tell you!" At this point she opened the door and twenty-seven United States veterans—Army, Navy, Air Force, and Marines—all in uniform, walked in, each carrying a desk. These vets placed the desks in rows, walked over, and stood at attention along the wall.

Martha said, "You didn't earn the right to sit at these desks. These heroes did it for you! Now it's up to you to sit in them. It's your responsibility to learn, to be good students, to be good citizens. They paid the price so that you could have the freedom to have an education. Don't ever forget it!"

Finally . . . whatever is true, whatever is noble, whatever is right, whatever is pure, whatever is lovely, whatever is admirable—if anything is excellent or praiseworthy—think about such things (Philippians 4:8).

306. JUST TWO HORSES

If we were to travel by pickup truck down a particular dusty road and pass a certain ranch in Argentina, we might see two special horses in a pasture that runs along the road. From a distance these two horses look much like any other pair of horses. But let's stop the pickup and get out for a closer look at these two. It's quite amazing.

Look carefully into the eyes of the larger horse. The eyes are nearly white, this horse is blind. The rancher has made a choice. This horse has served him well but now that it is blind, he has chosen to provide a good home for it and not put it down. But this is not the whole story. As we stand looking at the blind horse, we listen and hear the sound of a bell. We look around for the source and discover it comes from the smaller horse in the same pasture. Attached to the halter is a small bell. It lets the blind horse know where the other horse is so it can be followed.

Soon we notice the horse with the bell seems to always be checking on the blind one. Then the blind one listens to where the sound of the bell comes from and follows the sound to graze with the sighted horse. When the horse with the bell returns to the shelter of the barn for the night, it stops occasionally and looks back making sure the blind one isn't too far behind to hear the bell.

What a beautiful picture, a real live parable. Like the owner of these two horses, God doesn't throw us away just because we are not perfect or have been damaged. God watches over us and if needed, brings someone into our lives to help us.

Sometimes we are like the blind horse. Other times we become the guide horse to help others find their way. Remember, always be kind. Others may need you!

My command is this: Love each other as I have loved you. Greater love has no one than this, that he lay down his life for his friends (John 15:13).

307. THE REAL DAIRY QUEENS

Did you know that if you name a cow, she will produce on the average of sixty-eight more gallons of milk per year? Yes, you read correctly. Cows give more milk when they have a name! And I am aware that I'm talking largely to people who are not farmers and have not a single worry or thought about cows and how they give milk, other than that milk is good for all of us to drink.

Is this udder nonsense? Scientists don't think so. After studying the working relationships between dairy farmers and their cows, the researchers at Newcastle University in the United Kingdom found that farmers who gave Bessie and Gertrude and Millie tender loving care reaped the benefits of increased milk yield over a ten month period. Loved cows produced more milk than cows that were merely part of the herd.

Researchers found the average cow produced about 1,981 gallons of milk during this time span, but referring to their cows by name and treating them with TLC, farmers saw a spike in milk production.

Now get this: these scientists believe that personal attention to cows improves cows' comfort levels while lessening their fear of human contact. This just goes to show that cows don't like being herded or lumped with the crowd! How important a name is to a cow and to each of us.

Can you believe this? Even cows respond better when they are loved! Pretty good advice for all of us as we go through life. The Good Book is not so much out-of-date when it commanded us to love our neighbors as ourselves. It works on cows and works even better on people!

Do not seek revenge or bear a grudge against one of your people, but love your neighbor as yourself. I am the Lord (Leviticus 19:18).

308. 'TWAS THE NIGHT JESUS CAME

'Twas the night Jesus came and all through the house,
Not a person was praying, not one in the house.
The Bible was left on the shelf without care,
For no one thought Jesus would ever come there.
The children were dressing to crawl into bed,
Not once ever kneeling or bowing their head in prayer.
And Mom in the rocking chair with baby on her lap,

221

Was watching the Late Show as I took a nap.
When out of the East there rose such a clatter,
I sprang to my feet to see what was the matter.
Away to the window I flew like a flash,
Tore open the shutters and threw up sash.
When what to my wondering eyes should appear,
But angels proclaiming that Jesus was here!
The light of His face made me cover my head,
It was Jesus returning just like He had said.
And though I possessed worldly wisdom and lots of wealth,
I cried when I saw Him in spite of myself.
In the Book of Life that he held in His hand,
Was written the name of every saved man, woman, teen, and child.
He spoke not a word as He searched for my name,
When He said, "It's not here!" I hung my head in shame.
The people whose names had been written with love,
He gathered to take to His Father above.
With those who were ready He arose without a sound,
While all the others were left standing around.
I fell to my knees but it was too late,
I waited too long and so sealed my fate.
I stood and I cried as they rose out of sight,
Oh, if only I'd known that this was the night![38]

Now brothers, about times and dates we do not need to write to you, for you know very well that the day of the Lord will come like a thief in the night
(1 Thessalonians 5:1).

309. BLACKOUT

Dennis E. Hensley had a most interesting assignment and writes this:

When I was a newspaper reporter, I did a feature on training procedures for Air Force pilots. One flight condition a pilot must understand is hypoxia or oxygen starvation.

Students are paired off in an altitude simulation chamber. With their oxygen masks on, they are taken to simulated conditions at 30,000 feet.

Then one student removes his mask for a few minutes and begins to answer simple questions on a test paper. Suddenly, their partners will force the oxygen masks back on the uncovered mouths and noses of the people who are doing the writing.

After a few gulps of normal air, each writer is astounded at what he or she sees on the paper. The first few written lines are legible; the last few lines are unreadable.

One minute earlier, the participant was absolutely sure he had written his answers in perfectly legible script. In reality, he was on the verge of losing total consciousness. Remarkably, he didn't even know he was blacking out.

In just the same way, people can be spiritually starved. They may not know anything is wrong, but unless someone explains how to obtain the "breath of life," those disconnected from God will never gain spiritual consciousness."

The gospel of Jesus Christ has been described in many ways: the bread of life; the water of life; the river of life; the way, the truth and the life—but not the "breath of life." But what an excellent way to describe it. Without breath we do not live. However, in creation God breathed into human forms and they began to live. Have you had your breath of new life? It's time to take a deep breath!

The Lord God formed the man from the dust of the ground and breathed into his nostrils the breath of life, and the man became a living being (Genesis 2:7).

310. WHAT IS LIFE REALLY ALL ABOUT?

The most destructive habit of living is worry.

The greatest joy and happiness comes in giving.

The greatest loss you can suffer is your loss of self-respect.

The most satisfying life work is helping others.

The ugliest personality trait is selfishness or ego.

The most endangered human species is dedicated leaders.

The greatest of all natural resources is our youth.

The greatest shot in the arm is encouragement.

The greatest problem in living to overcome is fear.

The world's most effective sleeping pill is peace of mind.

The most crippling failure disease is excuses.

The most powerful force in life is love.

The most dangerous human being is a gossiper.

The world's most incredible computer is the human brain.

The worst thing to be without is hope.

The world's mostly deadly weapon is the human tongue.

The two most power-filled words are "I can."

The greatest asset to have is faith.

The most worthless emotion is self-pity.

The most beautiful thing you can wear to be well-dressed is a smile.

The most prized possession is eternal life in heaven.

The most powerful channel of communication is prayer.

The most contagious attitude is enthusiasm.

The people who really love you the most are family members.

Does this read like your life? If not, you still have time to change and live it to the fullest. Go for it!

Then he said to them, "Watch out! Be on your guard against all kinds of greed; a man's life does not consist in the abundance of his possessions"
(Luke 12:15).

311. WHAT IS A WIND ANCHOR?

Have you ever been to a major city such as New York, Singapore, Tokyo, or Hong Kong? Was the first thing you noticed as you came near the city the skyscrapers? Many of these reach as high as 1,000 feet into the air and more than 60 stories high. How do they manage to stand even in winds as high as 100 miles per hour?

The unseen secret to allow them to withstand wind pressure is something called wind anchors. These are not seen but they extend as many as seven stories into the earth until they are anchored in solid rock. These are huge steel rods on which the skyscraper is built; they form the foundation.

These wind anchors are not needed for a single story building, but if you want to build something magnificent that will last such as tall skyscrapers, you need this foundation. Life is much the same.

Sadly, almost every day we hear or read of some character building that has collapsed. It's another example of a person whose life was not built with a solid rock foundation of real character. The Bible tells us about a man who was going to build his house but there were two possibilities: he could build on the sand or on the rock. It makes no difference how it was built because the storms would be coming. The house without the proper foundation would collapse, but the house on the rock would last.

So my young friend, my recommendation is to build your life well. Start with Jesus Christ as the "wind anchor" of your life, and you'll build well and it will last!

Because God wanted to make the unchanging nature of his purpose
very clear . . . we have this hope as anchor for the soul, firm and secure
(Hebrews 6:17, 19).

312. WHAT AM I GOING TO DO WITH YOU?

A very successful businessman, who happened to be nearing retirement age, gave a fabulous wedding and reception for his only daughter. Following the wedding and the honeymoon, the father set aside some time to have a serious meeting with his son-in-law.

The two met in his private conference room and the businessman said, "I love my daughter and now I welcome you into the family. To show you how much we care for you, I'm offering you a fifty-fifty partnership in the family business. You are now half owner of a very successful and profitable family business!"

The proud father-in-law continued, "All you have to do is go down to the factory and learn the operation from the bottom up."

The son-in-law interrupted and said, "I hate factories. I can't stand the noise, the dirt, the dust, and the confusion."

The father-in-law replied, "I see. Well, then, you'll work out of this office. You'll be put in charge of some division."

The kid interrupted again, "I hate office work. I can't stand the thought of working at a desk."

The father-in-law said, "Wait a minute. I just made you half owner of a money-making organization. You can't stand factories; you can't stand offices; you hate desks. What am I going to do with you?"

The young man said, "Buy me out!"

Please understand, the only place where you find success before work is in the dictionary. The elevator to success is out of order so you'll have to climb the steps. Go for it!

Even when we were with you, we gave you this rule: "If a man will not
work, he shall not eat" (2 Thessalonians 3:10).

225

313. SOME SURPRISING BENEFITS OF BEING A COPYCAT

Imitation too often gets a bad rap! For example, take imitation leather. It's not comfortable or breathable. Or how about imitation crabmeat? It's not tasty or enjoyable. But in relationships, imitation can be very good. Why? It can make you seem more interesting and more appealing.

Take the experiments at Radboud University of Nijmegen in the Netherlands, where subjects were interviewed by someone who subtly mirrored their postures. These subjects subsequently gave bigger donations to the charity discussed and were more likely to help the interviewer.

And in research published in the Journal of Personality and Social Psychology, students rated interactions with mimickers as smoother than those with non-mimickers; they also considered mimickers more likable.

However, while imitation may seem simple, it can be very tricky, warns Robert Epstein, Ph.D., former editor of Psychology Today. If people notice what you're doing, they may think you are manipulative. Epstein's advice, "Think smaller: If someone crosses his or her legs, wait five to ten seconds, then cross your ankles." If subtlety's not your strongest suit, make note of a person's mannerisms, then try a few mini-versions the next time you're together. This works only on a simplistic level of influencing someone's behavior.

Is this being a good Christian? Paul the apostle provides an answer. He said that he was willing to do most anything in order to reach people with the gospel of Jesus Christ. If you want to influence someone on a deeper level, a good plan to share the gospel is to be willing to make friends first, of course not by imitating their actions but by genuinely being interested in them. Then they may be more willing to listen when you tell them about your personal relationship with Jesus Christ.

To the weak I became weak, to win the weak. I have become all things to all men so that by all possible means I might save some. I do all this for the sake of the gospel, that I may share in its blessings (1 Corinthians 9:22-23).

314. THE SPAGHETTI TREE

Have you ever fallen for a hoax? A hoax is a trick, a fraud, or a practical joke played on the innocent with the intent to deceive. These hoaxes perpetrated in history are as varied as humanity but can also show the shocking amounts of gullibility on the receiving end. How about the following?

On April Fools' Day, 1957, the British Broadcasting Corporation pulled this tom-foolery on their news show, Panorama. News reporter Richard Dimbleby offered viewers a tour of a "spaghetti harvest" in Ticino, Switzerland. Dimbleby reported, "The last two weeks of March are an anxious time for the spaghetti farmer" as a video of a family was shown picking strips of pasta off their trees. He also added, "There's the chance of a late frost, which, while not entirely ruining the crop, generally impairs the flavor." This report then concluded, "For those who love this dish, there's nothing like homegrown spaghetti!"

After this report was shown, the BBC was flooded with calls from people asking how and where they could also get a spaghetti tree. The BBC reportedly told each caller this simple message: "Place a sprig of spaghetti in a tin of tomato sauce and hope for the best!"

We laugh at how gullible people can be. However, an even more diabolical hoax has been perpetrated on humanity by the devil who tells us that there is no God, that there is no heaven or hell, that you can live like you want with no consequences. He talks about the pleasures of sin but not the price of eternal damnation that all of us will pay unless Jesus Christ has become our personal Savior.

For all have sinned and fall short of the glory of God, and are justified freely by his grace through the redemption that came by Christ Jesus
(Romans 3:23-24).

315. WHAT IS A CHURCH?

What is a church? First off, you and I need to know that a church is not a building or a cathedral or a mosque or a synagogue or even a denomination! Yes, you read correctly.

Okay. Again, what is a church? As simply as I can explain, a church is basically and simply the community of people who have a personal relationship with Jesus Christ. It is not an institution or a program, but a group of people who have heard about Him, who know Him in a personal way, who have responded and keep on responding to Him in such a way as to become His body of believers on this earth. This is the way His Spirit lives on and influences lives of all who believe all over the world.

The church is the loving and responsive community of believers. It's the community in which Christ is honored and followed. It's the group of people who continue to proclaim His love for all of mankind. It's a community who like Him, cares for the least and lowliest, the hungry, the hurting, and the lost.

When the church is really the church, it responds in faith to a God who can be trusted. It responds in celebration in acts of worship. It responds by sharing this faith way of living. It does His work in obedience and challenges the powers of evil. This community binds up the wounded; it gives itself in caring for others. It helps those who can't help themselves. It cares when no one else cares.

And this real church invites you to come and share in the celebration of life and love. There is plenty of room for you to become part of this exciting community of believers!

Now you are the body of Christ, and each one of you is a part of it
(1 Corinthians 12:27).

316. THE LATEST IN A CHURCH BUILDING

A Californian who had made a fortune in the computer business went to his pastor and offered, "Pastor, I know you would like to build a new church, so I have planned for you and your wife to take a six-month sabbatical and visit the Holy Land and other places. When you get back, I'll have a surprise for you. You need the break and I'll take care of the new building."

Six months later they returned and were met by this businessman, who told them that while they were gone he had had the new church built. He said, "It's the finest building money can buy, no expense was spared, and it has the latest in technology." And he was right—it was a magnificent new church inside and out.

But there was a difference; it contained only a single pew at the back of the sanctuary. The pastor said, "A church with one pew?"

"Just wait until Sunday," said the computer guru.

Sunday came and people filled the one pew and sat down. Then a switch clicked silently, a circuit breaker closed, a belt moved, and the pew moved forward and the next pew popped up. And it continued. Pews were filled and moved forward until the church was full from front to back.

"Wonderful!" said the preacher. "This is marvelous!"

The service began. Then the preacher launched into his sermon, and when noon came, he was still going strong with no end in sight. Again, a switch clicked, a circuit closed, gears meshed, and the pulpit with the longwinded preacher dropped out of sight!

"Wonderful!" said the congregation. "This is marvelous!"

And on this rock I will build my church, and the gates of Hades will not
overcome it. I will give you the keys of the kingdom of heaven
(Matthew 16:18-19).

317. MONKEY BUSINESS

Do you ever think about how this earth came into being? Did it happen, did it evolve, was it the result of a Big Bang? How did it all happen? Think with me about the following concept:

If you put a bunch of monkeys together in the same cage and gave each of them a computer to bang on, how long would it take them to turn out a literary masterpiece, such as Shakespeare's Hamlet, or a John Grisham novel, or even the Bible? Could it happen by chance? Could a bunch of monkeys make this happen?

Well, Dr. William Bennett, a professor of physics at Yale University, created a special program and put a computer to work on this proposition. His findings might be a discouragement to those who have contended that the intricate universe and existing life came into being through chance.

Here's the computer's response: if a trillion monkeys hammered away at a rate of ten characters per second, it would take a trillion times longer than the universe has been in existence to produce only a single line, "To be or not to be, that is the question."

If this is true, what do you think are the chances that this world and you are the product of chance?

Here's the real answer to how this world and you came into being. Read carefully:

In the beginning God created the heavens and the earth. And God said, "Let there be light," and there was light. Then God said, "Let the land produce vegetation . . . And it was so. And God said, "Let there be lights in the expanse of the sky." Then God said, "Let us make man in our image . . . so God created man in his own image . . . male and female he created them!"
(Genesis 1:1, 3, 11, 14, 26-27).

318. CHOOSE WISELY

She's nineteen and has launched a singing career. Her first single had made the charts and through this she had gained some fame in the music scene. She also happened to be a beautiful young lady, having been a runner-up in a beauty contest. Her talent and beauty had caught the eye of a Hollywood movie producer who offered her a role in an upcoming movie.

She carefully read the script of the proposed role and discovered her role called for a number of scenes of immorality. She quickly lost interest and refused the offer.

Her business manager pleaded, "Don't be foolish! Can't you see that this is the crossroad in your professional life? Pass up this picture and you've lost your big chance. Go ahead with it and your career will really take off! You'll have everything you want!"

She replied, "Yes, everything but my self-respect and peace of mind."

The choice between what would be acceptable and even desired in the eyes of the world and what is acceptable to God and a Christian are not always easy to make. Pride, goals, greed, or desire too often can blind us to any dangers involved in choices we make. On one side may be the glamour or material gain and on the other is the right, honest, and positive thing to do. It's not always easy or cut and dried.

How do we make the right choices that are pleasing to God and to a young Christian? First begin with a knowledge of the written Word of God. What does the Bible have to say about this particular choice? As we apply these standards to our choices, we discover the rewards of peace and the knowledge of right living.

Trust in the Lord and do good . . . Delight yourself in the Lord and he will give you the desires of your heart. Commit your way to the Lord; trust in him and he will do this: He will make your righteousness shine like the dawn (Psalm 37:3-6).

319. EVER BEEN TO A RODEO?

Rodeo's can be great fun! You'll find them in all parts of the world where there are ranches and cowboys. Let's read about a special performance at a rodeo.

We hear the announcer blare: "Ladies and gentlemen, Slim Cotton will now perform the dangerous, spectacular, breathtaking feat of galloping his horse Kayla up to his red bandanna lying on the arena dirt and with his teeth, pick up the bandanna as he rides past. Let 'er go, Slim!"

The drums roll, the chute opens, and out rides Slim on his beautiful, swift, golden palomino. Nearer and nearer to the handkerchief he gallops. Slim leans to the side and swings low from the saddle. Now he's almost at ground level, opens his mouth, and he and his horse speed past. But the red bandanna lay on the ground! An embarrassed silence grips the crowd.

Slim wheels his horse around and gallops over to the announcer's stand. A hasty conference takes place. Then the announcer returns to the microphone and says, "Ladies and gentlemen, Slim Cotton will now ride back and pick up his bandana and his teeth!"

Have you ever been really embarrassed in public? So what do you do? Hopefully you will have the opportunity, like Slim, to go back for a second attempt. Success in life comes in "can's" and failure comes in "cannot's." It's always too soon to give up, even if you have embarrassed yourself publicly or even in front of a friend. You may have stumbled and fallen, but get up one more time than you have fallen. That's real success in your living. Go for it! You can do it.

With you is the fountain of life; in your light we see light. Continue your love to those who know you, your righteousness to the upright in heart (Psalm 36:9-10).

320. CAN YOU HAVE FUN AS A CHRISTIAN?

Did you know that one of the best-kept secrets is how much fun life can be when you become a God-fearing Christian? Most of us have heard the lie about all the terrible sacrifices that come with being a Christian. Okay, so there may be some sacrifices involved. Think of it like this: any sacrifices we might make to have eternal life with Jesus are only short-term compared to the sacrifices a non-Christian makes that leads to eternal life in hell!

Or think of it like this: the fun non-Christians have is always about self-gratification. And the fun and joy of being a Christian centers around others and the excitement of sharing.

Paul wrote this: "Don't do anything out of selfish ambition or vain conceit, but in humility consider others better than yourselves" (Philippians 2:3). To do and share is such fulfilling fun when you do and share with others. Talk about real, lasting joy—this is it! You should give it a try. Believe it and live it!

That's not all. How about another quick note about sacrifice. This is not a reason to sacrifice, but it is a benefit. This is a promise made by Jesus Christ to all of us who are or will become His followers: "I tell you the truth . . . no one who has left home for me and gospel will not fail to receive a hundred times as much in this present age . . . and in the age to come, eternal life" (Mark 10:29-30).

How about that? The most fabulous reward in or out of this world is to be privileged to spend eternity with Jesus Christ and the family of God. Believe it and live it! Life as a Christian is fun and the rewards are out of this world.

Come, you who are blessed by my Father; take your inheritance, the kingdom prepared for you since the creation of the world (Matthew 25:34).

321. DO YOU KNOW THIS ABOUT IRAQ?

Israel is the nation most often written about in the Bible. Perhaps you already knew this, but Iraq is the second most often mentioned nation. But there's a whole lot more to consider:

• The garden of Eden was in the nation of Iraq.

• Mesopotamia, which currently is known as Iraq, was originally the cradle of civilization. Here is where it all began.

- Noah built the ark in Iraq, the Tower of Babel was built in Iraq, and Abraham was from Ur, which is in Southern Iraq.
- Isaac's wife, Rebekah, was from Nahor, which is in Iraq.
- Jacob met the beautiful Rachel in Iraq.
- Jonah preached his message of doom and revival in Nineveh, which is in Iraq. Assyria, in Iraq, conquered the ten tribes of Israel.
- Amos the prophet did his preaching in Babylon, which is in Iraq, and Babylon marched against Jerusalem and destroyed it.
- Daniel was thrown into the lion's den in Iraq, and the three Hebrew children were tossed into the fire in Iraq.
- Belshazzar, the King of Babylon, saw the handwriting on the wall in a palace in Iraq.
- King Nebuchadnezzar carried the Jews into captivity in Iraq.
- The wise men who came to see the baby Jesus came from Iraq.
- The name Iraq means the "country with deep roots." No other nation, except Israel has more biblical history or prophecy connected with it than Iraq. Bible history is certainly fascinating.

This is the text of the letter that the prophet Jeremiah sent from Jerusalem to the surviving elders among the exiles and to the priests, the prophets and all the other people Nebuchadnezzar had carried into exile from Jerusalem to Babylon (Jeremiah 29:1).

322. THE HOTTEST THING GOING

Are you a part of the very hottest thing going in this world? A majority of this world's population are! So, the real question is: Are you too cool to be a part of the hottest thing going?

Are you thinking, *What is this hottest thing going?* Or *What can be this hot?* The answer is in a simple four letter word: hell! Yes, the hottest thing going is hell. So let's think about it. The Bible says that the road to heaven is a narrow road, the road less traveled. But the road to hell is broad, and anybody can go to hell!

So let's get down to the bottom line. Are you going to follow the crowds or are you going to go upstream and fight the currents of sin and deception? When Jesus Christ died on the cross, the Bible tells us that He went to hell and conquered death and hell. Then He said it much like this: "Been there, done that, and I don't recommend it! How's that for an up-to-date eye witness report?

Jesus then reported to the world that hell is the place to avoid at all costs, even if you have to cut off your hand or put out your eye to avoid this place. Therefore, Jesus advised all of us to choose life—real, eternal life. When you choose eternal life, the promise is that God's Word gives you strength for this journey and God will part the waters of sin and deception so you can keep moving upstream. So jump in the water now and stay too cool for the hottest thing going!

> *The rich man died . . . in hell where he was in torment, he called: "Father Abraham, have pity on me and send Lazarus to dip the tip of his finger in water and cool my tongue, because I am in agony in this fire*
> (Luke 16:23-24).

323. WELCOME BACK TO SCHOOL

Despite popular opinion, school can be a wonderful place. It can also be a very funny place. The humorist Richard Benson has collected a bunch of student test blunders and dumb answers in his book, *F in Exams: The Funniest Test Paper Blunders*. Here are a bunch of samplings:

Question: "What is a nitrate?"
Answer: "Much cheaper than a day rate."

Question: "What did Mahatma Gandhi and Genghis Khan have in common?"
Answer: "Unusual names."

Question: "Name one of the early Romans' greatest achievements."
Answer: "Learning to speak Latin."

Question: "Where was the American Declaration of Independence signed?"
Answer: "At the bottom of the page."

Question: "What is a fibula?"
Answer: "A little lie."

Question: "Explain the phrase 'Free Press.'"
Answer: "When your Mom irons pants for you."

Question: "Name the wife of Orpheus, whom he attempted to save from the underworld."
Answer: "Mrs. Orpheus."

Okay, how did you do on this simple test? Fortunately, this test is not being graded. All of the above is shared to really say this: Study hard, apply yourself, make the best of the fabulous opportunity to learn. There's a statistic that says college graduates earn more than twice the amount of people who don't finish school. It pays to study!

Do your best to present yourself to God as one approved, a workman who does not need to be ashamed and who correctly handles the word of truth (2 Timothy 2:15).

324. DID YOU KNOW? (PART 1)

- Matthew suffered martyrdom in Ethiopia and was killed for the gospel of Jesus Christ when he was wounded with a sword.
- Mark died in Alexandria, Egypt, for preaching the gospel, and was dragged through the streets until he was dead.
- Luke became a missionary to the Greeks and as a result of his powerful preaching to sinners and the many conversions, he was hanged in Greece.
- John faced martyrdom when he was boiled in a huge basin of boiling oil during persecution in Rome. However, he was miraculously delivered from death and was then sentenced to the mines on the prison island of Patmos. While there, he wrote the prophetic book of Revelation and was freed and returned to serve as Bishop of Edessa in modern-day Turkey. He died as an old man, the only apostle to peacefully die a natural death.
- Peter was crucified upside down on an X-shaped cross. According to tradition, it was because he told his tormentors that he was unworthy to die in the same way that Jesus Christ had died.
- James the Just was leader of the church in Jerusalem and was thrown over a hundred feet down from the southeast pinnacle of the temple when he refused to deny his faith in Christ. When they discovered that he had survived the fall, his enemies beat James to death with a club. Incidentally, this was the same pinnacle where Satan had taken Jesus during his period of temptation.

These stories make us stop and think about our commitments.

I am the First and the Last. I am the Living One; I was dead, and behold I am alive for ever and ever! And I hold the keys of death and Hades (Revelation 1:17-18).

325. DID YOU KNOW? (PART 2)

- James the Great, the son of Zebedee, was a fisherman by trade when Jesus called him into a lifetime of ministry. He was the leader of the church at Jerusalem and was beheaded. The Roman officer who guarded James watched in amazement as James defended his faith at his trial. Later, this guard walked with him to the place of execution. He was overcome by conviction, so he declared his new faith to the judge and knelt beside James to also accept beheading as a new Christian.

- Bartholomew, also known as Nathaniel, was a missionary to Asia in present day Turkey. He was martyred when he was flayed to death with a whip.

- Andrew was crucified on an X-shaped cross in Patras, Greece. First he was whipped by seven soldiers, and then tied to the cross to prolong his agony. He survived for two days on this cross and continued preaching to his tormentors and spectators until he died.

- Thomas was thrust through with a spear in India during one of his many missionary trips to establish the church in this subcontinent.

- Jude was killed with arrows when he refused to deny his faith in Jesus and refused to stop his preaching.

- Matthias was the apostle chosen to replace the traitor Judas Iscariot and was stoned; when he didn't die, was then beheaded.

- Paul was tortured and then beheaded by Emperor Nero at Rome in AD 67. Paul endured a lengthy imprisonment that allowed him to write his many epistles.

Talk about a reminder to all of us who think life is too tough. Just think of the persecution and cold cruelty faced by these apostles. Without them, there would be no church today!

All men will hate you because of me, but he who stands firm to the end will be saved (Matthew 10:22).

326. KIDS CAN SAY THE FUNNIEST THINGS

Tina, a middle school teacher, attempted to explain Thanksgiving to her four-year-old nephew, who thought it was a boring holiday with no presents or treats.

She patiently told him that it was a time for appreciating all we have—a loving family, health, good food, and so forth.

At bedtime on Thanksgiving evening, Tina overheard the boy saying this prayer, "Dear God: I am thankful for my mommy and daddy and my sister, even though she breaks my toys, and my food and my warm house and my toys. I am thankful for my Aunt Tina, but could you tell her that she talks too much! I am only four!"[39]

The First United Methodist Church of Gilford, New Jersey, has a children's story time shortly before the children leave for Sunday school. One

Sunday after Easter, Rev. Victoria Wood Parrish told the children that after Jesus was resurrected, He saw His disciples fishing from the beach, helped them catch a net full of fish, and shared a breakfast that Jesus had prepared for them.

When the pastor asked the children what they thought the disciples ate for that breakfast that Jesus had prepared, the youngest child shouted, "Sushi!"[40]

A pastor who slept in late on a Monday morning, and his wife had some difficulty in waking him up. When he finally got up, he asked, "Why couldn't the Lord have rested two days instead of only one?"

The question is, do you think the Lord has a sense of humor? I do! Have you looked at some of His creations lately? How about checking out monkeys, elephants, giraffes, platypuses, and even me and you?

A cheerful heart is good medicine, but a crushed spirit dries up the bones
(Proverbs 17:22).

327. SEEING RED, BLUE, WHITE, OR PURPLE

Because they attended high school in Washington, D.C., the boys of Gonzaga College High School had a unique platform for their 1969 prank. They tricked the Department of the Interior into allowing them to turn the Washington Monument purple and white, their school's colors, just before the annual football game against their rivals, St. John's College High School.

Mark Smith, who led the caper, recalls, "We convinced the government that we were doing a science project to test the effects of casting light through a semipermeable membrane on a white oblique object." A forged letter on the headmaster's stationery could have been the tipping point that sealed the deal.

On the night of November 11, the boys brought yards of purple celluloid in wooden frames to many of the monument's gigantic spotlights. Park police kept visitors away and at 7:05 p.m., the boys set them over the spotlights. Two sides of the monument turned purple and stayed that way for thirty-five minutes! As city residents gaped at the transformation, Smith and his friends celebrated. "We thought, This is the greatest moment of our short lives," he remembers. Press coverage included dramatic photos.

What great fun! But what is it in your life that distorts the true light of God? What kind of a color screen is changing the light of your life? Is there something that prevents you from seeing the truth? Jesus said we are to be the light of the world, so what kind of light are you shining? Is it tinted or does it give the true light, the real light, the white hot light of God's love? Think about it.

Neither do people light a lamp and put it under a bowl. Instead they put it on its stand, and it gives light to everyone in the house. In the same way, let your light shine before men, that they may see your good deeds and praise your Father in heaven (Matthew 5:15-16).

328. THE WORLD'S DEADLIEST SNAKES

What snake in this world would you nominate as being the deadliest? Think about it as we consider some of the following:

- The FIERCE SNAKE lives in Australia and one bite from this killer contains enough venom to slaughter one hundred people.
- The BROWN SNAKE is also from Australia and one drop of its venom, as small as a grain of sand, can kill a human being.
- The MALAYAN KRAIT inhabits Southeast Asia, and 50 percent of the Malayan krait's victims die, even if they're treated.
- The TIGER SNAKE is another aggressive Australian snake that kills more people than any other Australian snake.
- The SAW-SCALED VIPER from Africa kills more people than all other African snakes combined.
- The BOOMSLANG is also from Africa, but stand back! This snake has very long fangs and can open its mouth to a full 180 degrees.

All right, what's your choice? My choice for the deadliest snake is the one found in the garden of Eden. Here's what the Bible has to say about the world's deadliest snake: "Now the serpent was more crafty than any of the wild animals the Lord God had made" (Genesis 3:1). This snake tempted Eve and Adam to sin. This serpent lied, distorted the truth, and called God a liar. A bite from the deadliest snake of all can cause you to spend an eternity with him in hell! This snake not only kills physically, this snake has the ability to send you to an eternity without God. Think about it.

So the Lord God said to the serpent, "Because you have done this, Cursed are you above all the livestock . . . You will crawl on your belly and you will eat dust all the days of your life (Genesis 3:14).

329. TAKE A TASTE OF HONEY

Let's take time to consider some very sweet facts about bees and honey.

- A single honey bee will make only one-twelfth of a teaspoon of honey during its entire lifetime, which is only about four months.

- Worker honeybees have the toughest job in the hive as they gather nectar for the honey. To make just one pound of honey, collectively, they will fly more than 55,000 miles and visit more than two million flowers.

- Even though their wings beat very fast, honeybees fly only about fifteen miles per hour.

- European colonists introduced the honeybee to North America in 1638. Native Americans called them the "white man's fly."

- Not only did ancient Egyptians use honey to sweeten their bread, they also fed it to sacred animals.

- In the Middle Ages, German peasants often paid their rent with honey and beeswax.

- Early American settlers used honey to make cement, varnish, medicine, and furniture polish. They also added it as an ingredient to food or drinks.

- Besides all that, honey is one of the most nourishing foods you can eat. It's no wonder the Bible has a lot to say about honey. The land of Israel was described as being wonderful because it flowed with milk and honey. It also tells us that the commands and words of God are more precious than gold and sweeter than honey. The Bible tells us to take a taste and see that the Lord is good. Have you had your taste today?

How sweet are your words to my taste, sweeter than honey to my mouth!
(Psalm 119:103).

330. THREE REASONS WHY YOU NEED JESUS

Let's start here: Jesus loves you! He wants to have a personal relationship with you and to give you a life that is full of joy and purpose! So, why do you need Him in your life?

1. Because you have a past. You can't go back but He can! The Bible promises, "Jesus Christ is the same yesterday and today and forever" (Hebrews 13:8). He can walk back into those places of your sin and failure, He can wipe your slate clean, and He can give you a new beginning!

2. Because you need a real friend who will always be your friend. Jesus knows the worst about you, yet He believes the best. Why? Because He sees

you not as you are but as you will be when He gets through with you. What a friend!

3. Because He knows and controls the future. Who else can you trust or are you going to trust? In His care you are safe and secure today, tomorrow, and for all eternity. The Bible promises: "For I know the plans I have for you" says the Lord. "They are plans for good and not for evil, to give you a future and a hope. In those days when you pray, I will listen" (Jeremiah 29:11-12, TLB).

If you have not, would you like to begin a personal relationship with Jesus today? It begins with a simple prayer you can pray right now:

Lord Jesus, I invite you into my life. I believe you died for me and that your blood pays for my sins and provides me with the gift of eternal life. By faith I receive this gift and acknowledge you as my Lord and Savior. Amen.

For the wages of sin is death, but the gift of God is eternal life in Christ Jesus our Lord (Romans 3:23).

331. ARE YOU A SUPERSTITIOUS PERSON?

This world seems to be full of strange types of superstitions. Let's look at some of them.

- In Tibet the number forty-two is considered to be a sacred number.
- The Mexican version of the tooth fairy is the "tooth mouse."
- The ancient Egyptians believed that black cats had magical divine powers.
- Phrenology is the belief that the size and shape of a person's head determines their character. According to phrenologists, the bumps on your head reveal forty-two different aspects of your personality.
- According to legend, emeralds have the power to chase off evil spirits.
- Many people believe that if you have a dream about a dove, this will bring you happiness.
- In Asia, cranes (the bird, not the machine) are symbols of long life.
- Superstitious people think an itchy nose means you'll have an argument with someone.
- According to Egyptian mythology, the fate of the dead is decided by a group of forty-two demons!

That last one is the one that I dislike the most; I do not want my eternal fate determined by demons of any kind! I don't know what you believe, but I believe my eternal destiny has been decided because I am a child of the King and a friend of Jesus, and I'm on my way to heaven. My eternal destiny does not hinge on some superstition but my faith in Jesus Christ!

Jesus answered, "I am the way and the truth and the life. No one comes to the Father except through me" (John 14:6).

332. HOW DO YOU GET THERE?

A Sunday school teacher attempts to teach a lesson to the six-year-olds about what do you do to get to heaven. So he asked some questions.

"If I sold my house and car and had a garage sale, then gave all the money to the church, would that get me to heaven?"

"No!" the kids answered.

"How about if I cleaned the church every day, mowed the yard, painted the rooms, and worked full-time at the church, would that get me to heaven?"

"No!" they shouted again.

"Okay, what if I were kind to animals and gave candy to all kids and loved my wife and kids, would that get me to heaven?"

Again, "No!"

"Well, then how can I get to heaven?"

A boy in the back stood up and shouted, "You gotta die to go to heaven!"

Yes, he's right. You do have to be dead to go to heaven, but only if you die right. It's going to take more than simply being good or doing good to get you to heaven. This is important but it's not enough! To go to heaven you must have a personal relationship with Jesus Christ, who gave His life that you might have heaven as your final, eternal home. Jesus told the thief on the cross that today, you will be with me in paradise because you asked forgiveness, "Jesus remember me" had been the thief's short, simple, honest prayer, and he went to heaven with Jesus!

Jesus answered him, "I tell you the truth, today you will be with me in paradise" (Luke 23:43).

333. TAKING OR GIVING?

T wo young guys, Max and Joe, were good friends who went fishing on a cloudy, overcast afternoon. About two hours into their outing, a thunderstorm came roaring across the lake and caught them. Their small boat tossed, turned, and finally flipped over in the lake. Max, a strong swimmer, shouted out in an attempt to save Joe who couldn't swim. But Joe didn't respond to his shouts and went down three times and drowned. Slowly, Max swam to shore to break the news to Joe's mother.

"What happened?" she wailed.

Max carefully told her in full detail what had happened.

"But what did you do to try to save my Joe?" she shrieked.

Max explained again, "I kept yelling to your son, 'Joe, give me your hand, give me your hand, give me your hand, please give me your hand!' But Joe just gave me a blank stare, drifted away, and went down."

"You fool," shouted Joe's mother. "You said the wrong thing. You should have said, 'Take my hand, Joe.' Joe never gave anything to anybody!"

Do you know Joe? Don't we all know a Joe, or two or three or dozens of Joes in this world? Unfortunately, the tragedy of this persona is pandemic to the human condition. It seems to make little difference if the Joe we know or have become is young or old. The mantra in our world seems to be: look out for number one!

God's Word is very clear about this kind of living when it says that it is more blessed to give than to receive. So, my young friend, are you a giver or a taker? Takers may have more stuff, but givers are people that are blessed!

Forgive and you will be forgiven. Give, and it will be given to you. A good measure, pressed down, shaken together and running over, will be poured into your lap (Luke 6:37-38).

334. DISTRACTIONS

There is a former police chief who travels the country, lecturing to law enforcement agencies about how some roving bands of thieves accomplish their crimes. His description goes something like this: usually they enter a store they plan to rob as a group. One or two of them will separate themselves from the rest of the group. The group will then begin a commotion in one section of the store—dropping items and breaking them on the floor, fighting, picking on another customer, or getting into an argument with a clerk, and such disturbances are loud and noisy. This disturbance immediately catches the full attention of the clerks and customers. As all eyes are focused on the disturbance by the group, and those who separated themselves are now free to fill their pockets with merchandise or cash! Often no one suspects there has been a crime committed until hours or even days later. By that time, it's too late.

Very clever!

How often has this same strategy been used on you by the evil one? By the devil or any of his demons? It is so easy for us to be distracted. We are seduced into paying attention to the distractions in our life, while the agents of evil are ransacking our life. When in times of well-publicized sins, which have captured our attention or been revealed in public, it would be good if we would check our own moral pockets to see if we have anything left. The enemy of our souls will stop at nothing to distract us from the important focus in life.

Do not be deceived: God cannot be mocked. A man reaps what he sows
(Galatians 6:7).

335. WRONG ENOUGH TO WIN

The home team was losing the football game. They were down to their last play. Only a miracle touchdown could win them the game. The quarterback stepped into the huddle, carefully looked at the other ten players, and confidently called for play number fifteen. The play was an unusual choice for the situation but it worked! The home team took the ball all the way and scored the touchdown; they won the game.

After this surprise victory, the coach pulled the quarterback aside and asked him why he had ever thought to call such a strange play. The quarterback carefully explained, "Well, coach, I saw player jersey number eight had not caught a pass the entire game, and then I saw jersey number six and realized he hadn't caught a pass either. I figured that if I could bring the two players together, I could find the winning combination. So I added eight plus six and came up with play fifteen."

The astonished coach answered, "That's an interesting strategy, but do you realize that eight plus six actually equals fourteen?"

The quarterback thought about the problem with his equation for a moment and responded, "Well, Coach, I guess if I were as smart as you are, we would have lost the game!"

Sometimes in games and in life it might be better to be lucky rather than too smart. But what is luck? I like to think that such kinds of coincidences are simply God at work while wishing to remain anonymous. Confidence is necessary when facing an impossible situation, but confidence based on solid facts is always better!

I can do everything through him who gives me strength (Philippians 4:13).

336. THE THINGS THAT MAKE US

We must learn to be grateful for everything in life. You might be thinking, *That's not possible!* The following is an easy way to help you begin the process:

The first step is to start giving thanks for the outstanding things—a great home, family, and friends. Then move to the more common things—everyday food, clothes, or a means of transportation to school, work, and recreation. Then move on to the not-so-good things, then to the very not-so-good. And finally, give thanks in the midst of downright horrible things.

Why should we be grateful for the tough things we sometimes experience in life? If we have an attitude of gratitude when we're faced with difficult circumstances, we will move away from negative thinking and be more ready to seek solutions for our problems at hand. We will also become stronger and more ready to take on the next challenge, for we all have them throughout life. If we're steadfast with maintaining a correct attitude, we'll come to a new understanding that the things which almost break us are, in reality, the things that make us.

Expressing gratitude is a powerful factor in healthy living. It's an attitude which sets us free to really live. One interesting idea is to throw a gratitude party in your mind. Bring people to mind and picture yourself thanking them for the contributions they have made to your life. Maybe next time you see them, you'll be ready to thank them in person! Wouldn't that bless them!

Give thanks to the Lord, for he is good; his love endures forever
(1 Chronicles 16:34).

337. CROSS OVER THE BRIDGE

David Whyte tells an interesting story about hiking with a group of older teens in the Himalayan Mountains. David studied the maps and decided he would do a three-day trek on his own and meet the rest of the group at a specific bridge in three days. He had the experience of a lifetime—teen against nature—as he slowly made his way to the bridge.

But when he arrived at the bridge, he was stunned! The chains that held the bridge were in disrepair; many boards were missing or broken. This rickety bridge was hanging four hundred feet over the valley below. He was afraid to cross it, but what was he to do now?

He looked at his maps and discovered no alternative bridge close to this gorge. It was either this bridge—and a possibility of death—or retrace his three-day walk and miss meeting with the other members of his team.

As he was groaning with indecision, an elderly mountain woman walked into the clearing carrying a heavy sack. She had been collecting the dry dung that she would use to build fires in her home. She greeting him with a simple word, "Nimaste," the Indian word for "Hello." Without waiting for an answer, she walked across the bridge to the other side. Inspired, David jumped up and with no more hesitation, followed her across.

When Jesus Christ died, was buried and resurrected on the third day. He showed us how to cross the rickety bridge of death. He walked it before us and crossed it with no problems. In fact, He did it without a worry, making it look easy. Confidence in facing death comes because of our hope in Jesus, the risen God of our faith. You can also give this hope to others who may fear death.

Even though I walk through the valley of the shadow of death, I will fear no evil for you are with me (Psalm 23:4).

338. HORSES CAN'T FLY

A young woman was once found guilty of a crime against the king, and he sentenced her to death. As the soldiers were taking her away to be executed, she shouted, "But Sire, I can teach your horse to fly!"

"Halt!" cried out the king. "What did you say?"

She replied, "Sire, if you give me but a year before executing me, I can teach your horse to fly."

"So be it," said the king. "You have one year to teach my horse to fly or else you will be executed. Let her go! Take her to a prison where she can teach my horse."

As this quick-thinking young lady was led away to her prison cell, one of the soldiers commented on how stupid she really was because it's impossible for a horse to learn how to fly.

"True," said she, "but a lot can happen in a year. The king could die or the horse could die or I might die, or the world could come to an end. Who knows, maybe the horse will learn to fly!"

A life lived like she lived hers, a life lived with a sense of the unknown but the possible potential is open to the fabulous possibilities of God. How do you know what might happen tomorrow? None of us knows that, only God knows what the future holds.

So why not live with faith and trust in God? You never know what the possibilities are when you place your faith and trust in the living, all-powerful, exciting, wonderful, loving God! I don't know about tomorrow, but I know who holds the key!

Now listen, you who say, "Today or tomorrow we will go to this or that city, spend a year there, carry on business and make money." Why, you do not even know what will happen tomorrow. What is your life? You are a mist that appears for a little while and then vanishes (James 4:14-15).

339. LIFE AS HOLLYWOOD FILMS IT

If you get your information and life values from Hollywood as they show it, this is what you can expect:

- During all police investigations, it will be necessary to visit a local strip club at least once while investigating.
- The Chief of Police will almost always suspend his star detective, or at least give him or her forty-eight hours to finish the job.
- The ventilation system of any building is the perfect hiding place. No one will ever think of looking for you in there, and you can travel to all parts of the building.
- All bombs are fitted with electronic timing devices with large red readouts so you know exactly when they are going off and can stop it at the last moment.
- A man will show no pain while taking the most ferocious beating but will wince when a woman tries to clean or treat his wounds.
- It is always possible in a busy city to park directly outside the building you are visiting so you can make a quick arrest.
- They will tell you there is no God, no moral values to life, and that you are free to indulge in any kind of sin you desire without any consequences.
- You will be told that there are no more normal families with a mother, a father, and normal kids who have high values and attend church on Sunday mornings.

From where are you getting your life values? I hope it's not popular culture or Hollywood but from God's Word!

I have hidden your word in my heart that I might not sin against you, praise be to you, O Lord (Psalm 119:11).

340. THE WORLD'S EASIEST QUIZ

Let's take a short a break and make this interactive test. Passing requires only four correct answers. Now be honest, keep track of your answers as I lead you through:

245

1) How long did the One Hundred Year War last?
2) Which country makes Panama hats?
3) From which animals do we get cat gut?
4) When do Russians celebrate October Revolution?
5) What is a camel's hairbrush made of?
6) The Canary Islands are named after what animal?
7) What was King George VI's first name?
8) What color is the purple finch?
9) Where are Chinese gooseberries from?
10) What is the color of the "black box" in a commercial airplane's cockpit?

All done? Here are the answers: 1) 116 years; 2) Ecuador; 3) Sheep and horses; 4) November; 5) Squirrel fur; 6) Dogs; 7) Albert; 8) Crimson; 9) New Zealand; 10) Orange. How many did you get correct? What do you mean you failed?

Some of them seemed obvious, but in reality were not. Not everything in life is as it seems on the surface. Which brings us to the bottom line. Exactly where are you getting the right answers to life's perplexing questions? I hope it's from people and sources you can trust. The most trustworthy source to life's tough questions is always the Bible, God's Word! Study it. You might be surprised what it has to say about life in the twenty-first century!

Do your best to present yourself to God as one approved, a workman who
does not need to be ashamed and who correctly handles the word of truth
(2 Timothy 2:15).

341. GOD IS GREATEST

God is greater than all the superlative statements of supremacy ever shared. No far-reaching telescope can bring into focus the shoreline of His unlimited supply. No deep digging dredge can discover the depth of His determination to deliver you. You can trust Him.

He doesn't need me and He doesn't need you. He stands alone on the solitary pinnacle of His omnipotence. He is enduringly strong and He is entirely sincere. He is eternally steadfast and He is impartial—impartially merciful. He is unparalleled and unprecedented. He is unique and inescapable. He is the cornerstone of all civilization. He is the central doctrine of all truth. He is God's Son, our Savior, and you can trust Him.

He can meet all your needs and He can do it simultaneously. He gives you hope when you are hopeless, help when you are helpless, peace when you are in pain, strength when you struggle, rest when you're restless, and courage when you cry! He sees and sympathizes. He guards and He guides. He heals the sick, cleanses the leper, sets the captives free, and forgives sinners! He's the Master of the masters, the Captain of the conquerors, the Head of the heroes and the Leader of legislators. He's the Governor of the governors, the Prince of Peace, the Prince of all princes! He is the King of kings! I'm telling you, you can trust Him!

You can't outlive Him; you can't live without Him! Pilate couldn't stop Him, Herod couldn't kill Him, death couldn't handle Him—and praise God—the grave couldn't hold Him. He is alive forevermore, and forevermore you can trust Him![41]

"I am the Alpha and the Omega," says the Lord God, "who is, and who was, and who is to come, the Almighty" (Revelation 1:8).

342. THE KISSING FISH

In the coral reefs of the Caribbean lives a small fish known as the kissing fish. It's only about two to three inches long. It's bright blue, and quick and fun to watch. Its kiss is fascinating. It's not uncommon to see two of these fish with lips pressed together and their fins thrashing. They give the appearance of a serious underwater romance.

You would think a fish like this would warm the heart of any aquarium lover's delight. They look energetic, vivid, illuminant, and affectionate. But looks are deceiving. For what appears to be a gentle friend in the sea is actually a pint-sized bully of the sea.

Ferociously territorial, the kissing fish has laid claim to its camp and wants no visitors. His square foot of coral is his and no one else's. He found it, he staked it out, and he wants no one of his own kind near it!

Challenge his boundaries and he'll take you, jaw to jaw. What appears to be a tryst is actually underwater martial arts. Mouth pushing, lip-locking, literal jaw-boning, and power moves with the tongue!

Does this sound funny? Does this sound familiar? We sure don't have to go scuba diving in the Caribbean to see this kind of a power struggle. Mouth-to-mouth manipulation is not limited to the Caribbean. Simply look at people around you, watch TV, read a blog, receive a twitter, read your emails, or check out the people in your school. Kissing fish aren't the first critters to use their mouth to make their point.

The tongue is a deadly weapon. Be careful how you use yours! How are you defending your territory? How about this? "A gentle answer turns away wrath" (Proverbs 15:1).

My brothers, take note of this: everyone should be quick to listen, slow to and slow to become angry, for man's anger does not bring about the righteous life that God desires (James 1:19).

247

343. LAUGHING IS GOOD MEDICINE

The wisest man who ever lived, King Solomon, wrote this about three thousand years ago, and it's still good advice for all of us today in the twenty-first century: "A cheerful heat is good medicine" (Proverbs 17:22). How true is this ancient advice? Scientists today have finally discovered the truth of what the Bible has said for thousands of years.

They have found that laughter is good for your physical health, and now they know why. Researchers at the University of Maryland found that when healthy volunteers smiled, laughed, and guffawed while watching the comedy, *Kingpin*, their blood flow increased by 22 percent. This is about the same increase you can expect when you do aerobic exercises!

But when these same healthy volunteers watched the tension-filled scenes from *Saving Private Ryan*, their blood flow decreased by 35 percent!

The researchers say that laughing apparently causes the endothelium, the tissue that lines blood vessels, to expand, which increases blood flow. Laughter may also improve arterial health by reducing mental stress that constricts vessels and cuts blood flow.

According to researcher Dr. Michael Miller, a healthy lifestyle should include thirty minutes of exercise three times a week and fifteen minutes of healthy, hearty, fun, joyful laughing daily.[42] This is good biblical advice, now confirmed by scientific study. So, have you had your fifteen minutes of laughing today?

There is a time for everything . . . a time to weep and a time to laugh, a time to mourn and a time to dance (Ecclesiastes 3:1, 4).

344. WHEN COWS FLY

A Mayday signal went out from a small Japanese trawler that they were sinking and needed to be rescued. The dazed crew was recovered by their Coast Guard as they were clinging to the wreckage of their boat. Their rescue, however, was followed by their being put in jail once the authorities were questioning them as to why their boat had sunk.

Every man of the crew claimed the same unbelievable story: a cow, falling out of a clear blue sky, had struck their small trawler mid-ship, shattered its hull, and sank their vessel within minutes. The authorities didn't believe their story and thought this farfetched lie was a cover-up for the real reason.

They remained in jail for several weeks awaiting their trial, until the Russian Air Force reluctantly informed the Japanese authorities that the crew of one of their cargo planes had apparently stolen a cow from the edge of a Siberian air field. They wanted to take it home to be butchered. So they forced the cow into the plane's cargo hold and hurriedly flew home. However, the plane and the crew were not equipped to manage a rampaging cow inside the cargo hold. To save the plane and themselves, they shoved the animal out of the cargo hold as they crossed the Sea of Japan at 30,000 feet!

Truth can be stranger than fiction. This is just another example of how unexpected life can be. Are you prepared for the unusual, the unexpected? The best insurance is to have your life anchored in the truth of a relationship with Jesus Christ.

When times are good be happy; but when times are bad, consider: God has made the one as well as the other. Therefore, a man cannot discover anything about his future (Ecclesiastes 7:14).

345. BABEMBA POSITIVE PUNISHMENT

The lifestyle of the Babemba tribe in South Africa was featured in a TV documentary on apartheid. Within this community of people, antisocial or criminal behavior is very rare. However, when it occurs, the Babemba have an interesting and beautiful way of dealing with it.

If a member of the tribe acts irresponsibly or criminally, he or she is placed at the center of the village. Work stops, and every person in the village—every adult and every child—gathers around the accused in a large circle. Then one at a time, each person, including children, call out all the good things the person in the center of the ring has done in the past. All the positive attributes and the kind acts are recited carefully and at length. No one is allowed to exaggerate or be sarcastic. It's a serious business!

This ceremony can often last for days until everyone is drained of every positive comment he or she can muster about the transgressor. Not one word of criticism is allowed. At the end, the tribal circle breaks up, a joyous celebration begins, and he or she is welcomed back into the community!

Apparently, this overwhelming, positive bombardment strengthens the self-esteem of the accused and causes that person to resolve to live up to the expectations of the tribe. Proof of the success of this creative response to wrongdoing seems evident in the fact that these ceremonies are very rare.[43]

This makes us wonder if, perhaps, borrowing this technique might be a great idea, especially in dealing with some family situations is which someone has gone astray.

By this all men will know that you are my disciples, if you have love for one another (John 13:35).

346. WOULD YOU LIKE TO BECOME A MILLIONAIRE?

This is what the website said, "Do you want to earn a million dollars? Then just click here!" Yes, really, that's what it said.

The next screen made this absolute guarantee: "We guarantee that you will make a million dollars if you follow our simple three-step method. There are no exceptions!"

Next the screen prompted the viewer to pay $100 for this secret guaranteed method. Only $100 for the chance to make a million? Sure, why not?

So after the viewer pays the nonrefundable amount of $100, then and only then is this secret to guaranteed wealth revealed.

The next screen reveals this $100 secret: "Send a request for $100 to ten thousand people who agree to send you the money. As soon as they send you the money, you are a millionaire! Please note: it may take a while, so please be patient."

I believe it was P. T. Barnum of "Barnum and Bailey Circus" fame who said, "There is a sucker born every minute."

Today the devil works on the same principle of bait and switch. The bait is so enticing, but the devil will eventually get his dues. Every sucker he can dupe is another sucker who will spend eternity in hell with him. On the other hand, the Lord invites you to come based on trust. Place your trust in Him and you will spend an eternity with Him in heaven! You pay the price first and enjoy the rewards later. With the devil you enjoy the pleasures first and pay with your eternal soul later.

I tell you, there is rejoicing in the presence of the angels of God over one sinner who repents (Luke 15:10).

347. ADAPTING TO CHANGE

Your generation has no recollection of World War II because it happened in the past. However, you may have studied it and some of the effects of this war to end all wars. Among the nations almost totally destroyed was Japan. Following the war, industry in Japan was devastated. The Japanese government hired Dr. Edward Deming, who was a capitalist, to help them rebuild their industrial infrastructure.

Dr. Deming's main theme was simply that they must "make it better and it will cost you less in the long run. It will increase demand for your products and cost you less to repair them if they malfunctioned."

Deming then presented his clients with a list of objectives that began with the simple notion that for a business to be successful, that business needed to know what business it was really in. He explained to them that buggy whip manufacturers were no longer in business because they thought they were in the buggy whip business. But they were actually in the business of vehicle acceleration.

If they would have understood that their real business was vehicle acceleration, they may have been able to adjust with a changing market. As modes of transportation changed, they could have adapted. They needed to see the big picture.

When you go out into the business world when you finish school, if you are to make real, lasting changes, always keep the big picture in mind. It's the same way in the spiritual world. What is the big picture? To prepare yourself to eventually make heaven your eternal home and to help as many other people also get to heaven with you.

Now all has been heard; here is the conclusion of the matter: Fear God and keep His commandments, for this is the whole duty of man
(Ecclesiastes 12:13).

348. WHAT IS A CURIOUS QUANDARY?

A quandary is described as being in a "state of uncertainty, or caught in a dilemma." Let's think about some of the following:

- Why is the third hand on a watch or clock called the "second hand?"
- If a word is misspelled in the dictionary, how will we ever know?
- Why does "slow down" and "slow up" mean the same thing?
- Doesn't "expecting the unexpected" make the unexpected expected?
- Why is it called "after dark" when it really is "after light?"
- Why do "tug" boats push their barges?
- If work is so terrific, why do they have to pay you to do it?
- Why do you press harder on the buttons of your remote control when you know the batteries are already dead?
- If you are cross-eyed and have dyslexia, can you read all right?
- How come "abbreviated" is such a long word?
- If Webster wrote the first dictionary, where did he find the words?
- Why do they call it a "TV set" when you only have one?
- Why, at Christmas, do you sit in front of a dead tree and eat candy out of your socks?
- Why does the Bible say it's harder for a rich person to get into heaven than it is for a camel to go through the eye of a needle?

- Why does the Bible say that if you want to be the leader, you must serve others?
- Why do we say we love God, yet do not keep His commandments?

The proverbs of Solomon . . . are for giving prudence to the simple, knowledge and discretion to the young. The fear of the Lord is the beginning of knowledge, but fools despise wisdom and discipline (Proverbs 1:1, 4-5, 7).

349. THE PUFFER FISH

The puffer fish is one of the most poisonous creatures in the sea. Its poison is 275 times more deadly than cyanide. In spite of its poisonous nature, many Japanese diners consider the raw flesh of the fugu, a type of puffer fish, the ultimate delicacy.

These Japanese gourmets will pay well over $300 per plate for a fugu meal. For the most discriminating diners, nothing can match the flavor of its liver. But it's also the liver where the poison can be most concentrated. Even though it is illegal to serve the puffer fish, chefs are sometimes begged, bribed, or bullied into serving this poisonous delicacy.

If the fish is very carefully prepared, then it is safe. A couple of problems arise, however. There is no way to tell if the fish has been properly prepared, and the only way to tell if there is still poison in the fish is to eat it. If the diner lives, then the fish is okay. If the diner dies, the fish is poisonous.

The death is grim. The toxin acts on the nervous system, first a tingling in the lips and mouth, then paralysis. You can still think clearly, but you are paralyzed and death may occur instantly or it may take six hours. No known antidote is available.

Why would anyone want to each such food? Why feast on things in this world that are just as deadly and will eventually kill you? Both spiritual poison and spiritual life-giving food are available to all of us. Life or death depends on which diet we choose! The best diet is recommended by the writer of Psalms, "Taste and see that the Lord is good" (Psalm 34:8). Oh, the joys of those who trust in Him! When you eat this good food, death will not occur, but eternal life and abundance.

Do not work for food that spoils, but for food that endures to eternal life, which the Son of Man will give you. On him God the Father has placed his seal of approval (John 6:27).

350. HAVE YOU TAKEN A TEST LATELY?

Test results can be very interesting, especially when kids take a Children's Science Exam. How interesting? The following are some real answers from real kids:

Question: Name the four seasons.
Answer: "Salt, pepper, mustard, and vinegar."

Question: Explain one of the processes by which water can be made safe to drink.
Answer: "Flirtation makes water safe to drink because it removes large pollutants like grit, sand, dead sheep, and canoeists."

Question: What happens to your body as you age?
Answer: "When you get old, so do your bowels and you get intercontinental."

Question: Name a major disease associated with cigarettes.
Answer: "Premature death."

Question: How are the main parts of the body categorized?
Answer: "The body is consisted into three parts: the cranium, the borax, and the abdominal cavity. The cranium contains of the brain; the borax contains the heart and lungs, and the abdominal cavity contains the five bowels, A,E,I,O, and U."

Question: What is the fibula?
Answer: "A small lie."

Kids are always good for some laughs. Our special thanks to Babs Eggleston for the questions and answers. Is there a life lesson to be learned from these test results? Be prepared before you take a test. The ultimate test will take place when we all, someday, stand before the judgment place with God as the judge. It's not too late to prepare.

Just as man is destined to die once, and after that to face judgment, so Christ was sacrificed once to take away the sins of many people (Hebrews 9:27).

351. PLAYING WITH ONE STRING

The colorful nineteenth century showman and gifted violinist Nicolo Paganini was playing a very difficult piece of music with a full orchestra supporting him. Suddenly, one string of his violin snapped and hung down from his violin. Beads of sweat popped out on his forehead. He frowned but kept playing, improvising beautifully. Then a second string broke and quickly a third string.

Now there were three limp strings dangling and to the conductor's surprise, this master performer completed this composition on the one remaining string! The audience jumped to their feet in good Italian fashion and filled the air with shouts and screams of "Bravo! Bravo!"

As the applause began to die down, the violinist motioned the people to sit back down. Even though they knew that there was no way they could expect an encore, he held the violin high for all to see. He nodded to the conductor to begin the encore. Then he turned to the crowd with a twinkle in his eye, smiled and shouted, "Paganini and one string!"

Then he placed the Stradivarius beneath his chin and played the final encore on one string. What an attitude! Paganini and one string. The conductor and crowd were transfixed.

Now it's your turn! What do you do when things go wrong? What do you do when the strings of your life begin to break? Give up or keep going? The next time you are tempted to give up or stop playing, remember Paganini and one string!

You have persevered and have endured hardships for my name and have not grown weary (Revelation 2:3).

352. RETURNED BECAUSE OF A HIGHER CALLING

It happened in the sixteenth century in the Netherlands where Dirk Willems had been labeled an Anabaptist during the rule of the Spanish Catholics and was imprisoned for his faith. He was running for his life. He had escaped out the tiny window in his cell and lowered himself on a rope made of old rags. Landing on a frozen pond alongside the prison wall, he stepped lightly onto the ice, wondering if he would fall through. But the months of starvation he had endured in prison now served him well. He barely weighed one hundred pounds.

Before reaching the other side of the pond, a scream broke the night's silence. "Halt, immediately!" yelled the guard as he was coming out the same window that Dirk had climbed through moments before. Dirk was too close to freedom. He kept going. The guard yelled again as he set foot on the ice. He began to chase Dirk but on his third step, there was a loud crack, a splash, as the guard fell through the ice. His screams turned to shrieks of cold and terror, "Help me, please! Help! Help me!"

Dirk paused, looking toward freedom. Then he turned and quickly made his way back to the prison pond. He lay on his stomach and stretched his arms to rescue the nearly frozen guard. In sarcastic attitude, the guard grabbed Dirk and forced him back to his prison cell.

Despite being a hero, Dirk was burned at the stake because of his faith!

Why? Committed Christians don't live according to common sense; they do the unthinkable, they do the impossible because they live according to a higher calling! To what are you committed?

For to me, to live is Christ and to die is gain (Philippians 1:21).

353. HIDDEN RICHES

Some of you, and how I wish it could be all of you, teens reading this are some of the richest people who have ever lived on the face of this planet. Really, I am talking to you and about you! Maybe you don't believe me? I challenge you to take the following simple, four-question test. I hope it will prove my point.

If you can answer three out of the four following questions with a yes, then you are among the 10 percent wealthiest teens who have ever lived on earth.

1. Do you own more than one pair of shoes?
2. Do you own more than one pair of underwear?
3. Do you have a choice of what to eat for at least one meal out of three?
4. Do you have your own transportation?

Perhaps you are richer than you thought. Right? You'll notice, however, that the test does not specify that you can find both shoes out of a pair, that the other pairs of your underwear are clean, folded, and in a drawer. And that the food tastes good and the transportation isn't covered in mud!

If you happen to be a part of the 10 percent wealthiest teens who have ever lived, what are you doing to help the other 90 percent who are not so fortunate? One of the real marks of a Christian is to be helping others not so well off. What did Jesus do for those in need? What would Jesus do today if He lived where you live and had what you have?

What good is it, my brothers, if a man claims to have faith but has no deeds?
Can such faith save him? Suppose a brother or sister is without clothes and
daily food. If one of you says to him, "Go, I wish you well; keep warm and
well fed" but does nothing about his physical needs, what good is it?
(James 2:14-16).

354. FROM WINNER TO LOSER

Jose Lima began his professional baseball career as a nineteen-year-old pitcher and starred as a pitcher for the Houston Astros for several years in the late 1990s. Jose was an outgoing, energetic, likable young ballplayer who usually had a positive outlook on life and his career.

But when the Astros built their new ball park known as Minute Maid Park, Jose became upset. The problem? The left field fence has one of the shortest distances from home plate to the left field fence in major league baseball. The hitters love it; the pitchers hate it. It was even tougher on pitchers when they faced right-handed batters who tended to hit the ball to left field.

The first time Jose stepped onto the new diamond he looked into the outfield and noticed the close proximity of the left field fence. He said, "I'll never be able to pitch in here."

Sure enough, despite the excitement of playing in a new ball field, Jose had the worst year of his career. He plummeted from being a twenty-game winner to being a sixteen-game loser. Never in the history of the Astros had any pitcher experienced such a negative turnaround.

What happened to Jose? The same thing that happens to many of us every day: we get what we say! Our words become self-fulfilling prophecies. If you allow your thoughts to defeat you and they give birth to negative ideas through what you say, your actions will follow. Thoughts and words have tremendous power, and if you want to or not, we give actions and life to what we say—good or bad!

As water reflects a face, so a man's heart reflects the man (Proverbs 27:19).

355. PESSIMISTIC LAWS OF THE NATURAL UNIVERSE

Von Fumbles Law: When you wish to unlock a door—any kind of a door—but have only one hand free, the keys are always in the opposite pocket.

Yale Law of Destiny: A door you have just opened will always snap shut only when you have left the keys on the other side of the door.

Cheney's Second Corollary: When things seem to be going really well, think again, you have probably forgotten to do something.

Destiny Awaits Law: When things seem easy to do, it's likely you haven't read and followed all the easy-to-follow instructions.

Law of Gravitas: If you are keeping your cool when everyone else is losing theirs, it's probably because you have not realized the seriousness of the problem.

Principle of Ding-a-Ling: If you have to run to answer your cell phone, you'll always pick it up just as the calling party hangs up on you.

Law of the Wasteland: If there are only two programs on TV that are worth your time, they will always be on at the same time.

Law of Campbell's Oops: The probability that you will spill food on your clothes is directly proportional to your need to be clean to make a good impression.

Law of Fatal Irreversibility: After throwing something away you haven't used for a long time, you will desperately need it one week later.

Theory of Absolute Certainty: Do not take yourself or life too seriously while you are taking your eternal destiny seriously because you won't come out alive in the end anyway!

For we must all before the judgment seat of Christ, that each one may receive what is due him for the things done while in the body, whether good or bad (2 Corinthians 5:10).

356. ARE CARS MENTIONED IN THE BIBLE?

Most people assume "WWJD" stands for "What Would Jesus Do?" But the initials really stand for "What Would Jesus Drive?"

- One theory is that Jesus would have tooled around in an old Plymouth because the Bible says God drove Adam and Eve out of the garden of Eden in a Fury.
- But in Psalm 38, the Almighty clearly owns a Pontiac and a Geo. The passage urges the Lord to "Pursue your enemies with your Tempest and glorify them with your Storm."
- Perhaps God also favors Dodge pickups because Moses' followers are warned not to go up a mountain "until the Ram's horn sounds a long blast."
- Some scholars insist that Jesus drove a Honda but didn't like to talk about it. They cite the following as proof, "For I did not speak of my own Accord."
- Meanwhile, Moses rode an old British motorcycle because, "the roar of Moses' Triumph is heard in the hills."
- But then Joshua drove a British sports car with a hole in the muffler, "Joshua's Triumph was heard throughout the land."
- And finally, following the Master's lead, the apostles carpooled in a Honda, "The Apostles were all in one Accord."

Oh well . . . just a bit of biblical fun. However, it goes to show how easy it is to misplace Scripture, to misread Scripture, to misinterpret Scripture, to misapply Scripture, or to twist Scripture. When hearing or reading the Word of God, make sure to rightly use it and always consider it in its context and get the big picture. Make sure you are a regular Bible reader!

Your Word is a lamp to my feet and a light for my path (Psalm 119:105).

357. MONKEYS AND BANANAS

Two college business professors, Gary Hamel and C. K. Prahalad, write about an experiment conducted with a group of monkeys. It's a story of failure.

Four monkeys were in a room that had a tall pole in the center, and suspended from the top was a bunch of bananas. The monkeys were hungry and one started climbing the pole; but just as he reached out to grab a banana, he was doused with ice cold water. Squealing, he scampered down the pole and gave up this attempt to feed himself. Each monkey made the same attempt and had the same drenching with cold water. After several attempts they all gave up.

Then researchers removed one monkey and replaced it with a new monkey. As the newcomer began to climb the pole, the other three grabbed him and pulled him back to the ground. Each time he tried, he was pulled back.

The researchers replaced the original monkeys one by one, and each time a new monkey was brought in he was dragged down by the others before he could reach the bananas. In time the room was filled with monkeys who had never received a cold shower; none of them would climb the pole, but none of them knew why!

Have you ever attempted some action but were discouraged by others who told you how it would not work? If you asked them why something will not work, none of them could tell you why. Ever had that experience? Did you eventually give up without giving it a try?

There's an old Chinese proverb: "Man who say it cannot be done should not interrupt man doing it!" Who do you listen to for your advice in life and living?

Listen, my son, to your father's instruction and do not forsake your mother's teaching (Proverbs 1:8).

358. THE POWER OF BAPTISM

William Willimon, in his book, *Remember Who You Are,* writes this: "Through baptism, a Christian first and finally learns who he or she is. It is the rite of identity. Baptism asserts rather than argues, it proclaims rather than explains, it commands rather than describes. When you ask in desperation, 'Who in God's name am I?' baptism will have you feel the water dripping from your head and say, 'You are, in God's name, royalty, God's own, claimed and ordained for serious and joyful business!"

Just like Jesus identified with us when He was baptized, when we are baptized, we identify ourselves with Jesus! We publicly declare our intention to become like Jesus and follow God's Word and will for our living.

Baptism is a very serious public announcement for all the world to hear and see. It's filled with joy, happiness, and celebration. It's a new beginning! From that point onward we see things differently than before. We see other people differently than before. We look through eyes of faith and the eyes of Jesus. Our baptism enables us and empowers us to do the things Jesus wants us to do.

Martin Luther said, "When I preach and teach, I adapt myself to the circumstances of the common people. I don't look at the doctors and masters but at the young people and children. It is to them I devote myself."

Jesus also devoted Himself to the young! So, you in your baptism are important to Christ and Christianity. If you have not experienced a baptism, go to a church that will help you and seek out a pastor that can explain it to you.

He said to them, "Go into all the world and preach the good news to all creation. Whoever believes and is baptized will be saved, but whoever does not believe will be condemned" (Mark 16:16).

359. THINK WITH ME ABOUT YOUR BODY

Physically speaking, your body and my body are made out of the dust of the earth. The chemist or biologist will analyze it and tell us it is made up of so much lime, magnesia, potash, soda, fluorine, silica, iron, and other trace minerals. Think of your body as something like a large city where people are dying and babies are being born at the same time. Just like this, the cells of the body are constantly breaking down and dying and being carried away in waste removal, while at the same time others come into being. What a process—constantly dying and living at the same.

Because of this process, scientists tell us that we will have practically a completely new body as far as the cell structure is concerned every seven years. If you are fourteen years old, you will have had two new bodies since birth. Awesome! But some parts of the body have been renewed even more frequently than that.

Yet, through all these changes, you and your personality haven't changed, and you have vivid images of the life you have already lived. Your real memory is not only in your brain; it's in your cell structure and nerves. So the real you is built on physical, material, and a spiritual dimensions as well as your lasting individuality.

But if you are a believer, the ultimate body change is yet to come. The Bible promises that one of these days there will be a body change of all changes. The Spirit of God will quicken your mortal body and change it into a body that is patterned after that of Jesus Christ! This is called the glorious hope for all believers. Are you really ready for this big change? If you are a believer, you are. If not, now is the time to get ready for the fabulous, unbelievable, incredible, ultimate body transformation!

Listen, I tell you a mystery: We will not all sleep, but we will all be changed—in a flash, in the twinkling of an eye, at the last trumpet. For the trumpet will sound, the dead will be raised imperishable, and we will be changed (1 Corinthians 15:51-52).

360. A JESUS THREE POINT LANDING

Howard County, Indiana, Sheriff Jerry Marr got a disturbing call one Saturday. His six-year-old grandson, Mikey, had been hit by a car while fishing with his dad. The father and son were near a bridge by the Kokomo Reservoir when a woman lost control of her car, slid off the bridge, and hit Mikey at about fifty miles per hour. The sheriff rushed to the emergency room at St. Joseph Hospital to find Mikey conscious and in fairly good spirits.

"Mikey, what happened?" Sheriff Marr asked.

Mikey replied, "Well, Pawpaw, I was fishin' with Dad and some lady runned me over. I flew into a mud puddle and broke my fishin' pole and I didn't get to catch no fish."

As it happened, the impact threw Mikey a few hundred feet, over some small trees, an embankment, and into a mud puddle. His only injury was a right femur bone that had broken in two places. Mikey had surgery. Otherwise he was fine.

Since all Mikey could talk about was his broken fishing pole, the sheriff went to Wal-Mart and bought him a new one. The next day, the sheriff sat with Mikey to keep him company.

Mikey enjoyed his new fishing pole and talking about going fishing. When they were alone, Mikey matter-of-factly said, "Pawpaw, did you know Jesus is real? Really real?"

"What do you mean?" asked the sheriff.

"I know He's real 'cause I saw Him," said Mikey. "Yep, when the lady runned me over and broke my fishin' pole, Jesus caught me in His arms and laid me down in the mud puddle!"[44]

For he will command his angels concerning you to guard you in all your ways; they will lift you up in their hands, so that you will not strike your foot against a stone (Psalm 91:11-12).

361. A LESSON ON LEADERSHIP

Part of being a good leader is to know when not to assert authority but instead inspire motivation to do what is best for everyone concerned. This concept of leadership can best be illustrated by the response of a commanding officer during a war game.

During this Army war game, a particular commanding officer's jeep got stuck in the mud. The officer saw a couple of eighteen-year-old soldiers sitting on the ground under a shade tree just a few feet away from the mud hole and asked them to help him get his jeep out of the mud.

These young soldiers respectfully declined to help him and explained, "Sorry, sir, but we've been classified as dead, and the umpire said we couldn't contribute in any way."

The commanding officer apologized to the men and told them he had not realized that they were dead soldiers. The officer then turned to his Jeep driver and gave him this direct order: "Soldier, go over to those dead men and drag their lifeless bodies over here. I then want you to put their dead bodies into the mud under the wheels of my Jeep to give us some needed traction."

Immediately the Jeep driver and his commanding officer witnessed a miraculous resurrection of two dead soldiers!

There's nothing like a good wakeup call to refresh our focus on the immediate necessity! Have you heard any kind of a wakeup call lately from our Commander-in- Chief, the Lord Jesus Christ? He commands us to be alert, awake, and ready at any moment to keep involved in the battle for right against the wrong.

> *Be self-controlled and alert. Your enemy the devil prowls around like a roaring lion looking for someone to devour. Resist him, standing firm in the faith* (1 Peter 5:8).

362. HOW MILITARY SPECS LIVE FOREVER

The USA standard railroad gauge, the distance between the rails, is four feet, eight and a half inches, which is a very odd number. Why was this gauge used? Because that's the way they built them in England, and the United States railroads were built by English expatriates.

Why did the English build them like that? Because their first rail lines were built by the same people who built the pre-rail tramways and that's the gauge they used.

Why did they use that gauge? Because the people who built the tramways used the same jigs and tools they used for building wagons, which used this wheel spacing.

Okay! Why did the wagons use this odd wheel spacing? Well, if they tried to use any other spacing, the wagons would break on some of the old long distance roads because that was the spacing of old wheel ruts.

So who built those old rutted roads? They were built in Europe by Imperial Rome for the benefits of their legions. The roads have been used ever since. And the ruts? These ruts were first made by Roman war chariots. Since the chariots were made for or by Imperial Rome, they were all alike in this matter of wheel spacing.

This brings us to the answer! The United States railroad gauge of four feet, eight and a half inches comes from the original military specs of an Imperial Roman Army war chariot. Military specs and bureaucracies of any kind live forever!

So the next time you are handed a specification, a bylaw, a custom, or a tradition, wonder where it came from. You're right, because the Imperial Roman chariots were made to be just wide enough to accommodate the back ends of two war horses!

You nullify the Word of God for the sake of your tradition. You hypocrites!
Isaiah was right when he prophesied about you: "These people honor me with
their lips, but their hearts are far from me" (Matthew 15:7-8).

363. THE UNBELIEVABLE SALARY

At the conclusion of a quite lengthy employment interview, the Human Resources Manager looked at the young graduate engineer, who was right out of college, and point blank asked him, "Now, what range of salary are you thinking you should have if we hire you at our company?"

The young, ambitious, confident job-seeking graduate thought for a moment or two and said, "Oh, I was thinking somewhere in the range of $150,000 depending, of course, on the size of the benefits package you will offer."

The manager sat back in his chair and responded, "Then what would you think about an offer that included six weeks vacation a year beginning with your first year? How about twenty days for holidays and personal days? How about a full health insurance package, including dental, paid in full by the company? And to top it off, you will receive a hefty bonus annually and a retirement fund that would continue to pay you a full salary, including all benefits, for the rest of your life? Oh, and one more thing, how would you like a signing bonus of a new Porsche 911 sports car including a credit card to cover all your expenses?"

The young college grad just about fell off his chair. He could not believe what he was hearing. He gasped and said, "That's really great! You've got to be kidding!"

The manager said, "Well, yes, I am kidding, but you started it."

Okay, when you begin job hunting for real, where will you start? Always keep this tidbit that I shared earlier in your mind: the only place where success comes before work is in the dictionary!

We hear that some among you are idle. They are not busy; they are busybodies. Such people we command and urge in the Lord Jesus Christ to settle down and earn the bread they eat (2 Thessalonians 3:12).

364. PRISONER OF WAR COMMUNICATIONS

Nothing can be as deadly as living without communications with other humans. During the Vietnam War a number of Americans were taken prisoners and some were detained in the infamous Hanoi Hilton and other prisons. These soldiers learned how to communicate with each other by tapping messages through the prison walls. Ron Bliss, former Air Force pilot, describes this communication method: "The Hanoi Hilton sounded like a den of runaway woodpeckers."

Their North Vietnamese captors never mastered the code. It went like this. The code laid out the alphabet on a simple five by five square grid. They omitted the K and substituted the C instead. It was five down and five across and left off the Z. They would tap the first time for the line and then the letter in that line. For example, for the letter B, they would tap once for the first line, then quickly tap, tap for the second letter, which is B. It would be tap . . . tap, tap.

This code flowed so fluently that the men told one another jokes, while kicks on the wall meant a laugh. They sent messages of encouragement to each other.

And every Sunday at a coded signal that went through the prisons, at a specific time, they would all stand and collectively recited the Lord's Prayer, the Twenty-third Psalm, and the Pledge of Allegiance. This drove their captors nuts. They knew something significant was happening, but not being able to break the code or understand English, all they could do was beat their prisoners. Through the power of communications they survived their imprisonments.

So then brothers, stand firm and hold to the teachings we passed on to you, whether by word of mouth or by letter (2 Thessalonians 2:13).

365. REMEMBERING CHRISTOPHER COLUMBUS

Edward Markham wrote a poem, "Courage," with the subtitle of "Remembering Christopher Columbus." It's really the story of a brave man who fought against overwhelming odds. He went to the Court of Spain with his dream that the world was round and the plan to find a short path to the Indies.

He cried even at the court of the king
His story of incredible things.
When they made fun of him in the Court, Columbus
Was not baffled, for . . .
He knew he was
A servant of the Holy Ghost.

Did Columbus actually think that he was called of God to do this important thing? Actually, "Yes," says Markham. "I have read every book available, including the Diary of Columbus, and it's clear to me that Columbus looked on himself as a servant of God on that eventful voyage."

Ultimately he got his financial support and set sail. It's a story of long days and nights, near mutinies, his crew wanted to turn back, but the sheer courage of Columbus kept them going on to the West. Markham ends his poem with four lines:

Now let this startling thing be said:
If land had not been on ahead,
So mighty had been his gallant dare,
God's glad hand would have put it there!

Markham was asked what he meant by these four lines. His reply, "I mean that God is in His heavens, the stars and planets in their courses, the sun and moon and stars, the seasons in their cycles, all history, time, and eternity, and the very angels in heaven are always on the side of the daring, the audacious, the courageous—the man or woman who catches the vision and goes ahead regardless of the obstacles!"

No one will be able to stand up against you all the days of your life. As I was with Moses, so I will be with you; I will never leave you nor forsake you. Be strong and courageous (Joshua 1:5-6).

ENDNOTES

1 Reuter's News Service
2 AP, News Leader, Springfield, MO
3 *USA Today*, 12/16/09
4 Ann Landers, Chicago Tribune
5 Teen-Aid curriculum by Steve Potter and Nancy Roach
6 *Citizenship in a Republic* is the title of this speech given by the former President of the United States, Theodore Roosevelt, at the Sorbonne in Paris, France on April 23, 1910.
7 Associated Press.
8 Dr. Dobson's "Family Bulletin"
9 *Sports Spectrum*
10 *The Sun Herald*
11 *Sports Spectrum*
12 Dr. David Gibbs, founder of Christian Legal Association
13 Jess Kenner, Pueblo, Colorado
14 Ted Engstrom, modified and expanded
15 Richard Hoffer, "Big Man on Campus" from *Sports Illustrated*, 9-28-92.
16 United Technologies Corporation
17 *TIME* magazine, 3/1/2010
18 Adapted from *Soul of a Citizen* by Paul Rogat Loeb
19 Adapted from Success, April 2010
20 Adapted from W. Clement Stone and Napoleon Hill
21 Sean Covey, *The 7 Habits of Highly Effective Teens,* a Fireside Book, Simon & Schuster
22 *USA TODAY*
23 Adapted from *Smart Money*, May 2010
24 Adapted from *You're Not Ready To Have Sex If. . .* (Journeyworks Publishing)
25 Adapted from *Sports Spectrum*, spring 2010
26 John McCaslin, *The Washington Times,* from "Inside the Beltway," 11/12/2003
27 Adapted, Leland H. Gregory III, Dell Publishing, New York
28 Adapted from Jennifer Taylor, *On Course*, Fall 2009/Winter 2010
29 Adapted from Erma Bombeck, *At Wit's End*
30 Adapted from the National Church Life Survey, Sydney, Australia
31 Adapted from Victoria Seltz and William Cohen, Business Forum, California State University
32 Condensed from Christian Clippings, April, 2009
33 Adapted from *Sports Illustrated,* May 24, 2010
34 Facts from Freeda Keet, a retired Israeli journalist from Jerusalem, who was known as the "Barbara Walters of Israel"
35 Ibid.
36 Statistics are from Teen Drug Abuse
37 Nationmaster.com, statements & statistics based on studies between 1998 and 2009
38 Author unknown, from Christian Clippings
39 Columnist Smiley Anders, Baton Rouge, LA, Advocate
40 Joyce Keyser, First United Methodist Church Secretary
41 Taken from a sermon preached by Dr. Shadrach Lockridge
42 Research findings adapted from *The Week* magazine
43 Jim Colaianni, Voicings Publications
44 *Uniting Men and Women,* the magazine of United Methodist Men, Vol. 5, #3, Summer 2002, condensed and adapted